Banning Transgender Conversion Practices

Law and Society Series
W. Wesley Pue, Founding Editor

We pay tribute to the late Wes Pue, under whose broad vision, extraordinary leadership, and unwavering commitment to socio-legal studies our Law and Society Series was established and rose to prominence.

The Law and Society Series explores law as a socially embedded phenomenon. It is premised on the understanding that the conventional division of law from society creates false dichotomies in thinking, scholarship, educational practice, and social life. Books in the series treat law and society as mutually constitutive and seek to bridge scholarship emerging from interdisciplinary engagement of law with disciplines such as politics, social theory, history, political economy, and gender studies.

Recent books in the series:

Kim Stanton, *Reconciling Truths: Reimagining Public Inquiries in Canada* (2021)

Daniel Rück, *The Laws and the Land: The Settler Colonial Invasion of Kahnawà:ke in Nineteenth-Century Canada* (2021)

Suzanne Bouclin, *Women, Film, and Law: Cinematic Representations of Female Incarceration* (2021)

Amanda Nelund, *A Better Justice? Community Programs for Criminalized Women* (2020)

Trevor C.W. Farrow and Lesley A. Jacobs, eds., *The Justice Crisis: The Cost and Value of Accessing Law* (2020)

Jamie Baxter, *Inalienable Properties: The Political Economy of Indigenous Land Reform* (2020)

Jeremy Patrick, *Faith or Fraud: Fortune-Telling, Spirituality, and the Law* (2020)

Obiora Chinedu Okafor, *Refugee Law after 9/11: Sanctuary and Security in Canada and the United States* (2020)

Anna Jane Samis Lund, *Trustees at Work: Financial Pressures, Emotional Labour, and Canadian Bankruptcy Law* (2019)

Shauna Labman, *Crossing Law's Border: Canada's Refugee Resettlement Program* (2019)

Peter McCormick and Marc D. Zanoni, *By the Court: Anonymous Judgments at the Supreme Court of Canada* (2019)

For a complete list of the titles in the series, see the UBC Press website, www.ubcpress.ca.

Banning Transgender Conversion Practices

A Legal and Policy Analysis

FLORENCE ASHLEY

UBCPress

1971–2021

Library and Archives Canada Cataloguing in Publication

Title: Banning transgender conversion practices : a legal and policy analysis / Florence Ashley.
Names: Ashley, Florence, author.
Series: Law and society series (Vancouver, B.C.)
Description: Series statement: Law and society, 1496–4953 | Includes bibliographical references and index.
Identifiers: Canadiana (print) 20220167486 | Canadiana (ebook) 2022016777X | ISBN 9780774866927 (hardcover) | ISBN 9780774866934 (paperback) | ISBN 9780774866941 (PDF) | ISBN 9780774866958 (EPUB)
Subjects: LCSH: Sexual reorientation programs—Law and legislation. | LCSH: Transgender people—Legal status, laws, etc.
Classification: LCC K3242.3 A84 2022 | DDC 342.08/7—dc23

Canada

UBC Press gratefully acknowledges the financial support for our publishing program of the Government of Canada (through the Canada Book Fund), the Canada Council for the Arts, and the British Columbia Arts Council.

Printed and bound in Canada by Friesens
Set in Sabon Next LT Pro and Myriad Pro by Apex CoVantage, LLC
Copy editor: Stacy Belden
Proofreader: Kristy Lynn Hankewitz
Indexer: Emily LeGrand
Cover designer: Alexa Love

UBC Press
The University of British Columbia
2029 West Mall
Vancouver, BC V6T 1Z2
www.ubcpress.ca

For Erika

*for those who survived
and those who didn't*

I love you for who you are

Contents

Foreword / ix

Acknowledgments / xi

Introduction / 3

1 What Are Trans Conversion Practices? / 22

2 Interpreting the Scope of Bans / 33

3 Legal Variants across the Globe / 53

4 Opposition and Constitutional Challenges to Bans / 71

5 Analyzing the Benefits and Limitations of Bans / 103

6 Developing an Affirmative Professional Culture / 119

7 Annotated Model Law for Prohibiting Conversion Practices / 130

Conclusion / 174

Appendix: Professional Organizations Opposing Trans Conversion Practices / 177

Glossary / 185

Notes / 191

Index / 239

Foreword

This book is published within the historical context created by the entry into force in Canada of Bill C-4 on January 7, 2022. The legislation bans conversion practices and has been hailed around the world as indicative of growing awareness of the heinous nature of these human rights violations and the irreparable and profound damage that they cause on their victims.

Indeed, practices of conversion perpetrated against trans and other gender diverse persons are the source of extreme suffering. That these practices creep within the deep grooves cut in societies around the world by pathologizing views of gender diversity is, however, only part of the explanation for their cruelty: they are part of patterns followed by States and other entities that perpetuate violence and discrimination and defend rancid social structures, such as patriarchy, upon which is built most of the injustice in the world.

This work of Florence Ashley is crafted at the intersection of the ethical, political, and legal narratives that exist within and around this existential battle. Meticulously deconstructing layer after layer, they place conversion practices under the lens of their analytical scrutiny and bring clarity to a debate that is most often waged on the basis of only prejudice, and in which the very lives of trans and other gender diverse persons are often used in a most despicable way with the sole purpose of galvanizing political bases.

A world free of conversion practices serves the goal of respecting fully the existence of trans and other gender diverse persons who lead their lives in full enjoyment of their rights – rights that they use to seek happiness and fulfilment and is the natural consequence of the international human rights imperative of legal recognition of gender identity based on self-identification.

I became aware of Ashley's scholarly work in 2018 during my own research on conversion practices for my report to the United Nations Human Rights Council, through which I concluded that under international human rights law, these practices are cruel, inhuman, and degrading treatment and must be regarded by States as creating significant risk of torture. I also based on that conclusion my global call for a world free of this heinous scourge; Ashley generously contributed evidence created through their research to that process. We have kept in touch, not least through their prolific social media activity, and I have constantly learned from their knowledge and been inspired by the richness of their observations. I am delighted that this book is written in the same key.

Early in the book, Ashley reveals the vantage point from where they carry out their scholarly work, an awareness of which we are reminded throughout our reading. They convey the power of a trans-affirmative stance from which, through rigorous legal analysis, they craft a persuasive proposal for legislative solutions. In so doing, they bring a text of inestimable relevance for the work of eradicating violence and discrimination based on gender identity.

Victor Madrigal-Borloz
United Nations Independent Expert on
protection from violence and discrimination
based on sexual orientation and gender identity
Washington, DC

Acknowledgments

Countless individuals deserve thanks for their contribution to this book. Thinking and writing are collective endeavours. Though I may have been the one to type words onto the page, the spirit of countless communities shines through the pages as I reread them.

I first want to thank the survivors of conversion practices who have confided in me and whose perspectives have helped me hone my analysis. Many of you remain anonymous. These words are for you. No one deserves more thanks than Erika Muse, whose insights and encouragements were unwavering over the last few years. I am a better scholar because of you. I am glad that we have met and become friends. I owe a debt of scholarly gratitude to Drs. Sé Sullivan and Karl Bryant for their outspoken scholarship on the harms of conversion practices.

Over the years, I have had no more consistent and enthusiastic supporter than Jay De Santi. You have always read my work, provided brilliant feedback, and been a wonderful, wonderful friend. Laura Cárdenas, thank you for being a family to me and thank you for your magical hugs. As for Rowan and Saleem, you deserve my deepest gratitude for being the cutest famfam I could ever hope for. The rest of my family also deserves thanks for their love, affection, and support. Béa, maman, papa, merci pour tout.

I wish to thank Dean Robert Leckey for his wonderful support as my master's supervisor and Alana Klein for her most insightful comments as my external reviewer. This book has come a long way since its inception as a master's thesis idea. Without your critical eyes and encouragements, this book would probably never have existed.

A great many of you deserve thanks for your feedback, your scholarly insight, and the many discussions we have had together regarding specific parts of the book. In reverse alphabetical order, I want to thank Ezra Young, Kristopher Wells, Rachel Slepoi, Travis Salway, Cianán Russell, Darren Rosenblum, Annie Pullen Sansfaçon, Pelecanos, Lou Morin, Xtine Milrod, Hans Lindahl, Diana Kuhl, Jaime Grant, Dylan Felt, Cary Gabriel Costello, Matt Caron Francino, Mauro Cabral Grinspan, Lauren Beach, Sam Ames, and the members of the Transgender Professional Association for Transgender Health. Utmost distinguished thanks to Jen Hites-Thomas for her amazing comments and editorial help on the penultimate draft of this book. I am also grateful to the brilliant and inspiring Victor Madrigal-Borloz for writing the foreword to this book. It is a great honour.

My work was supported by multiple awards and fellowships. I would like to thank the Centre for Human Rights and Legal Pluralism at McGill University for their O'Brien Fellowship in Human Rights and Legal Pluralism. Thanks go to the Social Sciences and Humanities Research Council of Canada for awarding me the Joseph-Armand Bombardier Graduate Scholarship. To the Conseil québécois LGBT for their Bourse Dorais-Ryan. Bill Ryan and Michel Dorais deserve my personal thanks not only for funding the award but also for the trust and interest they have shown in my scholarship. Thanks to Start Proud for awarding me their LGBTQ+ Student Leadership Scholarship and to the McGill University Research Group on Health and Law for warmly welcoming me as a fellow during my master's studies. I also wish to thank Peter A. Singer as well as the team at UBC Press for their support in bringing my book to publication.

I conducted most of the research for this book while living in Tiohtià:ke, also known as Montréal. Tiohtià:ke is unceded land, and the Kanien'kehá:ka are its custodians. Tiohtià:ke has been, and continues to be, a gathering place for many First Nations. The many Indigenous

People who live on the island suffer ongoing violence at the hands of the settler-colonial state of which I am a part. Much of the editing and revisions were done while I lived in Toronto, which sits on the traditional territory of many Indigenous Nations, including the Anishnaabeg, the Haudenosaunee, and the Wendat. The name for Toronto comes from the Kanienke'haka word "tkaronto," meaning "where there are trees standing in the water" – a reference to fishing weirs in the narrows of the river. The land is subject to Treaty 13 with the Mississaugas of the Credit and is part of the Dish With One Spoon territory, a treaty between the Anishinaabe and Haudenosaunee peoples that has incorporated newcomers over time. As a white settler, I come to the Dish With One Spoon through the 1764 Treaty of Fort Niagara. Symbolized by the Dish With One Spoon Wampum Belt, the treaty was designed to create peaceful hunting conditions for nations living in close proximity. The land was to be shared, used in common just as family members ate from one dish. Settlers did not respect the treaty. Colonial forces unilaterally appropriated the territory – a violent dispossession of the First Nations of this land that continues today.

McGill University and the University of Toronto should divest from fossil fuels, which are ravaging the planet, and financially commit themselves to address the underrepresentation of Indigenous students and scholars in higher education. I call on the Canadian, Québec, and Ontario governments to recognize and respect Indigenous sovereignty and custodianship of the land, to implement the *United Nations Declaration on the Rights of Indigenous Peoples,* and to follow all recommendations of the Truth and Reconciliation Commission. Reconciliation cannot begin until we dismantle the settler-colonial state.

Banning Transgender
Conversion Practices

Introduction

On December 15, 2015, the Toronto Centre for Addiction and Mental Health (CAMH) announced that it would be closing its Gender Identity Clinic for Children and Youth. For decades, the clinic had been plagued with critiques accusing it of engaging in conversion practices.[1] These critiques came from academics, scholars, and community members alike. Its antiquated approach to trans care was enshrined in a nickname: the Jurassic Clarke – a pun on the name of its precursor, the Clarke Institute. Amidst reignited accusations that the clinic engaged in conversion practices and in the wake of Ontario's Bill 77, the *Affirming Sexual Orientation and Gender Identity Act*, which came into force in June 2015 to prohibit conversion practices across the province, CAMH announced the clinic's closure.[2]

Trans communities welcomed this change. The CAMH clinic had played a leading role in trans health for nearly four decades.[3] It had long been the sole approved source of referrals for medical transition in Ontario and, indeed, some other provinces.[4] Some detractors painted it as an international exporter of trans conversion practices due to its prominence in clinical and research circles. The clinic's demise marked the end of an era not just for Ontario but also for trans health itself. Its closure in the wake of a new law prohibiting conversion practices offers insight into both the limitations and potential of banning conversion practices.

The CAMH clinic's history begins in the 1970s, when it operated as a specialized team of the Clarke Institute in Toronto under the supervision of Susan Bradley. In the 1980s, Kenneth Zucker succeeded Bradley as head of the clinic. When the Clarke Institute merged with other organizations to form CAMH, the clinic continued to operate under the new institution.[5] The clinic was for a long time "among the few clinics able to produce longitudinal data and comparative research" and "generated the most highly cited writing on the topic of childhood gender diversity."[6] It was among the first to prescribe puberty blockers to adolescents, allowing them to transition. However, as science and our understanding of transitude – the fact of being trans – morphed into our contemporary understanding of being trans as part of normal human variation rather than as a mental disorder, the clinic's practice proved resistant to change.[7] A comparison between the 1995 monograph *Gender Identity Disorder and Psychosexual Problems in Children and Adolescents* by Kenneth Zucker and Susan Bradley and contemporary works by the same authors reveals few substantial changes in clinical approach.[8] Although the authors are more cautious in their propositions today and acknowledge a plurality of practices, they continue to view the prevention of adult trans outcomes as an appropriate and ethical clinical goal.

An external review of the clinic's practice undertaken at the request of CAMH informed the decision to wind down services. The review was ordered after the community organization Rainbow Health Alliance submitted a review of the academic literature and clinical practices on trans youth care, raising concerns that the CAMH clinic was not following accepted practices.[9] At the time, Ontario's ban on conversion practices was under consideration by the legislature with support from the majority government. Rainbow Health Alliance suggested that the clinic's approach would run afoul of the upcoming law, prompting further concern. The external review was conducted by psychiatrists Suzanne Zinck and Antonio Pignatiello, who completed a literature review; interviewed staff, community stakeholders, and clients, former clients, and families; reviewed written submissions from former patients; and reviewed patients' medical records. The review made recommendations based on the findings.

The report described the head of the clinic, Kenneth Zucker, as a "Mecca of knowledge and information" but found that the clinic was "out of step with current clinical and operational practices."[10] According to the reviewers, there was concern and anger among stakeholders that clinicians and students affiliated with the clinic were being taught the clinic's corrective approach.[11] The reviewers expressed concern that the clinic's use of play therapy and cognitive-behavioural therapy was directive rather than exploratory and that the clinic's approach was grounded in an assumption that gender non-conforming behaviours require intervention.[12] The clinicians would set out "to reduce [the] child's desire to be of the other gender," notably by attempting to identify the desire's causes through individual and parental counselling, by directing parents to limit or disallow the child's gender non-conforming behaviours in day-to-day life, and by promoting relations with peers of the same sex assigned at birth.[13] It is not clear from the report whether all clinicians at the clinic employed a similar approach, though the description of the clinic's practices seems to suggest as much.

Some who worked at the clinic opined that Ontario's upcoming ban on conversion practices would not apply to their approach.[14] The report did not express any view regarding the law's application and did not confirm whether the clinic engaged in conversion practices. The authors nonetheless noted that "they cannot state that the clinic does not" engage in conversion practices, pointing to evidence that may suggest as much.[15] The external review's findings do indeed suggest that conversion practices were being employed. Parents reported their children being questioned about their gender in ways that implied a negative judgment of their way of being.[16] The report found that the clinic pathologized children and parents and suggested that it inappropriately positioned being "heterosexual [and] cisgender as the most acceptable treatment outcome."[17] The reviewers concurred with participants that promoting comfort with one's sex assigned at birth was wrong and not consistent with current standards of practices. According to them, attempting to "treat" normal human variation surrounding gender is unlikely to succeed or be ethical.[18] They further faulted the clinic for not engaging collaboratively with trans communities.[19]

The central recommendation of the review was for the clinic to revise its assessment and treatment approaches and align them with patient-centred, affirmative care. The report authors recommended that staff refrain from attempting to reduce gender non-conforming behaviours and avoid language that pathologizes such behaviours.[20] The external review's recommendations were not followed by CAMH, which chose to close the clinic and terminate Zucker's employment. As William Byne has stated, echoing the external review, "[c]losure of the Ontario clinic before making alternative provisions for gender-variant children and adolescents has left a void for many needing its services."[21] The gap in services continues today.

For conservative commentators, the closure of the clinic and termination of Zucker's employment was evidence that "trans militants" sought to "censor" scientists. Barbara Kay, writing for the *National Post,* Canada's leading conservative newspaper, characterized critiques of the clinic's practices as symptoms of the "aggressive activism in the trans movement," suggesting that emotionalism had overtaken rational dialogue.[22] This belief is shared by many of Zucker' supporters. A petition opposing Zucker's firing and concluding that it was primarily political was signed by 508 individuals, many of whom are academics and scientists.[23] The signatories include many individuals known for their anti-trans views and activism. According to the chair of the CAMH Board of Trustees, the petition does not "provide an accurate assessment of what occurred," the closure having been motivated by CAMH's commitment to improving services in collaboration with community partners.[24]

Following his dismissal, Zucker sued CAMH for defamation and wrongful dismissal. In October 2018, CAMH announced that it had reached a financial settlement with Zucker and released an apology. The apology stated:

> In 2015, the Centre for Addiction and Mental Health (CAMH) commissioned an external review of the Gender Identity Clinic within the Child, Youth and Family Program. The purpose of the review was to identify best practices and determine how CAMH can best serve children and adolescents with gender dysphoria and their families.

The review was not intended to examine Dr. Zucker's behaviour or specific clinical practices.

The review produced a report that was released publicly on December 15, 2015. Unfortunately, the report contained some errors about Dr. Zucker's clinical practice and interactions with patients. The report was released publicly without review or comment by Dr. Zucker. Among other errors, the report falsely states that Dr. Zucker called a patient a "hairy little vermin." That allegation is untrue.

CAMH apologizes without reservation to Dr. Zucker for the flaws in the process that led to errors in the report not being discovered and has entered into a settlement with Dr. Zucker that includes a financial payment to him.[25]

Many saw the settlement as a vindication of Zucker and as evidence that he was wrongfully fired. However, the attending context suggests that the implications of the settlement are narrower and, crucially, did not extend to the findings about the clinic's approach being out of line with current, non-psychopathologizing approaches to trans care. The impugning of the corrective approach employed at the CAMH clinic is certainly the most damning element of the external review. One would think that the apology would explicitly refer to any significant mischaracterizations of the approach, had there been any. Although the apology alluded to errors regarding Zucker's clinical practice, none were explicitly mentioned – a telltale silence. On the contrary, CAMH publicly stated upon the apology's release that it "stands by its decision to close the child and youth gender identity clinic following an external review which concluded the clinic was not meeting the needs of gender expansive and trans children and their families."[26]

It is important to understand that employment law contemplates compensation not only for the act of termination itself but also for the manner in which the person was terminated.[27] Even if CAMH is entitled to terminate Zucker and close the clinic for engaging in outdated and possibly unethical practices, it must do so without harming the employee's reputation and future employment prospects. Conduct and statements that are "untruthful, misleading or unduly insensitive" can lead to compensation.[28] Damages can also be separately sought for defamation. Making a report public without giving interested parties an opportunity to comment on it ahead of time is a risky endeavour. For long-standing employees whose reputations are at play, having no opportunity to comment could by itself be understood as unduly insensitive. To claim that someone called a patient a "hairy little vermin" is bound to harm their reputation, regardless of whether someone else at the clinic made the statement. The reputational injury and insensitive process may turn out to attract particularly large sums of money when the person is a long-standing, well-paid employee in a managerial position. Given the apology's emphasis on the manner of termination and the subsequent statement by CAMH reaffirming its decision to close the clinic because of its approach to care, I would caution against interpreting the settlement as a vindication of Zucker's and the clinic's practices.

Regardless of the legal reasons behind the settlement, many people interpreted it as evidence that critics of the clinic were politically motivated bullies seeking to suppress science. Given the volatile context in which the clinic was closed, CAMH's handling of the closure and its subsequent settlement with Zucker may well have done a disservice to trans youth. However, characterizing the sustained critiques levied towards the clinic as emotions over reason does not appear to be justified. Emotions do run high, and, as Tey Meadow notes, "[f]or many trans activists, Ken [Zucker] and CAMH represented the pathologizing impulses of past psychiatric practice."[29] It is plausible that Zucker, because of his prominence and influence within the scientific community, was disproportionately targeted by criticisms. Zucker is far from being the sole proponent of the corrective approach. Those who have criticized him and his work have not always been measured in their words. However, that does not mean that the critics are wrong. Critiques of the corrective approach find support in clinical and ethical reasoning and began appearing in the scientific literature over a decade before the clinic's closure.[30] To detractors, as Jake Pyne explains, the debate surrounding the corrective approach simply "no longer qualifies as a true debate," and a clear consensus has emerged against practices that seek to "correct" gender variance in favour of the gender-affirmative approach.[31]

Depicting the debate as a clash between professionals and trans activists is inaccurate. Within trans communities, some of the most vocal opponents of the clinic's practices have been scientists and academics.[32] For instance, Pyne is a professor of social work who contributed to the TransPULSE research project in Ontario and held the prestigious Trudeau Doctoral Scholarship and Banting Postdoctoral Fellowship. Jemma Tosh holds a doctorate in psychology and has authored multiple peer-reviewed publications, many of which were on trans issues. Julia Serano holds a doctorate in biochemistry and molecular biophysics from Columbia University and has conducted extensive scientific research on genetics and developmental and evolutionary biology at University of California, Berkeley. Their critiques in the public realm were grounded in expertise and published in scholarly journals and books.[33] Pyne, Tosh, and Serano are joined by countless cis academics who similarly see significant flaws in the corrective approach. The gender-affirmative approach, now the leading approach to trans youth care, was developed in parallel to critiques of the corrective approach. Scientific knowledge, clinical experience, and community wisdom have all played crucial roles in the formulation of critiques of the corrective approach practised at the CAMH clinic.

Ideology played a role in the closure of the CAMH clinic, but it would be a mistake to characterize controversies over the clinic's practices as an opposition between ideology and science. Debates over therapeutic ethics are not value-neutral. Choosing an ethical framework within which to evaluate practices is a value-laden exercise. Someone who is guided by a desire to avoid people being trans because they see being trans as a form of mental illness is likely to reach different conclusions from the available data than someone who sees being trans as a benign human variation and sees transition as an equally acceptable life path. The controversy in many ways mirrors the controversy over the place of homosexuality within the *Diagnostic and Statistical Manual of Mental Disorders*, which was similarly characterized as "a value judgment about heterosexuality, rather than a factual dispute about homosexuality."[34] Given the intertwined nature of ethical judgment and clinical practice, it would be more accurate to depict the controversy as one arising between different schools of thought on trans therapeutics.[35] The clinic and its clinicians' desire to prevent adult trans outcomes was criticized by trans communities and trans-affirmative clinicians for being harmful to gender-creative youth and grounded in prejudiced conceptions of trans existence. The clinic defended its view by referring to long-standing theorizations of the corrective approach.

The closure of the CAMH clinic in the wake of Ontario's Bill 77 stands as a testament to both the potential and limits of prohibiting conversion practices. It shows that these laws have some bite, even outside of the courts. Bans can discourage conversion practices not only through legal enforcement but also by encouraging peer accountability between professionals and fostering the development of an affirmative professional culture. While the external review of the CAMH clinic's services may have been partly motivated by the upcoming legal ban, it ultimately did not matter whether the practices fell under the scope of Bill 77 since the CAMH administration could dictate how the services should be rendered. On the other hand, the unclear scope of the law enabled the clinic staff's belief that it did not apply to their approach and freed them to fan out into private practice once the clinic closed. If their approach indeed constituted a conversion practice, this outcome is far from optimal.

The clinic's closure and surrounding controversy highlight some of the key fault lines of policy-making about trans conversion practices. It is one thing to ban conversion practices. It is quite another thing to effectively discourage them. Throughout this book, the need for clearer, more detailed bans and the importance of bolstering bans by developing an affirmative professional culture will be recurring themes. Clarifying our picture of what counts as trans conversion practices and how to best ban them is crucial to enlightened, effective policy-making.

~

Trans conversion practices refer to a range of practices seeking to discourage behaviours associated with a gender other than the person's sex assigned at birth and/or to promote gender identities that are aligned with their sex assigned at birth. They take many forms, including behavioural therapy, psychodynamic therapy, parental counselling, and interventions in a naturalistic environment.[36] These practices are recognized as harmful and unethical by professional, scientific, and human rights organizations. Trans conversion practices typically begin with the premise that there is something disordered, wrong, and/or undesirable about being trans or gender creative. From the premise that there is something wrong or undesirable about being trans, proponents of conversion practices conclude that they should prevent people from being trans and transitioning socially or medically to live in their desired body and gender.

For many of those who were subjected to unrelenting attempts to alter, repress, or discourage their gender identity, trans conversion practices carry the resounding promise of life-long psychological distress. Dr. Sé Sullivan, a survivor of conversion practices, explained:

> My "treatment" included stigmatizing me through a medical model of "illness," which bore far-reaching consequences in my life. ... The psychological "treatment" I had as a child did not have my best interests at heart. It was child abuse. I developed coping mechanisms of protecting myself by hurting others before they could hurt me. Anger, fighting, sex, and drugs were the best tools I found for this. These same behaviors I used as mechanisms of defense eventually created damage of their own in both my youth and adult life. Self-loathing and shame guided all of my decisions and suicide became a frequent thought. ... As an adult, I struggle with depression, self-care, and have considered suicide over the years, including during this research project.[37]

Sociologist Karl Bryant spoke in similar terms about his experience of trans conversion practices: "The study and the therapy that I received made me feel that I was wrong, that something about me at my core was bad, and instilled in me a sense of shame that stayed with me for a long time afterward."[38] I discuss the nature of trans conversion practies and what they include at greater length in Chapter 1.

The harms of conversion practices can be understood from multiple angles. Most gravely, conversion practices persistently invalidate a core aspect of one's personal identity and self-knowledge. People who experience conversion practices learn to be ashamed of themselves and of who they are, leading to anxiety, depression, and suicidality. For youths whose parents are involved in the conversion practices, the practices can have severe repercussions on family attachment, which is closely tied to long-term mental health outcomes, especially among marginalized communities that may find less support within the broader society.[39] Conversion practices also tend to delay social and medical transition, condemning trans people who experience significant gender dysphoria to the experience of ongoing suffering.[40] For those who undergo conversion practices before or during puberty, this can mean undergoing undesired, difficult-to-reverse, and deeply distressing bodily changes. While not all trans people experience gender dysphoria or wish to medically transition, many do, and withholding medical transition causes part of the harms of conversion practices. So harmful are conversion practices that researchers, international bodies, and survivors often liken them to torture.[41]

The harm of conversion practices is borne out in quantitative research. The harms of conversion practices compound the already extreme levels of harassment, discrimination, and violence suffered by trans communities. Overall, within trans communities, 39 percent have experienced psychological distress in the last month, 48 percent had serious suicidal ideations in the last year, 7 percent attempted suicide in the last year, and 40 percent attempted suicide at some point in their lifetime.[42] A study by Jack Turban and colleagues has found that trans people who experienced attempts to change their gender identity greatly increased the rate of severe psychological distress, suicidal ideations, and suicide attempts long after being subjected to them.[43] Compared to those who did not have such experiences, trans people who had experienced trans conversion practices were 1.56 times more likely to have experienced severe psychological distress in the last month, 1.52 times more likely to have planned suicide in the last year, 1.49 times more likely to have attempted suicide in the last year, and 2.27 times more likely to have attempted suicide in their lifetime. For those who experienced conversion practices before the age of ten years old, the numbers are even grimmer. They were 1.75 times more likely to have experienced severe psychological distress in the last month, 2.82 times more likely to have planned suicide in the last year, 2.40 times more likely to have attempted suicide in the last year, and 4.15 times more likely to have attempted suicide in their lifetime. Similar outcomes were reported in a study by Amy Green and colleagues.[44]

That is a lot of numbers. I spell them out to emphasize how pervasive and severe the harms of trans conversion practices are. And those numbers only capture the starkest of harms – recent severe psychological distress and suicidality. Those who have already healed with the help of therapy and social support and those who were hurt by conversion practices albeit not to the point of suicide are simply not captured by those numbers. While not everyone who experiences conversion practices will be gravely and irremediably harmed by them, it simply cannot be acceptable for practitioners to sacrifice their patients to demonstrably dangerous, degrading practices.

While patients are those most harmed by trans conversion practices, the harm does not stop there. As a transfeminine scholar, I am intimately cognizant of the disastrous reverberations of trans conversion practices on trans communities writ large. Trans conversion practices are part of a larger social project of oppressing and discrediting trans communities. The open engagement in conversion practices, especially by people in positions of authority, gives an air of legitimacy to antagonistic attitudes towards trans communities. It depicts being trans as a mental illness and something to be avoided, two common beliefs in mainstream society that underpin harassment, discrimination, and violence against trans people.[45] Conversion practices symbolize and perpetuate the devaluation of trans lives. Trans conversion practices are fundamentally transantag-onistic – that is to say, they are intolerant, prejudiced, hostile, and dis-criminatory towards trans people. As the sociological theory of symbolic interactionism teaches us, humans lead fundamentally symbolic lives.[46] Through interactions, humans (re-)create symbols and shape the social imaginary, which we then use to arrange and direct our lives. Trans conversion practices symbolize the dehumanization and devaluation of trans people, which takes a significant psychological toll on many members of trans communities, myself included.[47] Indeed, working on this book was difficult for me as I had to read countless articles express-ing such negative attitudes towards trans people.

As the closure of the CAMH clinic demonstrates, trans conversion practices are an ongoing concern in Canadian healthcare. Yet people often react with utter shock when I tell them that conversion practices are still common. In the United States, 13.5 percent of trans adults reported being subjected to conversion practices, a number that climbed to 18 percent among those who discussed their gender identity with a professional.[48] Recent Canadian studies found that between 11 and 19 percent of trans people had experienced conversion practices.[49] Despite public concern over conversion practices often being limited to minors, recent studies show that conversion practices are common across all age groups. In terms of age, around half of individuals experience conversion practices before they reach the age of eighteen and the other half at or after the age of eighteen, with estimates varying by country.[50]

The leading trans health organization worldwide, the World Professional Association for Transgender Health, affirms that "[t]reatment aimed at trying to change a person's gender identity and expression to become more congruent with sex assigned at birth [is] no longer considered ethical."[51] Countless leading professional associations have come out in opposition to trans conversion practices, and, recently, the United Nations Independent Expert on Sexual Orientation and Gender Identity called on governments to ban conversion practices.[52] The professional consensus is clear. But even though conversion practices have fallen into disfavour within trans health, many licensed professionals nonetheless engage in them, and a faction of indomitable therapists and theorists continue to profess their commitment to the corrective approach, an approach that was used at the defunct CAMH clinic and that seeks to prevent children from growing up transgender. Conversion practices appear not only more common among trans people than cisgender queer people, but they also seem more likely to be done by licensed professionals. Internationally and in Canada, between a third and half of all conversion practices are by a licensed professional.[53] Data from the United States suggests that, among trans survivors, close to two-thirds have experienced conversion practices at the hands of a licensed professional.[54]

It is easy to dismiss trans conversion practices as an antiquated, dying approach in a world that is rapidly growing more accepting of trans people. However, the reality is far different. In recent years, we have seen a resurgence of advocacy in favour of trans conversion practices. With the rising visibility of trans communities came a backlash against trans youth care. Anti-trans voices allege that society is in the midst of an unprecedented epidemic of youth falsely believing themselves to be transgender due to "social contagion" and unexamined mental illness and trauma. These allegations are spurious and wholly disconnected from the evidence. No data support the view that there is social contagion of any kind, and the rapid growth in referrals to gender identity clinics is most likely attributable to a growing public awareness of trans realities and the possibility of medical transition.[55] In other words, more and more people are realizing that being trans is a normal, healthy thing and that services exist to help those who wish to medically transition.

In a similar vein, some transantagonistic groups and academics have claimed that most trans children grow up to identify with the gender they were assigned at birth and that we should therefore encourage this reidentification. However, the argument is based on flawed studies that do not adequately distinguish between gender non-conforming and trans children.[56] Whereas trans children identify with a gender other than the one they were assigned at birth, gender non-conforming children who are not transgender identify with the gender they were assigned at birth but encroach on the social norms and expectations associated with it. Contrary to the argument, studies show that trans children and adolescents know themselves and their gender and that regret and re-transition are rare – between 0 percent and 3.8 percent – with larger studies often reporting regret and/or re-transition rates below 1 percent.[57] But however flawed the arguments may be, they are still being used to breathe new life into conversion practices by portraying being trans and transitioning as an undesirable, pathological outcome that should be discouraged.

As trans people become more visible, a backlash can be felt. As I write these words, conservative legislators in the United States are introducing bills to criminalize offering minors gender-affirming medical care, despite medical transition being recognized as the best practice for trans youth who desire it.[58] In the United Kingdom and Canada, we are seeing attempts to curtail access to medical transition for minors, led by people who view trans youth as mentally ill.[59] These efforts have been met with some success in the United Kingdom, where the trial decision in *Bell v Tavistock* required a court application to initiate puberty blockers.[60] The decision is being appealed. The same groups that are pushing for these rollbacks are often also advocating against anti-discrimination protections and trans-inclusive policies, notably when it comes to trans women's inclusion in sports and access to public facilities.[61] Anti-trans groups are actively pushing for the exclusion of trans people from the protection of bans on conversion practices, arguing that gender-affirmative care is dangerous, that youths are falsely believing themselves to be trans, and that, if anything, trans conversion practices should be encouraged. We have seen this phenomenon in Canada. When the federal government proposed Bill C-6, *An Act to Amend the Criminal Code (Conversion Therapy)*, to criminalize conversion practices, a deluge of submissions urged them to remove the protection of gender identity under the law, relying on unscientific tropes and transantagonistic philosophies to prop up their position.[62] They argued that conversion practices targeting cisgender queer people were unethical but that those targeting trans people were not. To many of those individuals, being queer was fine, but being trans was not. By contrast, professional and community organizations were overwhelmingly in favour of including trans people under the protective fold of the law.

As these transantagonistic philosophies and movements grow in cultural prominence in all areas of social life, we will likely see a resurgence of trans conversion practices under the guise of protecting trans people against themselves. As jurisdictions worldwide turn to ban conversion practices, they must consider the prevailing landscape of anti-trans animosity and tailor their bans to ensure adequate protections for trans people. Bans on conversion practices are not a rote expression of disapproval towards a bygone practice. Trans conversion practices are alive and continue to threaten trans well-being. Effective bans on trans conversion practices are more important than ever.

In 2015, Ontario became the first Canadian province to prohibit conversion practices; the legislature acting in response to professional bodies' failure to protect trans youth.[63] At the federal level, the government has recently adopted Bill C-4, criminalizing conversion practices across Canada.[64] The federal government initially rejected the suggestion of criminalizing conversion practices, arguing that the provinces were better positioned to discourage them, but it reverted course after a report from the House of Commons Standing Committee on Health recommended legislative action at the federal level.[65] Trans voices have been integral to this legislative push. Erika Muse, a trans woman who testified to experiencing conversion practices at the CAMH clinic, has played an integral role concerning both the Ontarian and federal bans.[66] Survivors of conversion practices have also made their voices and needs heard through grassroots coalitions such as No Conversion Canada.[67] In contrast to other jurisdictions where practices targeting sexual orientation have been the primary, if not the sole, focus of legislators, the Ontario ban and Canadian federal bill stand out by demonstrating serious concern, however imperfect, for the well-being of trans communities. However, even bans that were not adopted out of explicit concern over trans conversion practices usually include protections for gender identity and/or expression, recognizing the harmfulness of trans conversion practices and the deeply intertwined, inseparable histories of conversion practices targeting sexual orientation and gender identity.[68]

As a jurist, a bioethicist, and a concerned member of trans communities, I am interested in how bans on trans conversion practices work. What does a standard ban look like and what is its scope? What are the different variants that these laws take? Do these laws stand up to constitutional scrutiny? What are the advantages and disadvantages of legislative approaches to trans conversion practices? How may we improve (upon) them? These questions animate my writing. My goal in writing this book is to guide jurists, policy-makers, healthcare professionals, scholars, and advocates in their thinking about how to best ban conversion practices. I take as my starting point that trans conversion practices ought to be eliminated and that bans on trans conversion practices, although not a panacea, contribute towards that goal. Ebbing and flowing between interpretive, comparative, constitutional, policy, and sociological analysis, I attempt to unearth what bans on conversion practices do and how we can make them more effective.

I approach my research and writing from an openly trans-affirmative stance. Rather than extensively arguing that transantagonism is wrong – that it is wrong to seek to prevent people from being trans – I take it as a guiding premise of my book. My trans-affirmative stance is a by-product of my identity as a transfeminine scholar. An intimate understanding of the topic shapes my writing. I know that being trans is no ill and that it is no evil to be avoided. I know that being trans and living in community with other trans people is a desirable life, one that ought not to be discouraged. Much ink has been spilled debating whether trans conversion practices are wrong, and I do not attempt to exhaustively revisit those debates.[69] I write to those who already desire to eliminate trans conversion practices and wish to know how to best do so. Those readers who are curious about ethical and scientific debates surrounding trans conversion practices will nonetheless find extensive references to the relevant literature throughout the book and may be interested to read my other work on the topic.[70] Because of my trans-affirmative outlook and the trust that members of trans communities have in my work, I have benefited from the confidences and insights of individuals who have undergone trans conversion practices throughout the research and writing process. Their experiences have guided my process. I am grateful for survivors' teachings, and I hope to do them justice. The book would have been greatly lacking without their perspectives.

The book primarily focuses on the regulation of licensed professionals. While I am also attuned to the importance of discouraging conversion practices, I chose to focus on licensed professionals because I understand the law as an enabler of behaviour. Half or more of trans conversion practices are deployed by licensed professionals. Few psychiatrists, psychologists, and social workers could keep up a thriving practice without their membership in professional associations. Membership serves as a gauge of competence and authority for members of the public. Trans people and/or their parents are likely to seek out licensed professionals in good standing when seeking out information and support. They are often lost and blame themselves for their, or their child's, gender identity and non-conforming behaviour.[71] This context can make them unable to critically reflect or push back against the approach that practitioners propose, making them particularly vulnerable to the pull of authority. Yet the very licensure that exacerbates conversion practices can also serve to undermine them. By operating within the law – within licensure schemes that grant them social authority – conversion practitioners open themselves up to legal regulation and professional pressures. Just as the law can enable conversion practices, it can also be used to prevent harmful professional behaviour.

I write this book as a Canadian transfeminine scholar. I was trained in Canadian law and primarily derive my knowledge of trans health and issues from scholarship and community knowledge that emerges out of the English-speaking and French-speaking Global North. This positionality informs and limits my writing. When engaging in legal analysis throughout the book, I focus on Canadian law and, to a lesser extent, US law. Although I strive to generate generalizable knowledge that goes beyond jurisdictional idiosyncrasies, notably by engaging in comparative analysis, readers should remain aware of these limitations and how they may bias my analysis or limit its generalizability.

The book's greatest contribution to policy-making and the scholarly literature on the regulation of conversion practices lies in its suggestion of how to improve (upon) bans, which are explored in Chapters 6 and 7. I propose a two-pronged approach to discouraging conversion practices, which should be implemented in close collaboration with survivor communities. My proposed approach builds upon a twofold insight. The first insight is that self-regulation and peer accountability among professionals is difficult, if not impossible, unless the professionals know what behaviours are prohibited by the law. As we saw with the CAMH clinic, existing bans often leave substantial doubt as to their scope. Bans should be drafted under a pedagogical ethos that aims to clearly and comprehensively set out the prohibited behaviours. People should be able to tell, as much as possible, whether a practice is prohibited without going through an entire, lengthy trial. The second insight is that bans are not enough and may be bolstered by intervening at the level of professional culture. By integrating a thorough appreciation of the importance of gender-affirming care and the harmfulness of trans conversion practices within professional identity, we can change professional culture and further discourage conversion practices. My two-pronged approach offers guidance to policy-makers and professional organizations, guidance that will further the fight against trans conversion practices.

The book is divided into seven chapters. Chapter 1 sets out to define the notion of trans conversion practices and answers whether the corrective approach used at the CAMH clinic is a form of conversion practice. This chapter sets out the essential groundwork for the rest of the book. Chapter 2 elucidates the scope of laws prohibiting trans conversion practices by taking the Ontarian Bill 77 as an example. The chapter will be of greatest interest to trans health clinicians who wish to know what behaviour is prohibited by the law as well as lawyers and judges tasked with interpreting bans.

Chapter 3 delves into the diversity of bans at the international level, offering a comparative overview that groups laws based on textual lineage and sanctions to emphasize the similarities and differences between different bans. This overview not only helps tease out the extent to which the analysis found in Chapter 2 applies to other jurisdictions but also serves as a basis for analyzing the pros and cons of bans in Chapter 5. The chapter will be of greatest interest to lawyers and judges who are interpreting bans as well as policy-makers curious to know how other jurisdictions have drafted their bans.

Chapter 4 analyzes the political and constitutional arguments being deployed against bans on trans conversion practices. In it, I consider and rebut the suggestion that bans violate therapists' freedom of expression, that they are overbroad, and that they are contrary to familial religious freedom and parental authority. While centring on Canadian and US legal knowledge in rebutting these arguments, I nevertheless strive to analyze the arguments from a general standpoint that does not overly rely on the jurisdictional particularities of Canadian and US law. The chapter will be of greatest interest to advocates and policy-makers who desire to ensure that proposed bans pass constitutional muster as well as lawyers and judges faced with a contemplated or actual legal challenge.

Chapter 5 investigates the benefits and limitations of legislative bans on trans conversion practices. Although they have had some success in altering professional practices and have an undeniable symbolic reach, existing bans retain significant limitations. Bans are often restricted based on age and the appearance of consent. They are often insufficiently detailed. When drafted as criminal laws, they may raise additional evidentiary difficulties, disempower survivors, and contribute to the expansion of the carceral state. Bans are often limited to regulated professionals and may cause professional resentment in traditionally self-regulating professions. Bans frequently fail to provide for proper compensation of survivors and do not adequately prevent funding of conversion practices. Furthermore, many legislatures simply may be unwilling to pass bans. Taken together, these limits suggest the need for not only better bans but also multifaceted approaches that go beyond bans. This chapter will be of greatest interest to advocates and policy-makers who wish to promote measures that are most likely to discourage conversion practices.

Chapter 6 answers the call of the preceding chapter, delving into the reasons why existing bans fail to thoroughly alter professional practice. Drawing on the sociology of professions and moral psychology, I explain that effectively discouraging trans conversion practices among professionals requires (1) the creation of laws and/or professional guidelines that clearly and comprehensively identify what counts as a conversion practice; (2) the adoption of educational initiatives that integrate gender-affirming care and opposition to conversion practices in professional identity; and (3) the development of accountability structures that ensure the visible oversight and enforcement of bans on conversion practices. This chapter will be most interesting to healthcare professionals, advocates, and policy-makers who wish to supplement bans with other effective measures for abating conversion practices.

Chapter 7 synthesizes the teachings of the previous chapters as well as my in-depth knowledge of trans health to propose a model law for prohibiting conversion practices. The model law's distinctive features are its comprehensiveness and level of detail, as it builds on the understanding that insufficiently detailed laws are a barrier to effective self-enforcement and mutual accountability. This chapter includes lengthy annotations on each part of the model law, explaining the purpose and rationale behind every provision. It will be most interesting to policy-makers who wish to adopt as effective a ban as possible as well as lawyers, judges, and healthcare professionals who are interested in the scope that bans should have.

In addition to the seven chapters, the book contains an appendix listing statements from professional organizations that oppose trans conversion practices as well as a selection of excerpts. The list highlights the overwhelming condemnation of trans conversion practices, emphasizing the importance of bans. A glossary of terms related to trans issues and conversion practices is also included at the end of the book.

My deepest wish is for this book to support the work of those who are fighting against trans conversion practices and, in so doing, contribute to their elimination. These harmful and degrading practices have no place in our societies. They are a blight on the riches that trans people bring to the world. Trans people deserve to be respected and valued as they are.

Let's get down to business.[72]

What Are Trans Conversion Practices? **1**

Much of the decades-long controversy surrounding the Centre for Addiction and Mental Health (CAMH) Gender Identity Clinic for Children and Youth centred on the question of whether its approach, which I call the corrective approach, is a form of conversion practice. Disagreement abounds as to what is, or what should be, considered a conversion practice. These disagreements reverberate in the public sphere since the term "conversion practices" (and other related expressions) carries significant political weight. To engage in conversion practices is to do something that, in the eyes of most, is objectionable. In the introduction, I have suggested that the CAMH clinic engaged in conversion practices. What did I mean when I said that? This chapter lays the terminological groundwork for the rest of the book by answering these questions: what are conversion practices and do they include the corrective approach, which aims at preventing youth from growing up trans? As the following section explains, trans conversion practices should be understood as sustained efforts to promote gender identities that are aligned with one's sex assigned at birth and/or to discourage behaviours associated with a gender other than the one assigned at birth. Applying this definition, it is clear that the corrective approach that was employed at CAMH is a form of conversion practice.

Defining Trans Conversion Practices

Various definitions of conversion practices have been offered in the literature, though few have been extensively discussed, explained, and defended. Most commonly, the definitions foreground the attempt, through psychological intervention, to change gender identity and expression.[1] The definition often encompasses gender identity and sexual orientation.[2] After reviewing the limits of the existing definitions, I propose the one mentioned in the preceding paragraph. Definitions for conversion practices often focus on change to gender identity (or sexual orientation) and, in doing so, fail to accurately capture and communicate the practices' harm. Conversion practices often target gender-creative children not only because they may grow up to be transgender but also because their gender non-conformity is understood to indicate, or be constitutive of, being psychologically disordered. When I speak of gender-creative youth, I am referring to young people, especially of a prepubertal age, who exhibit strong, ongoing behaviour patterns associated with a gender other than the one they were assigned at birth. They are also called gender independent, gender variant, gender expansive, and gender diverse. Gender-creative youths who undergo conversion practices are routinely made to feel broken or wrong for being as they are, with practitioners acting as if they are trying to repair or fix them – as the alternative moniker "reparative therapy" suggests. It may be more helpful to understand conversion practices not as an attempt to convert gender identity or sexual orientation but, rather, to convert them into gender-normative subjects. Because they cast gender creativity as undesirable, trans conversion practices seek to promote identification with one's sex assigned at birth and to discourage behaviours that are associated with a different sex assigned at birth. In the conversion literature, queerness is traditionally viewed as a failure of masculinity or femininity – a "gender role problem."[3] Framing the issue around changes to gender identity fails to encapsulate the harm done to youth whose gender identities are difficult to identify and risks obscuring the harm of trans conversion practices to those gender-creative youth who grow up to be cisgender.

We often do not know how people, and especially children, identify. Although affirmations of gender by youth such as "I am a girl" are more strongly associated with growing up trans than statements such as

"I want to be a girl," distinguishing between the two types of affirmation is not a perfect litmus test.[4] Children repeatedly told by parents that they are of a certain gender ("you're a boy!") or taught that gender is based on anatomy ("girls have vaginas, boys have penises!") may internalize parental teachings and couch their gender identity as "I want to be" rather than "I am."[5] Conversely, and even though this phenomenon remains rare, children assigned male at birth who are prevented from wearing dresses and told that "dresses are for girls" may tell their parents "I am a girl" because they want to wear dresses. Only with further conversation can we clarify what the child means.

Even if we assume that people have a well-defined gender identity, which I do not believe to always be the case,[6] our ability to identify that gender identity is imperfect.[7] Practitioners must have a big-picture understanding of the child's familial and social context to adequately interpret the language of gender-creative children in less clear-cut cases. Children do not always speak the same language as adults. Focusing on change fails to account for practices applied to youth whose gender identity is ambiguous. We must hold space for those cases by focusing on the fact that gender creativity – which includes people whose gender identities remain unclear or undetermined – is seen as disorderly and warranting intervention and targeted for conversion into normativity. By shifting the focus from gender identity changes to the psychopathologization of gender creativity, we may avoid unnecessary debates as to the true meaning of individual children's affirmations and instead focus on the pressure to identify with one's sex assigned at birth.

Focusing on changes to gender identity risks erasing the harm of conversion practices on those who do not grow up to be trans. Not all gender-creative children express a gender identity that differs from the one they were assigned at birth. Not all of them grow up to be trans. Many children assigned male at birth who wear dresses grow up to be cis gay men. Even those who are diagnosed with either Gender Identity Disorder under the fourth edition of the *Diagnostic and Statistical Manual of Mental Disorders* or Gender Dysphoria under the fifth edition of the same book sometimes identify with the gender they were assigned at birth.[8] According to Diane Ehrensaft, some "protogay" children "find themselves exploring gender on the way to affirming their sexual orientation identities."[9]

Trans conversion practices are frequently applied indiscriminately to all gender-creative children – many of whom cannot reasonably be labelled trans. I call them "trans" conversion practices to draw attention to their goal of avoiding trans outcomes. I do not intend to suggest that only those who are trans or who would grow up to be trans are targeted and/or harmed. Children who do not grow up to be trans are also harmed by conversion practices. Karl Bryant, a cisgender sociologist who was a patient of the University of California Los Angeles Gender Identity Clinic, explains that "it's hard to overstate the harm that [knowing others see you as disordered for being gender creative] can inflict."[10] Being told that you are wrong in some fundamental sense because of your gender non-conformity is harmful, regardless of whether you are trans or not.

In his academic work, Bryant has also highlighted the close relationship between gay and trans conversion practices, helping us understand why the latter may be deeply harmful to children who grow up to be cisgender and gay.[11] Rather than replacing homoantagonism with transantagonism, trans conversion practices involve a symbiotic relationship between homoantagonism and transantagonism that places gender-conforming cisgender lives at the top of the hierarchy of desired outcomes (often regardless of whether they are straight or not), to the detriment of gender non-conforming cisgender and transgender lives.[12] Because gender non-conforming cisgender people are often gay, trans conversion practices disproportionately impact cisgender gay individuals compared to cisgender straight ones. Defining trans conversion practices solely by the purpose of changing gender identity – neglecting how they target behaviour – underestimates their harm since they are also harmful to children who are not trans and will not grow up to be trans. Our definition must be adapted to account for these experiences.

In response to the problems with defining trans conversion practices around change, other theorists have proposed definitions that centre on the prevention of transgender identification and of gender non-conforming behaviour.[13] Julia Temple Newhook and colleagues offer a nuanced definition of conversion practices, highlighting that it originally referred to faith-based practices that sought to change sexual orientation but has expanded in recent years to include practices that seek to change gender identity or promote a preferred gender identity outcome.[14] Their definition better captures the goals of conversion practices – such as the promotion of preferred gender identity outcomes – and acknowledges the historicity of language. Unspoken in the definition is the shared understanding that the preferred gender identity outcome is aligned with the child's sex assigned at birth – we would not typically speak of conversion practices if someone were trying to make children trans. This distinction is important given the possible ethical differences between encouraging conformity to social norms and discouraging it. Individuals are subject to societal pressures towards conformity, and encouraging conformity reinforces those pressures whereas discouraging conformity provides an alternative and counterweight to them. Actively promoting trans outcomes, although ethically questionable, would not typically be seen as conversion practices.

Building upon previous attempts to define conversion practices and the limitations of focusing on changes to gender identity, I propose the following definition of trans conversion practices. Trans conversion practices refer to sustained efforts to promote gender identities that are aligned with the person's sex assigned at birth and/or to discourage behaviours associated with a gender other than the person's sex assigned at birth. Trans conversion practices are not exclusively practised on trans people and are often applied to people exhibiting gender non-conforming behaviour independently of gender identity.[15] The belief that being trans or gender creative is undesirable underpins the practices and often comes hand in hand with the belief that being trans or gender creative is pathological. Trans conversion practices take many forms, including behavioural therapy, psychodynamic therapy, parental counselling, and interventions in a naturalistic environment.[16] Play psychotherapy, limit setting on gender non-conforming behaviour, and the encouragement of peer relations with children of the same sex assigned at birth are commonly used in contemporary forms of conversion practices.

Is the Corrective Approach a Conversion Practice?

How far does the notion of conversion practices extend? Does it extend to all practices that seek to discourage being trans or reducing the likelihood of growing up trans? The corrective approach, which was promulgated by clinicians at the now closed CAMH clinic, featured prominently in the Canadian conversation on trans conversion practices and in Ontario's Bill 77, the *Affirming Sexual Orientation and Gender Identity Act*.[17] Also known as the psychotherapeutic, therapeutic, or pathological response approach, it has long played a prominent role in trans health and continues to be defended today.[18] I chose to call it the corrective approach to avoid the positive connotations of "therapeutic" and because the term pithily encapsulates its motivation: to "correct" gender creative children's identities and/or behaviours. Does the corrective approach fall under the umbrella of conversion practices? If it does, as I suggest in this section, then it is a mark of quality for bans on conversion practices to prohibit it.

Whether the corrective approach amounts to conversion practices has been controversial in the academic literature. Opponents of the approach have frequently likened it to conversion practices, whereas proponents of the approach have denied the accusations.[19] The corrective approach is directed towards gender-creative youth: its proponents adopt different approaches for children, adolescents, and adults. The belief that gender identity is malleable in children but typically not in adolescents and adults underpins the division into three groups.[20] However, the belief that corrective approaches should not be directed at adolescents and adults is not an unwavering commitment. Challenging adolescents' and adults' gender identity and delaying transition are often predicated on the same view that being transgender is pathological and that transition should be avoided as much as possible. Debates on the proposed developmental pathway of "rapid-onset gender dysphoria," which purports that youth are coming out as trans out of the blue due to "social contagion," have additionally hinted at an expansion of conversion practices to adolescents, and some authors have recently argued in favour of allowing conversion practices for adults.[21]

The goal of the corrective approach is to "cure" or "correct" trans and gender creative youth. According to a recent chapter co-authored by Jack Turban, Annelou L.C. de Vries, and Kenneth Zucker, this approach seeks "to reduce the child's cross-gender identification and gender dysphoria" and to "facilitate a gender identity that is more congruent with the patient's [sex assigned at birth]" through psychosocial interventions.[22]

The work of Susan J. Bradley and Kenneth Zucker, closely associated with the corrective approach, identifies the prevention of adult trans outcomes as one justification for the approach. They state that "prevention of transsexualism in adulthood [is] so obviously clinically valid and consistent with the ethics of our time that they constitute sufficient justification for therapeutic intervention."[23] Other justifications include the elimination of peer ostracism through enforced gender conformity and the treatment of other mental illnesses.[24] The reference to "other" mental illnesses in the context of the corrective approach is explained by its underlying view that gender variance and transitude have pathological foundations. As aptly summarized by Turban and Ehrensaft, "[t]his treatment approach presumes cisgender identification to be desirable, preventing the future need for hormonal intervention and protecting the child from the stigma of being a transgender individual."[25]

The proposed descriptions for the approach have evolved and become more nuanced. Current explanations of the approach often centre on wanting children to become comfortable in their skin and in the gender/sex they were assigned at birth, a description that has demonstrated considerable staying power over the last few decades.[26] Though rarely stating outright that the aim is to prevent adult trans outcomes, proponents of the approach nonetheless note that they find no "particular quarrel with the prevention of transsexualism as a treatment goal for children."[27] Of course, comfort in one's body and gender/sex assigned at birth is little better as a goal. Ultimately, it is just another way of saying that they do not want children to be trans or to grow up to be trans. Despite evolving descriptions, the corrective approach remains intent on reducing "the likelihood of [Gender Identity Disorder] persistence."[28] The reduction in distress and discomfort towards gendered bodily features brought about by gender transition does not seem to satisfy the proponents of the corrective approach.[29] According to the corrective approach, Gender Dysphoria – as a diagnosis under the fifth edition of the *Diagnostic and Statistical Manual of Mental Disorders* – remains a clinical problem even though people who have transitioned may lead perfectly happy lives free of distress towards their bodies. Gender Dysphoria (and, before it, Gender Identity Disorder) not only persists if there is ongoing distress towards one's body but also if the person would be distressed if they had not medically transitioned.[30] Under this logic, reducing the likelihood of Gender Dysphoria (or Gender Identity Disorder) persisting is essentially the same as reducing the likelihood of someone continuing to be trans. As sociologist Tey Meadow explains, the corrective approach holds that "short of psychologically damaging treatments, children should be encouraged to avoid transition if at all possible."[31] Unfortunately, proponents of the approach do not believe that it is tantamount to psychologically damaging treatment. Nor do they place much weight on its inherently demeaning nature for transgender people.

The corrective approach departs from prominent forms of trans conversion practices that have preceded it, which used a classic behavioural approach to change children's behaviours and identities. Proponents of the corrective approach are critical of classical behavioural therapy. However, they are critical of it not because behavioural therapy, and especially aversion therapies, may be harmful and degrading but, rather, because targeting behaviours alone may not "fully alter internal gender schemas" and children could "revert to their cross-gender behavioural preferences in the absence of external cues or incentives."[32] Instead, they rely on regular play psychotherapy, parent counselling, and parental limit setting on gender non-conforming behaviour.[33] The identification of factors that are said to contribute to gender identity and gender nonconformity also plays a crucial role in the treatment plan, with parents (and especially mothers) frequently being identified as a contributing cause of gender creativity in children.[34]

As Meadow explains, contrasting older approaches to the more recent gender-affirmative model,

> [b]efore the emergence of the trans child as a recognizable social category, psychiatry enlisted a binaristic understanding of gender development; on the one hand, there was normative gender, scaffolded by appropriate heterosexual dyadic parenting, and on the other, there was disordered gender. Disordered gender, whether underwritten by deficient parenting or psychopathology, was, in effect, a misperception on the part of the child about the relationship between body and psyche. It was a simple, dichotomous system. Children were either normatively gendered or psychiatrically ill.[35]

This explanation adroitly captures the conceptual logic under which the corrective approach operates – though the assumption of parental heterosexuality may be slowly waning. Gender creativity and being transgender are seen as constitutive of mental illness, and this assumption is so deeply rooted that it is rarely spelled out by theorists of the corrective approach and, instead, simply assumed.

The corrective approach plainly falls under the definition of conversion practices that I have proposed. However, proponents of the approach have long rejected labels such as "reparative therapy" and "conversion therapy."[36] It is unclear whether their claim that the corrective approach is not a conversion practice reflects a genuine theoretical position or a desire not to be associated with the politically loaded connotations of terms like "conversion practices." As far as I am aware, proponents of the corrective approach have not detailed their reasons for rejecting the terms. Some have suggested that the corrective approach should be treated differently because while sexual orientation is fixed, gender identity is malleable before puberty.[37] However, this argument understates the malleability of sexual orientation while overstating the evidence of the malleability of gender identity. The 2009 American Psychological Association's report on conversion practices assumed that sexual orientation can change and evolve, and it built its recommendations around the lack of evidence of malleability rather than on evidence of fixedness.[38] With respect to gender identity, the data used to support the claim that gender identity is malleable in youth was criticized for failing to distinguish trans and gender-creative youth from gender non-conforming youth who are cisgender.[39] Had they been valid, the studies would not have established that gender identity is malleable, rather than naturally evolving or fluid, like sexual orientation. It is not the same to say that gender identity is prone to change over time and that gender identity is malleable. Drivers can change the course of their car, but it does not mean that ramming into it with a truck is an effective or safe way of changing its direction.

Although not a proponent of the approach, William Byne, a professor of psychiatry at the Icahn School of Medicine at Mount Sinai, has argued that the corrective approach should not be construed as conversion therapy because there is no consensus over appropriate treatment for gender-creative youth, unlike treatment regarding sexual orientation.[40]

This critique is not convincing. Expressions such as "conversion therapy," "reparative therapy," and "conversion practices" do not imply the presence of consensus and can be deployed in its absence. What stands at the philosophical heart of these terms is a distinctively negative stance towards queerness and, through extension, transitude. The presence of consensus is of little matter. On the contrary, the expressions were being used long before a consensus was reached that these practices were unethical. The expression "reparative therapy" appears in the 1965 book *Sexual Inversion: The Multiple Roots of Homosexuality,* nine years before the 1974 reprint of the second edition of the *Diagnostic and Statistical Manual of Mental Disorders* declassified homosexuality.[41] The term was still prominently used by proponents of conversion practices long after the practices became discredited. As for conversion therapy, the term was used in the 1970s and 1980s, a time of significant debate surrounding the treatment of people who sought out conversion practices.[42] Yet, even if consensus was required before saying that an approach constitutes a conversion practice, the relevant consensus exists: attempting to change people's gender identity or to prevent them from growing up trans is unethical. Although the consensus over the best treatment for gender-creative youth is still emerging, there is a consensus that treatments seeking to align individuals' gender identity and gender expression with their sex assigned at birth are unethical.[43] We may not yet have reached a clinical consensus over which approach is the best, but a consensus was reached over the inadequacy of the corrective approach and other attempts to discourage trans outcomes.

The label of "conversion practices" groups together a wide range of practices based on shared traits and assumptions. Since the corrective approach seeks to discourage behaviours associated with a gender other than the one assigned at birth and/or promote gender identities that are aligned with the person's sex assigned at birth, it falls under the umbrella of trans conversion practices. Whether the corrective approach is outlawed by bans on trans conversion practices will be considered in greater detail in the next chapter. Since the corrective approach is the most thoroughly theorized form of trans conversion practices, this book will frequently refer to the work of proponents of the corrective approach as exemplars of conversion practices.

~

What counts as conversion practices is controversial and perhaps nowhere more so than in trans health. During the decades-long contestation of the CAMH clinic's approach to care, what counts as a conversion practice and whether the clinic's corrective approach falls under the umbrella has remained at the heart of the public debate. As I understand them throughout this book, trans conversion practices are sustained efforts to promote gender identities that are aligned with one's sex assigned at birth and/or to discourage behaviours associated with a gender other than the one assigned at birth. Shared by these practices is the philosophy that being trans or transitioning is pathological, undesirable, and something to be avoided. They can involve attempting to change, discourage, or repress the person's gender identity. They can also involve attempting to discourage gender transition. Whatever their form, they are trans conversion practices.

Interpreting the Scope of Bans   2

When the Centre for Addiction and Mental Health (CAMH) Gender Identity Clinic for Children and Youth underwent an external review following Ontario's proposed ban on conversion practices, some of its clinicians opined that their approach would not be prohibited by the upcoming law. I would venture to guess that few professionals engaging in trans conversion practices would readily admit that their actions run afoul the law of the land. Was the clinic's corrective approach contrary to Bill 77, which had come into force at the time the clinic was closed?[1] Or, asking more broadly, what is the scope of a standard ban on trans conversion practices? This chapter aims to answer these questions, elucidating the scope of bans on trans conversion practices using the Ontarian law as an example.

Known commonly as Bill 77, Ontario's *Affirming Sexual Orientation and Gender Identity Act* offers a promising case study for our purposes. Not only was it the first ban in Canada and found in the most populated of the country's provinces and territories, but it bears the unique distinction of having been adopted principally amidst concerns for the well-being of transgender youth. Its passage is embedded in a rich history of contestation to the CAMH clinic, discussed earlier in this book. Whereas most other laws have had sexual orientation as their primary focus – with some jurisdictions failing to protect gender identity at all – the Ontarian law centred trans voices throughout, making it a sensible choice for our study in interpretation. Taking Bill 77 as an exemplar of bans, this chapter sets out to define their scope by applying the traditional tools of statutory interpretation to the law, delving into legislative history and social context to highlight its wide breadth. Despite a lack of surface details, the chapter reveals that, under a proper interpretation, bans on conversion practices extend far enough to encompass practices bearing the psychopathologizing animus of the corrective approach employed at the defunct CAMH clinic.

The Ontario legislature intervened in the therapeutic world when, on June 4, 2015, the *Affirming Sexual Orientation and Gender Identity Act* came into force.[2] The statute, Bill 77, amended the *Regulated Health Professions Act, 1991*[3] to prohibit conversion practices.[4] As amended, the *Regulated Health Professions Act, 1991* states:

> 29.1 (1) No person shall, in the course of providing health care services, provide any treatment that seeks to change the sexual orientation or gender identity of a person under 18 years of age.
>
> (2) The treatments mentioned in subsection (1) do not include,
>
> > (a) services that provide acceptance, support or understanding of a person or the facilitation of a person's coping, social support or identity exploration or development; and
> >
> > (b) sex-reassignment surgery or any services related to sex-reassignment surgery.
>
> (3) Subsection (1) does not apply if the person is capable with respect to the treatment and consents to the provision of the treatment.
>
> (4) Despite the *Health Care Consent Act, 1996*, a substitute decision-maker may not give consent on a person's behalf to the provision of any treatment described in subsection (1).
>
> (5) Subject to the approval of the Lieutenant Governor in Council, the Minister may make regulations,
>
> > (a) clarifying the meaning of "sexual orientation," "gender identity" or "seek to change" for the purposes of subsection (1);

(b) exempting any person or treatment from the application of subsection (1).

Situated in the *Regulated Health Professions Act,* the section is enforced through complaints and independent investigations by the
regulating bodies of the professions covered by the act.

Two notions must be elucidated if we wish to determine the reach of the
law: gender identity and change thereof. Figuring out those concepts is
an invitation to foray into legislative history, previous judicial determinations, the social context of the legislation, and external texts that informed
the drafting of the law. Throughout this chapter, we should interpret the
law's words "in their entire context and in their grammatical and ordinary sense harmoniously with the scheme of the [law], the object of the
[law], and the intention of [the legislature]."[5]

Defining "Gender Identity"

For Bill 77 to be effective in prohibiting conversion practices, "gender
identity" must be interpreted to include self-reported gender identity.
Interpreting "gender identity" as only referring to the person's "true"
gender identity, as assessed by the practitioner and independent of the
person's self-report, would prevent the bill from effectively prohibiting
trans conversion practices since any practitioner could defend against
a complaint by claiming that the patient or client's underlying gender
identity differs from their self-reported identity. Practitioners could simply claim that youth are deluded about their gender identity to justify
engaging in conversion practices.[6] In this section, I consider the history
of the term "gender identity," the definition provided by the Ontario
Human Rights Commission, the legislative history of Bill 77, and its
social context to conclude that "gender identity" refers to a person's
self-reported identity.

History of Gender Identity

Gender identity originated in US medical discourse and later made its
way into Canadian law through court and tribunal decisions, known
as case law. Although much of this case law arose outside of Ontario,

other provinces' case law interpreting gender identity is relevant to Ontario given the influence that this case law had on the development of Ontarian human rights law. Gender identity was coined in 1963 by Robert Stoller and Ralph Greeson at the International Psycho-Analytic Congress.[7] In 1964, Robert Stoller wrote that gender identity refers to the "the sense of knowing to which sex one belongs, that is, the awareness 'I am a male' or 'I am a female'," adding that it "clearly refers to one's self-image as regards belonging to a specific sex."[8] It began appearing in Canadian jurisprudence in the 1990s.[9]

In 1992, the Workers' Compensation Appeal Tribunal had to answer whether being trans precluded the worker from rehabilitation following ankle and shoulder injuries.[10] The implicated individual was an adult patient of the Clarke Institute's Gender Identity Clinic, which later merged into CAMH, and had been diagnosed with Gender Identity Disorder. Considering the question before it, the tribunal determined that she could engage in a rehabilitation program leading to employment. Her being trans did not impact her ability to work and, thus, to be rehabilitated. A few years later, the germinal case from British Columbia, *Sheridan v Sanctuary Investments Ltd*, established that trans people could access the washrooms corresponding to their gender identity.[11] It relied on a Québec decision that centred the notion of "identité sexuelle," the then common French term for gender identity.[12] In *Sheridan*, expert testimony explained gender identity as "the person's inner subjective experience of femininity or masculinity," analogizing a trans woman's gender identity to having "a female brain." This characterization was adopted by the tribunal. *Sheridan* has frequently been cited in Ontario human rights cases.[13] The term has since evolved in popular and legal usage, notably through the growing acknowledgment of non-binary genders.[14] The words "gender identity" can now be found in human rights instruments across Canada.

Contemporary definitions of gender identity are similar to the one provided by Stoller in 1963. The World Professional Association for Transgender Health's "Standards of Care" define gender identity as "[a] person's intrinsic sense of being male (a boy or a man), female (a girl or a woman), or an alternative gender (e.g., boygirl, girlboy, transgender, genderqueer, eunuch)."[15] The international *Yogyakarta Principles*, an authoritative international human rights document developed by human rights experts convened by the International Commission of Jurists and the International Service for Human Rights, understand gender identity as "each person's deeply felt internal and individual experience of gender, which may or may not correspond with the sex assigned at birth, including the personal sense of the body (which may involve, if freely chosen, modification of bodily appearance or function by medical, surgical or other means) and other expressions of gender, including dress, speech and mannerisms."[16]

The Ontario Human Rights Commission's (OHRC) Definition
The definition given by the OHRC in its *Policy on Preventing Discrimination because of Gender Identity and Gender Expression* reflects an understanding of gender identity that is largely in line with the initial coinage: "Gender identity is each person's internal and individual experience of gender."[17] The OHRC's definition helps to interpret Bill 77. Although they are not laws, the policies of the commission carry an unmistakable weight. The *Human Rights Code* requires that the Ontario Human Rights Tribunal consider the OHRC's policies when deciding a case if it is requested by one of the parties.[18] This requirement indicates that the legislature intends the OHRC's policies to be used as interpretive guides in judicial decision-making. Legislatures are presumed to be aware of the case law – and, presumably, their governmental bodies' policies – when they are interpreting a term.[19] In the absence of indications otherwise, adopting the language of "gender identity," which is also found in the Ontario *Human Rights Code*,[20] should be presumed to be an adoption of the interpretation of the concept in the OHRC's policies and under the law.

Legislative History
The legislative history of the bill complicates this picture. Bill 77 originally specified that gender identity was "the patient's self-identified ... gender identity," but the wording was removed. The significance of this removal is ambiguous. On the one hand, the original wording could be interpreted as evidence of legislative intent. In that reading, the goal of the law is to protect self-reported gender identity, preventing professionals

from arguing that they did not seek to change the patient's gender identity since the patient was merely mistaken in reporting their gender identity. The word "self-identified" may have been removed because it is unnecessary, "gender identity" already referring to self-identification.

On the other hand, its removal could be interpreted as evidence that legislators did not wish to extend protection to self-identification and only decided to protect the "real" underlying gender identity. Yet human rights law does not typically require proof of gender identity as a precondition of protection.[21] An assertion suffices in the absence of a serious reason to doubt the expressed gender identity.[22] It could be argued that mental health professionals are in a position to assess whether there are serious reasons to doubt the person's self-identification and that they are therefore in a unique position to assess the accuracy of self-reported gender identity. Unlike Québec, Ontario requires a letter from a licensed physician or psychologist attesting that they "are of the opinion that the change of sex designation on the birth registration is appropriate" before changing said sex designation.[23] The recognition of professionals' legitimacy in assessing whether a person is transgender, although questionable,[24] could be read as favouring an interpretation of Bill 77 that enables professionals to doubt gender self-identification and act upon that doubt. However, the legislature is presumed to know the case law interpreting the notion of gender identity, and, thus far, human rights law has relied on self-reporting.

Social Context
A different principle of interpretation is of aid here. Plainly stated, legislation is intended to address a problem. As Justice Ian Binnie stated in *Re Canada 3000*, "[t]he notion that a statute is to be interpreted in light of the problem it was intended to address is as old at least as the 16th century."[25] Conversion practices are commonly justified by the belief that the person's gender identity is not an expression of a true gendered self. Since it is impossible to externally confirm a person's gender identity, it will always be possible to claim that the person's self-reported gender identity is mistaken. To exclude from application instances of conversion practices where practitioners argue that the person's expressed gender identity reflected a false belief would deprive the law of its ability to

address the ill towards which it is directed. Taken together, the factors considered in this section suggest that "gender identity" in Bill 77 should be interpreted as including self-reported gender identity.

Defining "Seeks to Change"

Insofar as Bill 77 only applies to those who seek to change a person's gender identity, does it ban all forms of conversion practices? In this section, I interpret the scope of the words "seeks to change." Three aspects of the bill are informative when interpreting these words: the removal of "or direct" from earlier drafts of the bill, the Standing Committee on Justice Policy hearings, and the list of exceptions in section 29.1(2) of Bill 77. I conclude that "seeks to change" must be interpreted as extending to all forms of conversion practices, including the corrective approach.

Removing "or Direct" from Bill 77

The original version of the bill, as tabled by Cheri DiNovo, was not only limited to services that seek to change gender identity but also included services that seek to direct gender identity. The words "or direct" were removed from the final version of the bill at the request of members of the governing Liberal Party.[26] The removal of "or direct" could be interpreted as evidence of an intention not to ban practices that seek to direct gender identity. Under this interpretation, mere pressure or nudging – however strong – does not constitute prohibited conduct. It is necessary that the practice amount to attempting to change the identity. This interpretation fails to prohibit the full range of trans conversion practices and would leave many conversion practices legal, such as the corrective approach. It would void the bill of its ability to address the very ill that it seeks to prohibit. In Ontario, statutes "shall be interpreted as being remedial and shall be given such fair, large and liberal interpretation as best ensures the attainment of its objects,"[27] and this object includes all practices that seek to discourage identification with a gender other than the one assigned at birth, even if they primarily operate through interventions at the level of gender expression.

A second possible interpretation is that the shift from "change or direct" to "change" was motivated by a desire to tighten the language of the bill and avoid ambiguity. Under this interpretation, the fact that "or direct" was included in the original language indicates an intention to prohibit more than may be captured by a narrow reading of the word "change" but was later removed for fear that relatively trivial pressures could be said to direct gender identity. This is not unusual; laws are sometimes written with more terms just to be sure and subsequently pared down to reduce redundancy, the simpler language being believed to be broad enough. I believe that this second interpretation is more faithful to legislative intent, which I discuss in the following section, and better prohibits the full scope of trans conversion practices.

Prohibiting Therapies That Seek to Avoid Adult Trans Outcomes
The legislative history of the bill suggests that the legislature intended Bill 77 to include the corrective approach and other practices that aim at discouraging or reducing the likelihood of trans outcomes. Although legislative history does not constitute incontrovertible evidence of legislative intent, it is a relevant aid in determining the problem that the bill sought to address.[28] The Standing Committee on Justice Policy hearings, before the third reading of Bill 77, provided evidence of the legislative desire to prohibit therapies that aim at preventing or minimizing adult trans outcomes. Cheri DiNovo, who sponsored Bill 77, stated before the committee that the bill was proposed at the suggestion of the trans community organization TG Innerselves, among others, and was designed to lower suicidality among queer and especially trans youth.[29] Vincent Bolt spoke for the group TG Innerselves and framed conversion practices as practices that make patients "feel like [their] entire being [is] wrong," giving the example of Leelah Alcorn as a victim of trans conversion practices.[30] Leelah Alcorn was a transgender girl from the United States who died of suicide at seventeen years old after being subjected to conversion practices. A note she left on her Tumblr ended with the words: "Fix society. Please."

The testimony of Erika Muse, a trans woman who spoke of undergoing conversion practices as an adolescent and young adult, also highlights the broader understanding of conversion practices that motivated Bill 77. In her opening statement to the second reading of the bill, Cheri

DiNovo referred to Erika Muse's testimony as a motivation to adopt a ban.[31] Before the legislative committee tasked with studying the bill, Muse gave the following account:

> I was denied the medication I asked for that was appropriate for my age, but I had to return for more therapy. In each appointment that I came to, he would comment on newly masculinized parts of my body that had been changing due to puberty – parts he could have stopped from developing had he given me care – then asked me how I could possibly pass as a woman in my future life. He would berate me for not meeting unknown expectations and excoriated my life at that point. Sessions were not therapeutic, but abusive. ... Eventually, he relented and allowed me some care, but I think the only reason he did is that I proved to him I couldn't be fixed. ... I've been suicidal and depressed due to his treatment of me. My self-identity is ruined, and only in the past year have I gained any self-esteem. I live in a body I hate, due to him.[32]

Her emotional talk before the Standing Committee on Justice Policy provides important insight into the context that gave rise to Bill 77.[33] Given that she was invited to speak about her experience before the committee and that Cheri DiNovo specifically referred to her testimony during the second reading of the bill, we have good reasons to believe that avoiding experiences like those she spoke of was part of the *raison d'être* of Bill 77.

Erika Muse had been a patient of the CAMH clinic. As we saw, the clinic made use of the corrective approach, which aims at reducing the likelihood of youth growing up trans.[34] The corrective approach focuses on prepubertal youth, and clinicians using the approach have often claimed to employ a different one for older individuals, believing their gender identity to be less malleable.[35] However, Muse's statements before the legislature gestured towards a similar approach being applied to adolescents and young adults. It is unnecessary for us to delve into whether clinicians at the CAMH clinic indeed applied a similar approach to adolescents and young adults. For statutory interpretation, what matters is the language used before the legislature. Muse spoke of attempts to discourage her from being trans and transitioning. For the law to address the practices that legislators had in mind, it must include clinical approaches that aim at discouraging or reducing the likelihood of trans outcomes. That was how Muse described the conversion practices she experienced in testimony that was emphasized at the bill's second reading by its sponsor. Interpreting "seeks to change" narrowly and excluding practices that demonstrate hostility to trans outcomes from the ban would mean failing to prohibit approaches that were part and parcel of the ban's inspiration.

The intent to prohibit the corrective approach was also evidenced when Cheri DiNovo, Bill 77's sponsor, quoted Jake Pyne at second reading, saying: "If your practice does not respect gender diversity, if in fact, you insist on treating gender diversity in young people as a disorder to be cured or prevented, then you will no longer have the use of public funds to do so."[36] This quote was taken from an article in *NOW Toronto* that questioned the ethicality of the practices at the CAMH clinic.[37] Before the Standing Committee, Pyne later framed the practices targeted by the bill as "treatment that seeks to correct young people," a framing that is reminiscent of the definition proposed in the introduction and that invites us to adopt a broad and liberal interpretation of "change" so as to include practices that seek to prevent or minimize the likelihood of adult trans outcomes.

Legislative history suggests that the legislature intended for Bill 77 to be interpreted broadly to include all forms of conversion practices. The term "seeks to change" should be interpreted in light of this intent and include approaches that discourage behaviours associated with a gender other than the one assigned at birth and/or promote gender identities that are aligned with the person's sex assigned at birth. Seeking to alter the development of the gender identity of a child who did not yet report it and attempting to change their eventual gender identity so that it aligns with the gender they were assigned at birth in adolescence and adulthood – these are no less attempts to impress a change onto the child's gender identity. If it were otherwise, gay conversion practices targeting young children would be legal since sexual orientation often develops in adolescence – an equally absurd result. Insofar as there is no unmediated access to gender identity, change to it can only operate (if at all) by interfering in the psychological processes through which gender identity is developed and consolidated.[38] In this light, the distinction between seeking to alter a present gender identity and preventing an eventual gender identity falls by the wayside. To the practitioners who say "I didn't try to change your gender identity! I just tried to change the gender identity you would have had if I hadn't interfered," I can only respond: that is no better. Nor is the fact that some children may not have grown up trans provide much of a defence, given that the practices are, at their core, directed towards those who would. Others are merely casualties. And, here too, I would respond: that is no better.

Interpreting Subsection 29.1(1) Together with Subsection 29.1(2)

Subsection 29.1(2) is indicative of legislative intent. Reading subsections 29.1(1) and 29.1(2) of the law together suggests that the prohibition of conversion practices should be interpreted broadly as including all forms of conversion practices, including the corrective approach. I begin by arguing that subsection 29.1(2) suggests that subsection 29.1(1) should be interpreted broadly and that all forms of conversion practices are therefore prohibited. I then consider two possible counterarguments. The first counterargument advances that if the legislature wanted to include the corrective approach under the prohibition, it would have done so explicitly. The second counterargument advances that many forms of conversion practices, such as the corrective approach, fall under an exception set out in subsection 29.1(2). As I will show, neither of these counterarguments is plausible.

For convenience, I reproduce the subsections of the act:

29.1 (1) No person shall, in the course of providing health care services, provide any treatment that seeks to change the sexual orientation or gender identity of a person under 18 years of age.

(2) The treatments mentioned in subsection (1) do not include,

(a) services that provide acceptance, support or understanding of a person or the facilitation of a person's coping, social support or identity exploration or development; and

(b) sex-reassignment surgery or any services related to sex-reassignment surgery.

If subsection 29.1(1) was to be interpreted narrowly, it would be unnecessary to exclude affirmative practices in subsection 29.1(2), as they would plainly not be included in the notion of conversion practices. This exclusion provision shows legislative awareness that subsection 29.1(1) is phrased broadly, including such a wide range of practices that they found it wise to specify that affirmative practices are not prohibited. They did not provide an exception for practices that seek to prevent adult trans outcomes, even though they would surely be prohibited under any interpretation of subsection 29.1(1) that would also prohibit the affirmative practices set out under subsection 29.1(2). If the legislature had wanted to only prohibit practices that narrowly seek to change gender identity, but not those that seek to prevent, discourage, or minimize the likelihood of adult trans outcomes, they would have explicitly excluded those practices. We must therefore infer that all forms of conversion practices, including the corrective approach, are prohibited by subsection 29.1(1).

A first possible counterargument is that if the legislature wanted to prohibit the corrective approach – which seeks to discourage or minimize the likelihood of trans outcomes – it would have done so explicitly. This counterargument is related to the argument, considered earlier in this chapter, that removing "or direct" from Bill 77 is evidence that the legislature did not intend for merely directing or discouraging gender identities to be prohibited. As I have pointed out, removing these terms is equally compatible with an understanding that "seeks to change" is already sufficiently broad to capture all forms of conversion practices. An analogous response can be given here. Subsection 29.1(2) suggests that the legislature intended subsection 29.1(1) to be interpreted broadly. If subsection 29.1(1) is broadly and liberally interpreted, it is unnecessary to specify that all forms of conversion practices, including the corrective approach, are prohibited since that is what subsection 29.1(1) already does. This counterargument would have been more convincing had Bill 77 included a list of practices included under the prohibition. Since it does not and since subsection 29.1(1) is to be interpreted broadly, the counterargument fails.

A second possible counterargument is that some forms of conversion practices, and especially the corrective approach, fall under an exception set out in subsection 29.1(2). However, interpreting the exceptions set out in that subsection as shielding some forms of conversion practices is inconsistent with both the spirit and letter of these exclusions. As I argue below, the textual source of subsection 29.1(2) makes it clear that it only excludes affirmative approaches. This conclusion obtains whether subsection 29.1(2) is interpreted as an exhaustive or as an illustrative list.

Subsection 29.1(2) can be interpreted as either an exhaustive list or an illustrative list. When one or more instances are mentioned that fall within a given class of things – in the present case, therapeutic practices – other instances are implicitly excluded. This is the principle of *expressio unius est exclusio alterius*.[39] The principle, however, only applies where the list is exhaustive. A list is exhaustive when it lists all of the possibilities, and nothing outside the list is allowed. It is instead illustrative if it gives some examples but leaves open the possibility of other options. For instance, "pets are dogs and cats" suggests exhaustiveness, whereas "pets include dogs and cats" suggests that the list is illustrative. Exhaustive lists are sometimes called closed lists, and illustrative lists are sometimes called open lists. The application of the *expression unius* principle can be rejected if, with regard to the context as a whole, the list is best interpreted as illustrative – as is the case when the *ejusdem generis* principle is applied. The *ejusdem generis* principle pulls in the other direction. When illustrative examples are given alongside general wording that expands from those examples, further instances should only be interpreted as falling under the provision if they are of the same type as the illustrative examples.[40] For example, if one were to interpret "other foodstuffs" in a statute referring to "bananas, apples, peaches, and other foodstuffs," the *ejusdem generis* rule would invite us to restrict "other foodstuffs" to fruits.

Both principles are relevant to interpreting subsection 29.1(2). Under the *ejusdem generis* principle, conversion practices may be excluded from the subsection 29.1(1) prohibition if they are in the spirit of listed exclusions, whereas under the *expressio unius* principle, they may only be excluded from the prohibition if they fall within the letter of an exclusion listed under 29.1(2). Although, at first glance, subsection 29.1(2) does not appear to have the type of general wording that would invite an application of the *ejusdem generis* principle, the subsection itself can be interpreted either as an interpretive guide to subsection 29.1(1) or as an exhaustive list of exclusions to it. Put more simply, the subsections can be read together either as "conversion practices are prohibited, and by conversion practices we do not mean gender-affirmative care" or as "conversion practices are prohibited but we exclude the following practices from the prohibition." The fact that the heading between subsections 29.1(1) and 29.1(2) reads "Exception" seems to lend credence to the interpretation that the latter states an exception. However, the choice of wording "do not include," instead of a clearer statement of exception, such as "[s]ubsection (1) does not apply with respect to," as found in subsection 30(1) of the same statute,[41] points in the opposite direction.

It is unnecessary to determine whether subsection 29.1(2) should be read as an exhaustive or an illustrative list because all conversion practices including the corrective approach are contrary to both the letter and the spirit of subsection 29.1(2). Thus, even if the *ejusdem generis* principle is the applicable one, the corrective approach remains prohibited. The textual source of subsection 29.1(2) makes it clear that both the spirit of subsection 29.1(2) and the meaning of each individual exclusion are geared towards practices that are gender affirmative and neutral with regard to gender identity outcomes. Taking the textual source of subsection 29.1(2) into consideration, it appears that all psychosocial interventions that fall under the notion of conversion practices are prohibited by Bill 77. Subsection 29.1(2) is textually lifted from the *Report of the American Psychological Association Task Force on Appropriate Therapeutic Responses to Sexual Orientation (Task Force report)*.[42] It is also found in each of the US state laws on conversion practices. The similarity of the texts is relevant to interpretation. In *R. v McIntosh*, the Supreme Court of Canada was faced with interpreting the self-defence provisions under the *Criminal Code*.[43] At the time, the provisions bore a striking textual similarity to the homologous New Zealand provision. Speaking for the majority, Justice Antonio Lamer relied on this similarity to interpret the Canadian law:

> If Parliament's intention is to be implied from its legislative actions, then there is a compelling argument that Parliament intended s. 34(2) to be available to initial aggressors. When Parliament revised the *Criminal Code* in 1955, it could have included a provocation

requirement in s. 34(2). ... The fact that Parliament did not choose this route is the best and only evidence we have of legislative intention, and this evidence certainly does not support the Crown's position.[44]

It seems reasonable to think that such an inference of legislative intention would also be available where the source text is non-legislative in nature. The reasoning of the Supreme Court of Canada relied not on the fact that the law's text was lifted from another statute but, rather, that it was lifted at all. The decision implies that a law's meaning should be presumed to be the same as its source material except for the parts where the two texts differ. Unlike the situation in *McIntosh,* however, subsection 29.1(2) does not significantly differ from the language of the *Task Force report.* The substitution of "and" for "or" is largely stylistic and does not alter the meaning of the listed interventions.

Given the close relationship between the two texts, the *Task Force report* is a powerful textual aid in interpreting the meaning of the legal provision. The exclusions set out in subsection 29.1(2) are grouped together in the report under the label of "affirmative therapeutic interventions."[45] Although the *Task Force report* explicates affirmative interventions within the context of sexual orientation, their descriptions apply *mutatis mutandis* to gender identity. For instance, they state that "same-sex sexual attractions, behavior, and orientations per se are normal and positive variants of human sexuality; in other words, they are not indicators of mental or developmental disorders" would apply equally to gender identity.[46] Having a gender identity that differs from the gender we were assigned at birth is a normal and positive variant of human gender subjectivity and is not an indicator of mental disorder, as confirmed by the *Diagnostic and Statistical Manual of Mental Disorders*'s shift in language from Gender Identity Disorder to Gender Dysphoria.[47]

The label is indicative of the spirit binding together the various subsection 29.1(2) exclusions. Under the *ejusdem generis* principle, the corrective approach would only be excluded if it can be termed an affirmative therapeutic intervention, which it cannot. The label is also useful when applying the *expressio unius* principle since it can help us interpret the meaning of listed exclusions: they must be interpreted in a way that is compatible with the label "affirmative therapeutic intervention." I now turn to the meaning of listed exclusions and conclude that none of them can be read to include the corrective approach or any other form of conversion practices. All forms of conversion practices are prohibited from subsection 29.1(1) and cannot be saved by subsection 29.1(2).

Based on the *Task Force report*, subsection 29.1(2)(a) can be subdivided into (1) acceptance and support; (2) understanding; (3) coping; (4) social support; and (5) identity exploration and development. Since subsection 29.1(2)(b) is not primarily concerned with psychotherapeutic interventions, I do not concern myself with elucidating the precise meaning of "sex-reassignment surgery or any services related to sex-reassignment surgery." The subsection may be there to prevent people from arguing that supporting transition is a conversion practice because people's sexual orientation labels may change (for example, from a lesbian to a straight man) with transition. While ludicrous, this argument has been deployed in bad faith by some anti-trans advocates.[48] It may also be a holdover from bans in the United States, which protect against attempts to change gender expression. Without a provision like subsection 29.1(2)(b), supporting someone's transition would risk being interpreted as an attempt to change their gender expression in violation of the law. In either case, the subsection is concerned with services that are integral to the person's medical transition – services that have nothing to do with trans conversion practices as understood in this book.

The notion of acceptance and support in subsection 29.1(2)(a) is grounded in the client-centred approach to therapeutic care. It is practised through "unconditional positive regard for and congruence and empathy with the client," "openness to the client's perspective as a means of understanding their concerns," and "encouragement of the client's positive self-concept."[49] The practice is non-judgmental and thus cannot exhibit any preference of outcome and primarily aims at reducing distress brought on by stigma, isolation, and internalized shame.[50] In the context of clients who wish to change their gender identity, acceptance and support mean addressing the conflict between identity and desire in a non-judgmental manner – the therapist must not judge the person for having difficulty accepting themselves – by exploring why they want to change their identity.

The provision of understanding in subsection 29.1(2)(a) corresponds in the report to comprehensive assessments. A comprehensive assessment is undertaken "in order to obtain a fuller understanding of the multiple issues that influence" the trans or gender-creative person's desire not to be trans, foregrounding the interconnectedness of gender identity and the whole person.[51] Depression, anxiety, post-traumatic stress, risky sexual practices, substance abuse, and intimate partner violence are common among trans people, in large part due to stigma and poor self-image.[52] Past traumatic experiences as well as cultural and family context are also crucial to gain a full picture of the person. This assessment is not geared towards identifying factors that may lead people to be trans or gender creative, as is the case under the corrective approach.[53] Approaches that seek to understand why a person identifies the way they do, especially in the hopes of acting upon that identification, would not fall under the notion of understanding as set out in the *Task Force report* and, thus, subsection 29.1(2). Understanding why someone is trans is fundamentally distinct from understanding why someone does not want to be trans, which is the goal of a comprehensive assessment, as set out in the report.

The *Task Force report* encourages mental health professionals to empower patients with strategies that "resolve, endure, or diminish stressful life experiences" because being trans or gender creative can be a difficult experience due to the pervasiveness of transantagonism.[54] This section of the report corresponds to the notion of coping in subsection 29.1(2)(a). A range of coping strategies is proposed, including multiple common therapeutic interventions such as cognitive-behavioural therapy,[55] mindfulness-based therapy, and narrative therapy. Like acceptance and support, these interventions aim at reducing distress brought on by stigma, isolation, and shame. While coping could sometimes be achieved by adopting a gender expression aligned with one's sex assigned at birth, the exception would not be satisfied by clinical approaches that are grounded in negative attitudes towards being transgender, that seek to align gender identity with sex assigned at birth, or that fail to appreciate the negative psychological impact of staying closeted.

The inclusion of social support in subsection 29.1(2)(a) reflects the task force's recognition that "struggling with a devalued identity without adequate social support has the potential to erode psychological well-being."[56] Access to mutual support groups, self-help groups, welcoming communities, and psychotherapy are all encouraged by the *Task Force report* for their positive impact on minority stress, marginalization, and isolation. The gender-affirmative approach to trans youth care has indeed long foregrounded the importance of support groups and group treatment for gender creative youth and their parents.[57]

The facilitation of identity exploration and development, the final intervention in subsection 29.1(2)(a), is also detailed in the *Task Force report*. According to the report, these interventions are predicated on the idea that "conflicts among disparate elements of identity appear to play a major role in the distress of those seeking" conversion practices.[58] Identity is understood holistically and is not limited to gender identity: "[I]dentity comprises a coherent sense of one's needs, beliefs, values, and roles, including those aspects of oneself that are the bases of social stigma, such as age, gender, race, ethnicity, disability, national origin, socioeconomic status, religion, spirituality, and sexuality."[59] Identity development refers to a specific, active manner of "exploring and assessing one's identity," in light of its various components, "and establishing a commitment to an integrated identity."[60] In line with the gender-affirmative model, the role of mental health professionals is to facilitate this process without preference for the end outcome. As the report clearly sets out, "the treatment does not differ, although the outcome does."[61]

Gender-creative youth may grow up female, male, or non-binary. They may have a clear relationship to various components of gender – identity, expression, norms, and roles – or not.[62] Contrary to the oft-repeated distinction made by proponents of the corrective approach between the malleability of gender identity and the fixedness of sexual orientation, the *Task Force report* assumes that sexual orientation can evolve and change over time.[63] Their discussion of identity exploration and development, though set out in the context of sexual orientation, is equally applicable to gender identity and would preclude interventions that seek to discourage, prevent, or minimize the chance of developing or maintaining a certain gender identity.

All of the subdivisions of the *Task Force report* that inform subsection 29.1(2)(a) share a vision of therapeutic interventions that endeavour to help the person accept their gender identity and develop a positive self-image and help them manage the difficulties and distress associated with being trans or gender non-conforming in a transantagonistic society. The list can be best summarized as "affirmative therapeutic interventions" for those who are struggling with their gender identity. Conversion practices are inconsistent with these goals. The corrective approach's avowed goal of preventing trans outcomes – whether couched in terms of "prevention of transsexualism in adulthood"[64] or reducing "the likelihood of GID [gender identity disorder] persistence"[65] – through psychosocial interventions is diametrically contrary to the affirmative view espoused in the *Task Force report* and Bill 77.

Psychosocial interventions that are part of conversion practices, such as the corrective approach, are prohibited by subsection 29.1(1). This conclusion can be reached whether we interpret subsection 29.1(2) as a closed or open list. Neither the *ejusdem generis* nor the *expressio unius est exclusio alterius* principles save the corrective approach, as it does not fall under the listed exclusions and does not comport with the affirmative spirit that underpins them. If the legislature wished to exclude some conversion practices from the scope of the prohibition, it would have done so. The fact that it chose to provide an exception for affirmative practices but not the corrective approach – despite the latter falling much closer to the language of "seeks to change gender identity" – is evidence of the legislative intent to prohibit all forms of conversion practices.

~

Based on the foregoing, it seems that the best reading of Bill 77 is one under which all forms of trans conversion practices are prohibited, including the corrective approach practised at the defunct CAMH clinic. The legislative history, social context, external co-texts, and previous judicial determinations all point towards that conclusion, as does a holistic reading of the law. If Bill 77 is any indication, bans on trans conversion practices may well achieve their goal. It makes sense to wonder, at this point, whether my analysis would transfer well to other jurisdictions. I drew a lot on the detailed legislative history of Bill 77, which centred on trans conversion practices and Erika Muse's testimony regarding her experiences at the CAMH clinic. This legislative history is specific to Bill 77, and other jurisdictions cannot borrow from it. In most jurisdictions, legislative history centres on sexual orientation rather than on gender identity. While that is a significant contextual difference, the interpretive arguments that I deployed towards gender identity have close analogues for sexual orientation. To the extent that the histories and forms of conversion practices targeting sexual orientation and gender identity are similar, the arguments applicable to one should also apply *mutatis mutandis* to the other.

The task of legal interpretation unfolds in ways that are specific to each jurisdiction. The Canadian approach to interpretation is informative because of the breadth of its outlook. Judges must read words "in their entire context and in their grammatical and ordinary sense harmoniously with the scheme of the [law], the object of the [law], and the intention of [the legislature]."[66] We have to consider the traditional plain meaning rule ("according to their grammatical and ordinary sense") and the mischief rule ("according to the object of the law"). Regardless of which considerations attract emphasis in other jurisdictions, this chapter probably discussed them.

Different interpretive difficulties will emerge in different jurisdictions. Interpreting laws in Canada places significant emphasis on their goal. How would jurisdictions employing a more textualist approach decide among the multiple meanings and scope of terms such as "gender identity" and "change"? Looking at the listed exceptions, as I did with subsection 29.1(2), can be helpful, but it only goes so far. The more considerations we take out from Canada's purposive and holistic approach, the more difficult interpreting bans becomes. The social, moral, and clinical concerns that motivated the Ontario legislature to adopt Bill 77 spread far beyond its borders. Though there will be differences between bans, my analysis of Ontario's law offers a blueprint for how to read legislation addressing the same mischief: trans conversion practices. In the next chapter, I zoom out from Ontario and look at the shape of bans worldwide. This comparative exercise reveals the many similarities shared by Ontario's and other jurisdictions' bans, pointing towards a shared purpose and, one would hope, interpretation.

Legal Variants across the Globe   **3**

Having defined the scope of an archetypical ban on trans conversion practices, I now zoom out to a comparative perspective that will help us to tease out the similarities and differences among bans worldwide. Comparing the different laws helps us predict how well the analysis proposed in the preceding chapter might apply to other laws. More importantly, surveying the field offers an empirical basis for Chapter 5's policy analysis and provides inspiration for the supplement and improvements to the bans proposed in Chapters 6 and 7.

Despite the large number of jurisdictions that have adopted bans, clear trends can be identified, gesturing towards a roughly shared scope. Accordingly, my analysis of Bill 77, the *Affirming Sexual Orientation and Gender Identity Act,* may be partly portable to other jurisdictions.[1] I propose a dual typology of bans on trans conversion practices based on textual lineage and sanctions. This dual typology highlights two distinct but important aspects of bans: the scope of behaviours they apply to and the means they employ to discourage these behaviours. I have chosen to highlight textual lineage because of the importance of the law's text in ascertaining its scope. As I highlight, many of the laws draw some of their language from the *Report of the American Psychological Association Task Force on Appropriate Therapeutic Responses to Sexual Orientation* (*Task Force report*).[2] Textual similarities also lead to shared definitional benefits and limitations, which are considered in Chapter 5. Whereas textual groupings point to definitional limitations, grouping bans based on whom the law applies to and how it targets their behaviour emphasizes their benefits and limits with regard to the means they employ in banning trans conversion practices.

Methodologically, the bans were collated by conducting a review of the legal, healthcare, and social sciences literature on conversion practices, extensively searching for news reports using web and scholarly search engines, keeping track of new bans that were reported in my social network (which includes many survivors, advocates, scholars, and policy-makers interested in the regulation of conversion practices), and setting up alerts for new content mentioning conversion practices on the Internet and in the scholarly literature. My search was strongly limited by my linguistic abilities and social network. I am a resident of Canada who is fluent in French and English and has some understanding of Spanish. My social network centres on Canada, the United States, and the United Kingdom, although it also includes advocates and scholars from Europe, Asia, and South America. Because of linguistic limitations, laws that are not published in French, English, or Spanish were excluded from my analysis, such as the German law. This is a significant limitation.

English-speaking countries from the Global North are often assumed to be human rights leaders. I would caution against assuming that lists centring on English, French, and Spanish and biased towards the Global North are exhaustive or nearly exhaustive. Argentina, a South American Spanish-speaking country, is frequently noted as a leader on trans rights. Argentina hosts "one of the world's most comprehensive transgender rights laws under which people can legally change their gender without surgery."[3] Pakistan, a South Asian country where Urdu and English are co-official languages, has one of the most progressive laws for name and gender marker changes in the world.[4] We should resist the assumption that countries from the Global South are necessarily less legislatively advanced when it comes to trans rights.

To be included in the analysis, bans had to come into force by July 2020, had to take an enforceable legislative or executive form, had to be adopted at the national or subnational level, and had to ban trans conversion practices. For practical reasons, I had to stop updating the list at some point and chose July 2020 as the end date of my research. I did not include bans that do not apply to the entire country or to a large subdivision of it (such as a state or province). I did not include municipal bans – except for the District of Columbia because I'm feeling spicy.[5] Municipal bans often have a more limited legal reach, and including them would have been too unwieldy for analysis due to their large number. Most bans that I included are statutes, but some of them, like the one from Puerto Rico, are executive orders. I did not include general, non-enforceable guidance to professional associations or bans that were led by professional associations.[6] Jurisdictions that banned conversion practices targeting sexual orientation but not gender identity, such as California and Illinois, were excluded. Also excluded from the list were laws that prohibited mental health diagnoses solely based on gender identity, such as the law found in Uruguay, because of their uncertain legal impact on trans conversion practices.[7] These laws emphasize a commitment to the de-pathologization of trans people, undermining a core premise of conversion practices, which sees transitude as disordered. The laws also highlight the inseparability of human rights, human dignity, and mental healthcare: "Human dignity and human rights principles constitute the primary frame of reference for all legislative, judicial, administrative, educational and other measures and in all fields of application relating to mental health."[8] While Uruguay's law is laudable in many respects, it does not expressly refer to conversion practices, and its legal incidence on trans conversion practices is difficult to assess.

As of July 2020, three Canadian provinces, twenty US jurisdictions, four Spanish autonomous communities, and one country have legislated against anti-trans conversion practices.[9] In Canada, trans conversion practices are banned in Nova Scotia, Ontario, and Prince Edward Island.[10] In the United States, trans conversion practices are banned in Colorado, Connecticut, Delaware, the District of Columbia, Hawaii, Maine, Maryland, Massachusetts, Nevada, New Hampshire, New Jersey, New Mexico, New York State, Oregon, Puerto Rico, Rhode Island, Utah, Vermont, Virginia, and Washington State.[11] In Spain, the autonomous communities of Andalucía, Madrid, Murcia, and València have prohibited trans conversion practices.[12] The country of Malta has also prohibited conversion practices.[13]

Grouped by Textual Lineage

The first typology of bans I suggest is based on the textual similarity between the statutes. Textual similarity is important for interpretation since it points to a shared meaning and purpose. Approaching bans from this angle, we can discern four broad groups that are tied together by geography. The first group is composed of Canadian bans. The second is found in Spanish bans. The third is composed of US bans. And the fourth is Malta's national ban.

Canadian Bans

Laws from the first group, which includes Nova Scotia, Ontario, and Prince Edward Island, prohibit practices whose goal is to change the gender identity of a minor. Of the three provinces, only Prince Edward Island uses the term "conversion therapy." The other two refer directly to the practices without grouping them under a specific term. The Canadian bans do not include attempts at changing gender expression. Ontario and Prince Edward Island further include exceptions for transition-related surgeries and "services that provide acceptance, support or understanding of a person or the facilitation of a person's coping, social support or identity exploration or development" – terminology that is textually lifted from the *Task Force report*.[14]

Spanish Bans

The second group of bans includes those found in the Spanish autonomous communities of Andalucía, Madrid, Murcia, and València. These laws prohibit conversion practices under the terminology of aversion, conversion, or reconditioning therapies that aim at modifying gender identity. Unlike the bans found in Canada and the United States, conversion practices are banned for people of all ages. With the exception of València, the Spanish bans adopt a more expansive understanding of conversion practices that includes not only attempting to change gender identity but also pressuring, coercing, or forcing a person to hide, suppress, or deny their gender identity. They each include a definition of gender identity. Andalucía, Madrid, and Murcia adopt a definition directly inspired by the *Yogyakarta Principles*.[15] The definition they use is expansive, understanding changes in bodily traits that occur through gender transition to be part of gender identity. It is nonetheless somewhat narrower than the definition in the

Yogyakarta Principles, which includes all expressions of gender under the notion of gender identity – a definition that was changed in the 2017 supplement to the *Yogyakarta Principles,* which separates gender identity and gender expression. In comparison to the three other autonomous communities, València defines gender identity in simpler terms and separates it from gender expression. Gender identity is understood as an internal and individual experience of gender, which is self-determined and may not correspond to one's sex assigned at birth. Gender expression is understood as the person's manifestation of their gender identity.

The Andalucian law includes a clear drafting confusion, prohibiting attempts to change gender identity to a "heterosexual and/or bisexual pattern," concepts that have nothing to do with gender identity.[16] This wording was likely a drafting oversight but one that could create serious impediments to enforcing the ban in relation to trans conversion practices. The autonomous communities of Andalucía and Madrid expressly define conversion practices to include medical, psychiatric, psychological, and religious interventions, foreclosing any doubt as to their application to faith-based approaches. Unlike bans in the other three groups, the Spanish bans include no further specification of what counts as conversion practices – such as the language of the *Task Force report,* which was adopted in the Canadian and US bans. While they do not specifically state that transition-related surgeries are not conversion practices, unlike bans from Canada and the United States, Spanish law protects access to transition-related surgeries. Since people have a right to medical transition, it could hardly be argued that supporting medical transition runs afoul of the protections against trans conversion practices. Significantly, bans in this second group are placed within a comprehensive law that protects lesbian, gay, bisexual, trans, and intersex equality. These comprehensive laws go far beyond merely prohibiting conversion practices and include a whole slew of rights and protections including rights relating to healthcare and access to transition-related interventions.

US Bans

The third and largest group of bans is found in the United States and includes the states of Colorado, Connecticut, Delaware, the District of Columbia, Hawaii, Maine, Maryland, Massachusetts, Nevada, New

Hampshire, New Jersey, New Mexico, New York State, Oregon, Puerto Rico, Rhode Island, Utah, Vermont, Virginia, and Washington.[17] These laws exclusively protect minors, target conversion therapy by name, prohibit attempts to change gender expression, and provide exclusions for the practices set out in the *Task Force report* as well as practices targeting unlawful conduct and unsafe sexual practices. Some states – namely, Hawaii, Maine, Massachusetts, and Rhode Island – also prohibit advertising conversion practices. A small subgroup comprising Delaware, Massachusetts, and New Mexico includes a definition for gender identity.

Oregon's law is representative of the laws in this third group. The Oregonian law states:

(1)   A mental health care or social health professional may not practice conversion therapy if the recipient of the conversion therapy is under 18 years of age.

(2)   As used in this section:

    (A)   "Conversion therapy" means providing professional services for the purpose of attempting to change a person's sexual orientation or gender identity, including attempting to change behaviors or expressions of self or to reduce sexual or romantic attractions or feelings toward individuals of the same gender.

    (B)   "Conversion therapy" does not mean:

        (i)   Counseling that assists a client who is seeking to undergo a gender transition or who is in the process of undergoing a gender transition; or

        (ii)   Counseling that provides a client with acceptance, support and understanding, or counseling that facilitates a client's coping, social support and identity exploration or development, including counseling in the form of sexual orientation-neutral or gender identity-neutral interventions provided for the purpose of preventing or addressing unlawful conduct or unsafe sexual practices, as long as the counseling is not provided for the purpose of attempting to change the client's sexual orientation or gender identity.[18]

Oregon's law specifically refers to conversion practices under the term "conversion therapy." All bans in this group refer to conversion practices directly and proceed to define the term they use. The vast majority of bans refer to conversion practices as "conversion therapy." However, the District of Columbia, Hawaii, Massachusetts, New Jersey, and New York opted for the language of "sexual orientation change efforts" or "sexual orientation and gender identity change efforts," and Puerto Rico refers to "conversion and reparative therapies." It is worth noting that Puerto Rico's executive order is much less specific than other US bans, likely due to legal restrictions on the scope of executive orders.

Bans in this third group overwhelmingly include gender expression within the scope of protection. Most refer directly to gender expression, though some states like Oregon and Utah use more oblique language such as "attempting to change behaviors or expressions of self" or "behaviors, expressions ... related to a patient or client's sexual orientation or gender identity." Even in these somewhat ambiguous forms, the references to gender expression demonstrate an awareness of how many conversion practices operate through attempts at behavioural modifications and through the imposition of normative gender expression (for example, "dresses are for girls").

Bans on conversion practices in the United States reproduce the *Task Force report*'s language of "acceptance, support and understanding" and of "coping, social support and identity exploration or development." The laws add a further exception for practices that seek to address unlawful conduct or unsafe sexual practices, so long as they are neutral towards sexual orientation and/or gender identity. On a surface-level analysis, this additional exception might invite a rebranding of conversion practices around the prevention of anally transmitted human immunodeficiency viruses (HIV). HIV is an oft-mentioned facially neutral (that is, superficially, without looking to social context) reason to oppose same-sex intercourse between people assigned male at birth by proponents of gay conversion practices. Though neutral on their face, these practices are certainly not neutral in their substance. Whether or not this rebranding would fall under the exception is uncertain.

Delaware, Massachusetts, and New Mexico bans include a definition of gender identity. Their definitions seem to conflate gender identity and gender expression. Take, for instance, Delaware, which defines gender identity as

> a gender-related identity, appearance, expression or behavior of a person, regardless of the person's assigned sex at birth. Gender identity may be demonstrated by consistent and uniform assertion of the gender identity or any other evidence that the gender identity is sincerely held as part of a person's core identity; provided, however, that gender identity shall not be asserted for any improper purpose.[19]

This definition is partly self-referential: gender identity is a gender-related identity. It can be proven by consistent and uniform assertion – which is good – as well as by "any other evidence that the gender identity is sincerely held as a part of a person's core identity." While proof by self-report is beneficial, it is unclear how it belongs in a definition. Additionally, the requirement of consistent and uniform assertions may be prohibitively difficult to establish in young children, opening the door to the corrective approach. It is not altogether clear what constitutes consistent and uniform assertion – some trans people could potentially face charges of inconsistency for only being out as trans in some contexts but not in others. Outside of proof by consistent and uniform assertion, the definition sheds little light on what sort of evidence is required or what this evidence is evidence of in the first place. Massachusetts's definition of gender identity is similar to Delaware's.

Unlike the other two states, New Mexico's definition reads far more like a definition. Under New Mexico's ban, gender identity is "a person's self-perception, or perception of that person by another, of the person's identity as a male or female based upon the person's appearance, behavior or physical characteristics that are in accord with or opposed to the person's physical anatomy, chromosomal sex or sex at birth."[20] Like Delaware and Massachusetts, New Mexico's definition conflates gender identity and gender expression. Given the wording, I would even suggest that New Mexico understands gender identity exclusively through gender expression. The ban defines gender identity not only through self-perception but also in reference to others' perceptions. Both self-perception and other perception must relate to appearance, behaviour, or physical traits.

A deeply felt psychological sense of belonging to a gender or another – an archetypical definition of gender identity – would seemingly not constitute gender identity under this law. Defining gender identity through gender expression may create significant difficulties in enforcing trans conversion practices. People subjected to conversion practices may not have changed their appearances or physical characteristics yet, though they wish to do so. This situation may be especially true for younger children. It is far from clear whether the definition would effectively prohibit practices that seek to change gender identity but not gender expression. The definitions in Delaware and Massachusetts or the approach of the majority of jurisdictions of simply not defining gender identity strike me as preferable. No definition is often better than a bad definition.

Maltese Ban

Malta's ban alone constitutes the fourth group. Malta was the first country to legislate against conversion practices. Its ban targets conversion practices by name, applies regardless of age, defines conversion practices broadly and liberally, defines gender identity, drafts its own set of exclusions instead of using the *Task Force report*'s language, and permits the treatment of mental disorders that are not predicated on a psychopathologizing understanding of sexual orientation, gender identity, or gender expression. Under Maltese law,

> "conversion practices" refers to any treatment, practice or sustained effort that aims to change, repress and, or eliminate a person's sexual orientation, gender identity and, or gender expression; such practices do not include:
>
> (a) any services and, or interventions related to the exploration and, or free development of a person and, or affirmation of one's identity with regard to one or more of the characteristics being affirmed by this Act, through counselling, psychotherapeutic services and, or similar services; or
> (b) any healthcare service related to the free development and, or affirmation of one's gender identity and, or gender expression of a person; and, or
> (c) any healthcare service related to the treatment of a mental disorder.[21]

The Maltese law's definition of conversion practices is much broader than that offered in the other three groups of bans. It includes not only attempts to change gender identity but also attempts to "repress and, or eliminate" it. Such wording certainly facilitates interpretation, immediately clarifying that practices such as, for example, the corrective approach fall under the scope of the prohibition. This broader language is certainly helpful against attempts to define away bans based on pointed semantic distinctions.

Unlike the bans found in Canada and the United States, Malta prohibits conversion practices regardless of age. However, practices targeted at minors under sixteen years of age come with greater punishment.[22] Instead of exclusions drawn from the *Task Force report*, which are common in the North American bans, Malta drafted its own list of services and interventions that do not count as conversion practices. While the language is not the same as in the *Task Force report*, it certainly shares a similar spirit. Thus, services directed at the "exploration and, or free development of a person and, or affirmation of one's identity," healthcare services relating to the "free development and, or affirmation of one's gender identity and, or gender expression of a person," or healthcare services relating to the treatment of a mental disorder are not conversion practices. Although the divergence in language means that Maltese judges are not able to rely directly on the *Task Force report* to clarify the meaning of these exclusions, the emphasis on free development should prevent most faith arguments by conversion practitioners.

Given the similar spirit underpinning the Maltese exceptions and exceptions based on the *Task Force report*, the analysis of subsection 29.1(2) of the *Regulated Health Professions Act, 1991* proposed in Chapter 2 remains informative.[23] Within this list of exceptions, we find a major departure from the *Task Force report*'s exclusions in the form of a reference to "any healthcare service related to the treatment of a mental disorder." While worrisome in isolation, the exception must be read side by side with the Maltese ban's definition of mental disorder:

"[M]ental disorder" means a significant mental or behavioural dysfunction, exhibited by signs and, or symptoms indicating a distortion of mental functioning, including disturbances in one or more of the areas of thought, mood, volition, perception, cognition, orientation or memory which are present to such a degree as to be considered pathological in accordance with internationally accepted medical and diagnostic standards, with the exclusion of any form of pathologisation of sexual orientation, gender identity and, or gender expression.[24]

Thus, interventions predicated on the view that being trans is pathological and undesirable, such as the corrective approach, would not fall under this exception. Seeking to minimize the likelihood of youths growing up trans is tantamount to psychopathologizing gender identity, whether overtly embraced or adopted indirectly through the language of "likelihood of Gender Dysphoria or Gender Identity Disorder persisting."[25] The law's wording emphasizes that Malta disavows any form of psychopathologization of gender identity and/or expression. Theories that obliquely target trans people by depicting core components of trans subjectivity (for example, gender dysphoria) as pathological would plainly be captured by the ban.

Malta further distinguishes itself by the quality of its definition of gender identity, a feature that it shares with the bans from Spain. Drawn from the *Yogyakarta Principles*, the definition is far better written than those found in Delaware, Massachusetts, or New Mexico and genuinely adds clarity for practitioners and members of the public who are less familiar with trans realities. Under the Maltese law,

> "gender identity" refers to each person's internal and individual experience of gender, which may or may not correspond with the sex assigned at birth, including the personal sense of the body (which may involve, if freely chosen, modification of bodily appearance and, or functions by medical, surgical or other means) and other expressions of gender, including name, dress, speech and mannerisms.[26]

This definition is exactly the same as the one found in the *Yogyakarta Principles*. Unlike the Spanish jurisdictions, Malta did not remove "other expressions of gender, including name, dress, speech and mannerisms" from the definition. The definition partly conflates gender identity and gender expression, drawing from the 2006 version of the *Yogyakarta Principles* instead of the 2017 version, which introduced a definitional distinction between gender identity and gender expression. This conceptual merger is legally benign, and the degree of precision of the Maltese definition is laudable in the context of a law that will have to be interpreted by judges and disciplinary bodies that may not be very familiar with trans realities.

~

From this discussion, a few salient features may be highlighted in each of the four groupings. The Canadian bans prohibit changes to gender identity, but they do not prohibit targeting gender expression or behaviours, they do not define gender identity, and they have adopted a list of exclusions inspired by the *Task Force report*. The Spanish bans set out the prohibition of conversion practices in a minimalistic manner, but they do take care to define gender identity and situate bans within a comprehensive law protecting lesbian, gay, bisexual, transgender, and intersex rights, including access to trans healthcare. The US bans prohibit changing gender identity, prohibit practices targeting gender expression and behaviours, borrow a list of exclusions from the *Task Force report*, and add an exclusion for sexual orientation-neutral practices that target unlawful conduct or unsafe sexual practices. Though most of the US bans do not define gender identity, some do, but they do not do so particularly well. The Maltese ban, which is the only one in its group, uses broad language to prohibit conversion practices regardless of age, carefully defines gender identity, and drafts its own set of exclusions instead of adopting the *Task Force report*'s language. The core differences between these bans include whether they demonstrate a broad understanding of conversion practices that goes beyond mere change, whether they cover all ages, whether they include a definition of gender identity, and whether they contain a list of excluded practices and, if they do, which practices they exclude.

Grouped by Sanctions

Besides grouping bans by how similar their texts are, I also suggest grouping them based on what types of sanctions apply and to whom. Whereas grouping bans based on textual lineage gave us clear geographical clusters, groupings based on the kind of sanctions created by the law are fuzzier. Nevertheless, some general observations can be made. Bans from Canada and the United States, by and large, centre on disciplinary sanctions against licensed professionals. While Malta also contemplates disciplinary sanctions, the bans of Malta and Spain include severe penal sanctions, which are imposed administratively or through the criminal system. In terms of to whom the laws apply, the dominant trend is to restrict bans to licensed professionals. However, many jurisdictions also target unlicensed practitioners of conversion practices.

Type of Sanctions

Disciplinary Sanctions

Most bans surveyed provide for disciplinary sanctions meted out by professional bodies against licensed professionals. Procedurally, this will generally mean that those who experience conversion practices will lodge a complaint with the conversion practitioner's professional order, which will be followed by an inquiry and a hearing. If the practitioner is found to have engaged in conversion practices, they will receive a fine and/or lose their professional licence – either temporarily or permanently. Disciplinary sanctions do not typically come with compensation for complainants, though having a disciplinary decision in hand can help in subsequent malpractice lawsuits.

Jurisdictions vary as to whether the unlicensed practice of psychotherapy is legal. Where unlicensed practice is prohibited, conversion practices through psychotherapy will be *de facto* illegal, even when done by unlicensed practitioners, because they are not allowed to engage in psychotherapy or counselling at all. In jurisdictions where it is legal, however, disciplinary bans may not preclude conversion practices done by unlicensed individuals, which poses some concerns in the context of faith-based conversion practices, which more often include unlicensed practitioners.

Penal Sanctions

Some jurisdictions enforce the prohibition on trans conversion practices through penal sanctions. Penal law refers to legal frameworks focused on punishment through administrative, regulatory, or criminal sanctions – notably, monetary fines and/or prison sentences. Penal sanctions are included under both Malta's and Spain's bans, though they take significantly different forms. Spain punishes conversion practices through administrative sanctions enforced by the government in each autonomous community. The sanctions do not include imprisonment but can still be severe. In Andalucía, for instance, conversion practices can be punished with a fine of up to 120,000 euros; a prohibition from contracting with, or receiving public aid from, the government for up to five years, and a prohibition from dispensing public services for up to five years. Both Madrid's and Murcia's bans specify that they prohibit conversion practices within the public health system. However, other portions of the law do not specifically mention the public system – notably, the ban on pressuring, coercing, or forcing a person to hide, suppress, or deny their gender identity. Accordingly, the statutes would seemingly create sanctions for practitioners – licensed or unlicensed – operating outside of the public health system. The main difference between disciplinary sanctions and these penal sanctions is the legal and procedural framework within which they operate. Spanish fines are administrative in nature, being enforced by the government through administrative tribunals. By contrast, disciplinary sanctions are enforced by semi-independent licensing bodies.

The Maltese law is not just penal in nature but also criminal. Engaging in conversion practices does not only mean a disciplinary sanction or a fine – though both are contemplated – but also imprisonment. Professionals who engage in conversion practices can be subject to fines of up to ten thousand euros and/or imprisonment for three to twenty-four months. Unlicensed individuals who engage in forced conversion practices can be fined up to five thousand euros and/or imprisoned for up to five months and fined and/or imprisoned even more for any conversion practices on minors and certain vulnerable adults regardless of whether it was forced.

Deceptive or Unfair Trade Practices

Some bans classify conversion practices done in the conduct of trade or commerce – that is, those who engage in conversion practices for money – as deceptive or unfair trade practices. For instance, Connecticut law states:

(a) It shall be unlawful for any person who practices or administers conversion therapy to practice or administer such therapy while in the conduct of trade or commerce.

(b) A violation of subsection (a) of this section shall be considered an unfair or deceptive trade practice pursuant to section 42-110b of the general statutes and shall be subject to the same enforcement, liabilities and penalties as set forth in sections 42-110a to 42-110q, inclusive, of the general statutes.[27]

This qualification is in addition to disciplinary sanctions rather than instead of them. Sanctions against deceptive and unfair trade practices are peculiar, being a hybrid between a penal sanction and a private right of action. Under Connecticut law, the government can investigate deceptive and unfair trade practices and ask a court to impose a monetary fine.[28] But, in addition, anyone who suffers a monetary loss as a result of a deceptive or unfair trade practice can sue for damages in court.[29] This distinction can be good because it means survivors of conversion practices can receive some compensation and can pursue a remedy even if a licensing body or government fails to adequately enforce the law. A similar scheme exists under Massachusetts's law, though it only applies to healthcare professionals.

Trans conversion practices offered free of cost would fall outside of schemes targeting deceptive or unfair trade practices. While these schemes do not capture all trans conversion practices, they are not negligible either. Trans conversion practices are often paid, and over half of conversion practices in Canada involve an exchange of money.[30]

Restrictions on Funding and Public Benefits

Not all sanctions take the form of a cost positively imposed upon those who engage in conversion practices. They can also take away something to which conversion practitioners would normally be entitled. Besides threatening to take away conversion practitioners' money and freedom, bans also frequently prevent them from benefiting from insurance coverage, at least in theory. Bans on conversion practices frequently prohibit public insurance coverage of conversion practices. However, since conversion practitioners rarely bill their services as "conversion practices" to healthcare insurance providers, the impact of this restriction is likely minor in the absence of rigorous enforcement mechanisms. It is not a bad addition, to be sure, but it is not one that will be greatly consequential.

With regard to restrictions on funding and public benefits, Puerto Rico stands out. Going much further than merely prohibiting insurance coverage, it also requires that no institution holding a state-issued licence engage in conversion practices. Refraining from conversion practices is a condition of all state-issued licences. To enforce this requirement, Puerto Rico's executive order tasks governmental agencies with creating mechanisms to ensure compliance with this rule. The effectiveness of Puerto Rico's restriction on state-issued licences will largely depend on the strength of the enforcement mechanisms implemented by its agencies. The restriction could potentially reach far wider than restrictions on public insurance coverage, applying to all institutions that need a governmental licence to operate regardless of whether they depend on insurance funding for their continued existence.

Target of Sanction

Besides the nature of the sanction, bans also vary based on whose conduct is targeted. Not all bans target conversion practices regardless of who engages in them – quite the contrary. A large majority of the bans found in Canada and the United States only target licensed professionals, leaving unlicensed practitioners free to engage in conversion practices. Usually, the bans' focus on licensed professionals is a by-product of the fact that they operate through disciplinary sanctions. However, this is not always the case. Massachusetts, for instance, prohibits conversion practices as deceptive or unfair trade practices but only when done by a healthcare professional. Some bans target conduct by everyone and not just licensed professionals – for example, the bans in Nova Scotia, Connecticut, Malta, and Spain. Some of them apply to everyone, such as the Maltese ban, though Malta increases the penalty when conversion practices are done by a licensed professional. Nova Scotia, on the other hand, prohibits conversion practices by persons in a position of trust or authority, demonstrating an intermediate position between only targeting licensed professionals and targeting any person who engages in conversion practices.

Just because a jurisdiction does not expressly ban conversion practices by unlicensed practitioners does not necessarily mean that these practices are allowed. As mentioned earlier, many jurisdictions prohibit the unlicensed practice of psychotherapy or counselling. However, sanctions for engaging in a reserved act without a licence usually differ from the sanctions for engaging in conversion practices, and they may be weaker. Furthermore, it can be difficult to prove that trans conversion practices by an unlicensed practitioner cross the line into, say, psychotherapy. In many jurisdictions, psychotherapy and counselling are not reserved acts, and there is no sanction for people who engage in them without a licence. Most US states do not reserve the practice of psychotherapy or counselling.[31] In Canadian provinces and territories, it is common for mental health diagnoses to be reserved for licensed professionals and not psychotherapy or counselling. The effectiveness of bans will therefore depend in part on how a given jurisdiction deals with unlicensed practitioners. Conversion practices may also constitute negligence and give rise to civil liability, regardless of licensure.

In some jurisdictions – primarily the United States – it may be more difficult to prohibit trans conversion practices by unlicensed practitioners. The regulation of conversion practices in the United States relies in part on states' long-recognized power to regulate "certain trades and callings, particularly those which closely concern the public health."[32] Bans may have more difficulty passing constitutional muster if they target people who are not licensed professionals since they come closer to impinging upon private relations. This distinction has led some states to carve out additional people from their bans. Utah, for instance, excludes from its ban on conversion practices members of the clergy, religious counselling, and family members so long as they are not acting "in the capacity of a mental health therapist," even if they may otherwise be licensed professionals.[33] It may be that bans extending to everyone can nonetheless withstand a constitutional challenge. They are, after all, less restrictive than banning conversion practices by licensed practitioners and all unlicensed practice of psychotherapy and counselling. Courts have previously recognized states' power to prohibit the unlicensed practice of psychotherapy.[34] But because it only prohibits some forms of unlicensed psychotherapy and not others, bans targeting everyone – licensed or not – could run into constitutional difficulties in the United States. I explore the question of the constitutional status of bans at greater length in Chapter 4.

~

Grouped by sanctions, bans differ along two axes. First, they differ in the types of sanctions they provide. Do they contemplate disciplinary sanctions, penal sanctions, hybrid sanctions, and/or restrictions on funding and public benefits? Second, they differ in terms of who they target. Do they prohibit trans conversion practices by licensed professionals, by people in a position of authority, or by any practitioner regardless of authority or licensure? These differences lead to substantial differences not only in terms of scope but also in terms of how readily enforceable they are. In turn, these differences shape the benefits and limits of bans in effectively discouraging trans conversion practices. Most worrisome is perhaps the tendency to restrict bans to licensed professionals since many conversion practitioners are not licensed, which is a limitation that I make note of in Chapter 5's policy analysis.

In Chapter 2, I have argued that the scope of Ontario's law is quite broad – broad enough to cover all trans conversion practices, including those more insidious practices, such as the corrective approach, that try to prevent youths from growing up trans. Grouping bans together based on textual lineage offers some insight as to how the analysis from Chapter 2 might apply elsewhere. Bans may not all share the same genealogy or strike the same pose as Ontario's law, but they are not that different from it either – their goals and affirmative spirit are the same. Features may be added or removed here and there, but there is a recognizable core that all bans have in common. They share a similar recognition that trans conversion practices are psychopathologizing, transantagonistic, and have no place in the contemporary clinical apparatus.

Opposition and Constitutional Challenges to Bans

4

What would have happened if the Centre for Addiction and Mental Health (CAMH) had left its Gender Identity Clinic for Children and Youth open and been the subject of a complaint under the Ontarian ban on trans conversion practices? As Chapter 2 emphasized, their approach falls under the scope of the law and would seemingly be prohibited. However, the analysis cannot end there: bans would do very little good if they were found unconstitutional and struck down as soon as they were applied. Quite unsurprisingly given the explosive intersection of trans lives, conservative values, and parenting, a fierce opposition to bans has made itself heard in the public and legislative sphere. Many proponents of conversion practices have claimed that bans violate therapists' freedom of expression, are so overbroad as to run afoul of constitutional protections, and violate patients' autonomy and/or families' freedom of religion. In this chapter, I consider whether bans on trans conversion practices can withstand legal challenges and conclude in the affirmative. While the analysis varies by jurisdictions, legal challenges of bans should generally fail, especially outside the United States where freedom of expression plays less of an inflated role.

I attempt to address the three primary legal arguments levied against bans on conversion practices at a general level, without being too closely tied to jurisdictional idiosyncrasies that would risk muddying the waters for readers outside of the legal systems that I have chosen. To guide my analysis, I centre on Canadian and US law as examples: Canadian law because of its familiarity to me and US law because of its illuminating court decisions on the constitutionality of bans on conversion practices. Throughout the chapter, I seek to detail and rebut the different arguments that are deployed against bans on conversion practices.

Therapist Freedom of Expression

Therapists have criticized bans on conversion practices for curtailing their freedom of expression.[1] These critiques have been central to US challenges of bans, failing before two courts of appeal and succeeding before another.[2] In this section, I contrast how the claim would be analyzed under Canadian and US law, which adopt vastly different approaches to freedom of expression. Whereas Canadian constitutional law tends to be more flexible and focused on proportionality, US protections of free speech are more rigid and category based. In both Canada and the United States, alleged violations of freedom of expression are analyzed under a two-step argumentative structure, which will be familiar to many other jurisdictions. The first step is to determine how much the law impedes upon freedom of expression and, accordingly, what level of legal protection it attracts. This is done by looking at the nature of the prohibited act: the "speechier" it is, the greater the protection. The second step is to establish whether the beneficial effects of the law justify the impact on freedom of expression. There is good reason to believe that conversion practices attract little legal protection because they are best understood as non-expressive conduct rather than as speech. Even if they attracted a higher level of protection, the bans fulfill an important purpose by prohibiting actions proven to be harmful and would be justified despite their impact on speech.

Despite a shared overarching argumentative structure, Canada and the United States take vastly different approaches to expressive freedom. In Canada, freedom of expression (not speech) is protected under section 2(b) of the *Canadian Charter of Rights and Freedoms*.[3] Establishing that a prohibition impacts freedom of expression is easy: the Supreme Court of Canada has (in)famously said that even parking a car could be a protected form of expression if it was done in public protest.[4] So long as the act seeks to convey meaning, even an activity that is not inherently expressive can fall under the umbrella of expression.[5] Unlike the approach adopted in the United States, which I will discuss shortly, in Canada, relatively little turns on whether conversion practices are expression at all. What matters more is the extent to which the activity fulfills the ends that the *Charter*'s freedom of expression protections are directed towards: (1) the search for truth; (2) participation in political decision-making; and (3) the pursuit of self-fulfillment and human flourishing.[6] A restriction on freedom of expression will be justified and, thus, constitutional if its benefits are proportional to the negative impact on freedom of expression and if it restricts expression no more than necessary to fulfill its objective.[7] Since the negative impact on freedom of expression is evaluated based on the values underlying the protection, forms of expression that do not significantly implicate these values will be relatively easy to justify.

In the United States, the First Amendment's protection of free speech is applied through a category-based approach. Instead of a fluid approach that recognizes a continuous spectrum from non-expressive conduct to the most socially valuable forms of expression in a liberal democracy, the prohibition must be slotted into discrete categories of conduct or speech that each attracts a different level of protection.[8] While the United States uses the language of "speech" rather than "expression," expressive acts are included under the First Amendment.[9] Significant debate exists over which categories exist and which acts fall under them. Each level of protection is embodied in a different legal test. At the lowest level of protection, laws that regulate professional conduct and only incidentally impact speech will be constitutional if they bear "a rational relationship to a legitimate state interest," a level of protection known as rational basis scrutiny.[10] Some types of law attract an intermediate level of protection and will be justified if they directly advance a significant governmental interest, restrict speech no more than necessary, and leave open significant avenues of communication.[11] Laws that regulate commercial speech and laws that apply regardless of content – notably, by setting out the time, place, and manner in which speech must be conveyed – fall under this intermediary category.

Some courts have suggested that professional speech also falls under this category, but the Supreme Court of the United States (US Supreme

Court) has recently shed significant doubt as to the existence of a professional speech category.[12] At the highest level of protection, laws that regulate speech based on its content attract what is known as strict scrutiny and will only be justified if they are "narrowly tailored to serve compelling state interests."[13] Laws that are overbroad or under-inclusive and laws that do not use the least restrictive means of furthering the governmental interest will be unconstitutional. I take it for granted that bans on conversion practices are predicated upon a compelling interest, such as preventing psychological harm to its population, especially minors.[14] Preventing harm strikes me as one of the most compelling of governmental interests. The harm principle is long-standing as the quintessential liberal justification for governmental action. Bans arguably further other valid interests such as equality,[15] but, for my purposes, I restrict myself to harm.

How should we characterize laws that prohibit conversion practices? In my view, conversion practices are best understood as conduct rather than speech. Conversion practices are not inherently expressive; they do not fundamentally seek to communicate a point of view. As such, they do not deserve significant legal protection.[16] Even when conducted solely through talk therapy, conversion practices deploy psychological methods in a systematic manner that is deliberately tailored to effect a psychological change in the subject. They are not predicated on persuasion or education. Indeed, patients may already believe that they "truly" are the gender they were assigned at birth, that gender cannot be changed, that there is "no such thing" as being transgender, that it is a mental illness or perversion, and/or that it would be far preferable for them not to be transgender or transition. What is there for them to be persuaded of? Characterizing conversion practices as speech rather than action is irreconcilable with the theoretical apparatus that underpins psychotherapy. From a purely theoretical standpoint, there is no fundamental difference in expressive content between talk therapy and aversive treatments, despite the latter being undoubtedly a type of conduct.

Just as we can express ourselves through conduct, we can also act through speech. The fact that an activity is carried on exclusively through speech does not entail that it is necessarily speech. Many activities are regulated as conduct despite involving nothing but words. Contracts are formed through offer and acceptance, which are both forms of communication. Yet the formation of a contract in the United States is not regulated as speech but, rather, as conduct – the impact on speech being merely incidental.[17] The act of prescribing medication, too, is merely words. Even the preceding diagnosis may involve nothing but words, as is often the case when prescribing antidepressants. Yet prescribing is understood as conduct, not speech, though it is conduct carried out through words.[18] In the same way, conversion practices should be understood as conduct even though they are sometimes carried out solely through words.

It is true that we sometimes say that conversion practices communicate transantagonistic or homoantagonistic views – notably, the view that it is undesirable to be trans or queer. When thinking about freedom of expression, however, we must distinguish conduct motivated by a view from conduct expressing that view. Eating an orange may be motivated by the view that oranges are tasty and nutritious or that humans will die if they do not eat, yet we would be hard-pressed to claim that it expresses those views and therefore becomes a form of expression for the purpose of constitutional protections. Conversion practices are predicated upon negative views of queerness and transitude but do not inherently seek to communicate such views – rather, the aim is to make the subject of the practices heterosexual and/or cisgender. The goal is to prevent an outcome – to enact a change in the world.

It is not the content of speech that is prohibited by bans on conversion practices but, rather, the systematic deployment of psychological techniques to effect a change in the psyche. Indeed, the precise words matter little. If proponents of conversion practices believed that sexual orientation or gender identity could be changed or repressed by repeating an incantation of the word "banana" ten thousand times, that is what they would do. Indeed, it would often be difficult to discern whether a given practice aims at changing or repressing gender identity or sexual orientation without looking at the speech that accompanies the conversion practices. An analogy to forms of conversion practices that do not involve talking may be helpful. Electroshock therapy as a psychiatric technique can be deployed towards a range of different aims. Simply knowing that electroshock therapy was used does not tell you whether it was used as a conversion practice as it is compatible with other aims such as treating depression. To establish whether it was a conversion practice, we must look at ancillary speech and infer the aim towards which it was deployed.

For example, practitioners may readily admit that they have used electroshock therapy to change a person's gender identity. Such accompanying speech is not itself prohibited. Stating the intent to use electroshock therapy to "cure" someone's transitude, but not subsequently engaging in electroshock therapy, would be legal since it is the electroshock therapy itself that is prohibited. The same can be said for talk therapy. Challenging someone's self-understanding as trans may not be recognized as good psychological practice, but it is compatible with many goals besides changing or repressing the person's gender identity. It could be part of an assessment to ensure that the person is trans and thus eligible for medical transition. It could seek to teach the person to stand up for themselves in the face of family members challenging their gender identity. It could be an attempt to ascertain the person's psychosocial resilience. To establish that it is a conversion practice, it will be necessary to look at the context surrounding the practices. How did the practitioner explain the treatment plan and its purpose? Why did the patient or patient's parent seek out the practitioner, and how did the practitioner respond to the request?

Techniques themselves will sometimes be recognizable as conversion practices without reference to ancillary speech by the practitioner. We could infer that electroshock therapy is used to change the person's sexual orientation if the patient has no condition for which electroshock therapy is a recognized treatment and if the practitioner did not express an intent to use it for another, experimental purpose. Crucially, however, this form of inference relies on outside psychological knowledge and is rebuttable by evidence of another purpose. Without this additional psychological knowledge, the technique itself cannot be ascertained as a conversion practice. This point is reminiscent of the distinction drawn by the US Supreme Court in *Rumsfeld v Forum for Academic & Institutional Rights* between inherently expressive actions and actions that require explanatory speech to acquire meaning.[19] However, I am suggesting not that conversion practices acquire meaning through explanatory speech and context but, rather, that explanatory speech and context support inferences to the non-expressive purpose of a practice. Given the need to refer to explanatory speech and context, conversion practices through talk therapy cannot be said to be defined by the content of the words or even by the words at all. You could know nothing about what was said, bracketing the therapy itself, and still prove that it constituted conversion practices because of the context and what was said about the talk therapy. And when the content of the talk therapy must be looked at, it is only because the psychological techniques that constitute conversion practices are interwoven with admissions of purpose or bear similarity with recognizable techniques that are used towards an identifiable purpose. If saying "banana" five hundred times was known to solely be used to change or repress someone's sexual orientation or gender identity, it could support an inference that the practitioner engaged in conversion practices. The expressive content of the words – or whether the acts are words at all – matters not.

The preceding discussion suggests not only that bans on conversion practices regulate conduct rather than speech but also that they would be content neutral even if we were to understand them as regulating speech. It is regulated not because of disagreement with the message conveyed but, rather, because attempting to change someone's psyche through the structured application of psychological techniques is known to be harmful.[20] Indeed, as I have argued, conversion practices are not expressive. Crucially, the views that motivate conversion practices can still be expressed, including to the patient. Practitioners remain not only free to voice their disapproval of bans on conversion practices but also to express a plethora of negative attitudes towards queer and trans people.[21] Practitioners can still tell patients that they believe being trans is a mental illness, that it would be more desirable if they did not transition, that they believe their gender identity can be changed through psychological techniques, and that they would be happier if they stopped being trans. What they cannot do is deploy psychological techniques in a structured manner with the aim of altering the patient's gender identity.

For speech that is about expressing transantagonistic and homoantagonistic views, more speech may well offer a solution. It is, at the very least, the legally sanctioned response. As Justice Louis Brandeis of the US

Supreme Court famously said in *Whitney v California:* "If there be time to expose through discussion the falsehood and fallacies, to avert the evil by the processes of education, the remedy to be applied is more speech, not enforced silence."[22] Conversion practices being first and foremost conduct rather than speech, more speech offers little aid. No amount of positive speech can undo the harms already suffered by those subjected to conversion practices. They may heal – though it is no guarantee – but to be made whole is far from never having been injured. I hold out the inadequacies of additional speech as validating evidence that conversion practices are conduct rather than speech.

Moving to a more Canadian logic, the question is no longer whether it is conduct rather than speech, but how much it pursues the ends that motivate the constitutionalizing of freedom of expression. Because of the law's flexible approach to balancing restrictions on freedom of expression against other governmental interests, less turns on whether the prohibited acts are speech, and governments may at times even concede that freedom of expression is restricted.[23] For the sake of argument, let us assume that conversion practices are sufficiently expressive to attract some protection under the *Charter.* Freedom of expression is directed towards three ends: (1) the pursuit of truth; (2) participation in social and political decision-making; and (3) individual self-fulfillment and human flourishing.[24] The more the regulated acts contribute to these ends, the harder it will be to justify the impugned law. Conversion practices do not significantly contribute to any of them.

Conversion practices are not substantially in pursuit of truth. Any expressive content is incidental to the aim of altering someone's psyche through the structured deployment of psychological methods. Conversion practices are directed towards a goal – the cisgender and/or heterosexual subject – rather than the uncovering or construction of knowledge. Indeed, as pointed out earlier, patients may already believe that they are "truly" the gender they were assigned at birth and that it would be preferable for them not to be transgender. But, for other patients, it could be argued that conversion practices aim at unearthing their inner self, conversion practitioners often believing that queerness and transitude are disorders – maladaptive states that obscure their underlying natural truth as cisgender and heterosexual. While conversion practices could be said to pursue truth in some ways, this pursuit is tainted by the relationship of authority and trust between practitioner and patient. The patient is not positioned to effectively offer countervailing viewpoints due to the disparity in knowledge and authority between the two individuals.

The patient is not offered a diversity of viewpoints on their queerness or transitude from which to choose but, instead, is dogmatically instructed to be cisgender and/or heterosexual. There is no marketplace of ideas in the conversion practitioner's office. If freedom of expression seeks to empower individuals to decide for themselves the ideas and beliefs deserving of adherence, then conversion practices cannot be said to be particularly well suited for that purpose since they do not act through dialogue and persuasion but, rather, through structured psychological methods.[25] Nor are they explorative, having a fixed end goal. Would we say that brainwashing is substantially in pursuit of truth? I would not. It should be again emphasized that bans on conversion practices do not prohibit expressing negative attitudes towards queer and trans people. The pursuit of truth on these matters, especially in the marketplace of ideas, is only slightly hindered by the prohibition of conversion practices, which hold little to no inherent expressive content. While conversion practices contribute to the pursuit of truth to some degree, it is not a high degree.

Plainly, conversion practices are not a form of participation in social and political decision-making. Conversion practices are at the heart of heated social and political debates, but they are not themselves a participation in those debates. They do not bear on issues of governance. They typically have an audience of a single person. Importantly, bans on conversion practices do not prohibit discussing social and political issues surrounding queer and trans lives whether within or outside the therapeutic relationship, so long as conversion practices are not used. If anything, I would argue that conversion practices undermine queer and trans participation in social and political decision-making and thus frustrate freedom of expression.[26] The practices collaborate with the negative social landscape to discourage people from openly living as a queer or trans. And because they injure the mental health of individuals subjected to it, many of those who have experienced them will struggle to participate in social and political decision-making.

The last sanctioned end underlying freedom of expression is individual self-fulfillment and human flourishing. More precisely, freedom of expression seeks to promote "diversity in the forms of individual self-fulfillment and human flourishing [which] ought to be cultivated in a tolerant and welcoming environment for the sake of both those who convey a meaning and those to whom the meaning is conveyed."[27] The self-fulfillment and human flourishing of practitioners are not meaningfully in play as conversion practices aim to enact a change not in the practitioner but, rather, in the subject of the practices. The self-fulfillment and human flourishing of those subjected to conversion practices stand as perhaps the strongest defence of conversion practices. These practices could be claimed to pursue self-fulfillment and human flourishing if, in certain situations, they could be properly characterized as consensual, as flowing from the patient's free and enlightened will and untainted by internalized homoantagonism or transantagonism. In those cases, the end goal of conversion practices – that of a cisgender and/or heterosexual life – would be freely adopted by the person rather than imposed or urged by the practitioner.

It is difficult to imagine a neutral reason for pursuing conversion practices. If possible at all, situations of genuine consent would be incredibly rare given the position of authority and trust of practitioners, the pervasiveness of homoantagonism and transantagonism, and how conversion practitioners rarely appear to disclose the severe risks of conversion practices and the current professional consensus that they are ineffective, harmful, and unethical.[28] This purported contribution to self-fulfillment and human flourishing is predicated on conversion practices being effective and perhaps harmless. If they are fruitless endeavours, if they cannot succeed in effecting the desired psychological changes, then the patient's self-fulfillment and human flourishing lie unchanged. Sisyphus is no paragon of human flourishing.[29] Harmful endeavours may also undermine human flourishing, though the harm may at times be outweighed by a deeper satisfaction or happiness. This contribution to self-fulfillment and human flourishing will be readily thwarted by evidence that conversion practices are ineffective and harmful, and it will be limited by the fact that bans do not prevent practitioners from supporting someone who authentically wishes to live celibate or without transitioning, especially once social pressures and internalized homoantagonism and/or transantagonism have been explored and addressed.[30]

On the other hand, conversion practices are inimical to diversity in forms of self-fulfillment and human flourishing because they are predicated on degrading and demeaning queer and trans lives. Conversion practices are motivated by an understanding of queer and trans lives as disordered, sinful, and/or inherently less desirable. In so doing, they undercut the self-fulfillment and flourishing of countless queer and trans people by reinforcing their marginalization and attempting to erase them from public life.[31] Thus, though conversion practices contribute in some narrow cases to self-fulfillment and human flourishing, they also tend to undermine the diversity of forms of self-fulfillment and human flourishing that underpins the protection of freedom of expression, suggesting a lesser degree of protection.

Whether under a category-based approach as found in United States law or under the flexible spectrum approach like Canada's, there is considerable reason to accord little protection to conversion practices on account of freedom of expression. Conversion practices are not very "speechy." They are best understood as conduct, and the minimal expressive content that is incidental to such conduct contributes little to the ends that underlie freedom of expression. So, now that the level of legal protection that conversion practices attract is determined, we must establish whether the beneficial effects of the bans justify their restrictive impact on freedom of expression. Scientific evidence and consensus bear witness to the harm of conversion practices. No alternative, less restrictive means would equally further the government's interest in protecting queer and trans communities – as pointed out earlier, this is not a situation where more speech offers solace. Offering expanded training and funding for gender-affirming care would not repair the harm done to those who experience conversion practices. Offering them free, affirming therapy after the fact would not be an adequate alternative either. Healing is not the same as having never been injured. Nor is the law overbroad, a topic that I discuss more at length in the next section. Whether under Canadian law's flexible approach to justification or the US approach based on tiers of scrutiny, bans on conversion practices should be justified even if a high level of protection applies.

The literature is rife with reports of individuals being harmed by conversion practices, and many survivors have spoken out about the grave psychological suffering they have experienced.[32] So harmful and dehumanizing are conversion practices that researchers, international bodies, and survivors often liken them to torture.[33] Negative experiences are not limited to those who were forced to undergo conversion practices; they are reported even by individuals who sought out and/or ostensibly consented to conversion practices.[34] Reports of harm as a result of conversion practices are not exceptions. Depression and suicidality are common outcomes of conversion practices. A recent study by Amy Green and colleagues reports that 62.6 percent of lesbian, gay, bisexual, transgender, and queer (LGBTQ) individuals having undergone conversion practices seriously considered suicide, compared to 37.6 percent of those who had not undergone conversion practices.[35] A worrisome 43.6 percent of those who underwent conversion practices attempted suicide at least once, and 29.0 percent attempted more than once, compared to 17.3 percent and 8.3 percent of those who had not undergone conversion practices. Among trans individuals more specifically, Jack Turban and colleagues found that those having experienced conversion practices were 1.56 times more likely to have experienced severe psychological distress in the last month, 1.49 times more likely to have attempted suicide in the last year, and 2.27 times more likely to have attempted suicide in their lifetime.[36] The disparities are even worse among those who experienced conversion practices before the age of ten. Both studies included aversive and non-aversive forms of conversion practices alike. The odds reported by Turban and colleagues were adjusted for demographic variables to limit the risk of spurious correlations due to coincidence or the influence of a third variable. For example, a spurious correlation might appear if people who had experienced conversion practices were much older and older people had poorer mental health.

The harms of conversion practices are severe and common. If one hundred people who underwent conversion practices had instead not undergone them, twenty-seven would not have considered suicide, twenty-four would not have attempted suicide, and eighteen would not have attempted suicide multiple times. I am basing these estimates on the prevalence and adjusted odds ratios reported by Green and colleagues.[37]

It simply is not acceptable for a practitioner to sacrifice over a quarter of their 2SLGBTQIA+ (Two-Spirit, lesbian, gay, bisexual, transgender, queer, intersex, asexual, and others) patients to suicidal ideations, over a third of them to suicidal attempts, or more than an eighth of them to multiple suicidal attempts. Without compelling countervailing evidence of the effectiveness, let alone benefits, of conversion practices, these studies are strong enough to justify bans even if they are not randomized controlled trials – often understood as the gold standard in science.

Randomized controlled trials, which randomly assign participants to either undergo an intervention or not, are not always possible or desirable.[38] Even though no randomized controlled trial has ever been held on whether parachutes prevent death when jumping out of an airplane, I doubt anyone would call them unproven.[39] No randomized controlled trial has been done on the harms of child pornography either because it would be ethically abhorrent and even monstrous to conduct such a study. Weaker scientific evidence of concrete harm has been held to satisfy the highest of free speech protections in the past. In *New York v Ferber*,[40] the US Supreme Court upheld a ban on the sale of child pornography based on case studies, theoretical writing, and limited cross-sectional studies on predominantly physical injuries experienced by survivors of child sexual assault.[41] The strongest evidence bore on sexual assault rather than child pornography, and the reported rates of physical injury from sexual assault were not out of proportion with the rates of grave psychological harm reported in studies of conversion practices. None of the sources were controlled retrospective studies, let alone randomized controlled trials, for obvious reasons, yet the judges had little difficulty upholding the bans based on the harms of child pornography. Some individuals have suggested that the harm of child pornography and child sexual assault, like the harm of conversion practices, are overstated and that some have positive experiences – to no avail.[42] Under the evidentiary standards set by *Ferber*, bans on conversion practices should readily be justified under even the highest level of constitutional protection.

The harmfulness of conversion practices is further confirmed by the impressive number of professional organizations that have openly opposed conversion practices against queer and trans people alike on the grounds that they are harmful and unethical. The Appendix lists over fifty organizations that have taken a stance against conversion practices. Among the organizations that oppose conversion practices are the American Academy of Pediatrics, the American Medical Association, the American Psychological Association, the Australian and New Zealand Professional Association for Transgender Health, the British Psychological Society, the Canadian Professional Association for Transgender Health, the Canadian Psychiatric Association, the Canadian Psychological Association, the International Federation of Social Workers, the Royal College of Psychiatrists, the World Professional Association for Transgender Health – to name but a few of the most respected organizations.

The opinions of professional bodies are not incontrovertible evidence. In the past, negative views on queer and trans individuals have been tolerated or supported due to pervasive social animus rather than evidence. The statements of professional bodies also vary in relevance, some focusing more on the ineffectiveness of conversion practices, whereas others focus more on harmfulness. However, nearly all statements listed in the Appendix remark on the harmfulness of conversion practices, and there is no evidence that these opinions are based on animus or divorced from scientific evidence. For example, the American Psychological Association's resolution on conversion practices affirms not only that conversion practices show no evidence of alleviating gender dysphoria but also that they "can cause undue stress and suffering and interfere with healthy sexual and gender identity development" and are associated with "depression, anxiety, suicidality, loss of sexual feeling, impotence, deteriorated family relationships, a range of post-traumatic responses, and substance abuse."[43] None of the statements are limited to aversive forms of conversion practices; they oppose all forms of conversion practices as harmful. I am unaware of any widely respected professional organization that supports the use of conversion practices. Such a strong consensus provides powerful confirmatory evidence that conversion practices are harmful and that banning them is justified. Just as governments are owed some degree of deference in weighing scientific evidence, so should the scientific community upon whose considered evaluations laws are based.[44] They are far better positioned to consider, evaluate, and synthesize scientific evidence than courts. This is not to say that the opinions of professional bodies are legally conclusive. But judges should demonstrate humility in the face of far superior expertise.

Conversion practices are harmful. They cause harm to a significant proportion of those subjected to them, with no evidence of redeeming qualities or even effectiveness.[45] Given the magnitude and prevalence of the harm shown to be caused by conversion practices, it would be unethical to make individuals undergo conversion practices for a randomized controlled trial. No scientist or review board with a moral sensibility would allow such a study, as the American Psychological Association has emphasized in its submission in *Otto*.[46] This fact is due to the requirement of equipoise in research ethics.[47] Research is only allowable if there is genuine uncertainty in the scientific community as to the therapeutic merits of the interventions compared in the experiment. This state of uncertainty is known as equipoise. Without it, a study cannot be conducted. There is no equipoise when it comes to conversion practices. The evidence of harm is strong, and prominent professional organizations are uniform in their view that conversion practices are harmful and unethical.[48]

Whatever the standard of justification that the law uses in freedom of expression cases, it cannot be so high a threshold that proof is impossible. Yet proof becomes impossible if courts ask for more scientific evidence of harm than the scientific community asks for before disallowing randomized controlled trials. Randomized controlled trials of conversion practices cannot be conducted and nor can other forms of experimental studies where scientists engage in, or encourage, conversion practices for research purposes. Outside of the free speech context, the US Supreme Court has observed that

> [o]ne cannot demand a multiyear controlled study, in which some children are intentionally exposed to indecent broadcasts (and insulated from all other indecency), and others are shielded from all indecency. It is one thing to set aside agency action under the Administrative Procedure Act because of failure to adduce empirical data that can readily be obtained. ... It is something else to insist upon obtaining the unobtainable.[49]

The reasoning is all the more compelling in the context of conversion practices, which have been shown to be harmful through rigorous observational studies and thus cannot be ethically subjected to randomized controlled trials.[50] As a rule of thumb, courts should not ask for evidence beyond that which can be ethically obtained, even when the highest level of protection applies. Otherwise, some practices would be permanently shielded from regulation no matter how harmful they are.

Given the harmfulness of conversion practices, prohibiting them can be readily justified whether under a flexible or categorical approach. The harm of conversion practices is demonstrable and far greater than the ills of restricting practices that have little to no expressive content. Even if conversion practices held great expressive content, their harms should satisfy the strict scrutiny requirement of being "narrowly tailored to serve compelling state interests." But how conversion practices should be viewed may differ from how they will be viewed by the courts. The role of judicial and political culture in producing legal outcomes cannot be ignored. This is particularly worrisome in jurisdictions combining a strict category-based approach to freedom of expression with a strong conservative legal culture.

In the United States, little consistency exists among appellate courts when it comes to bans on conversion practices. In *Pickup v Brown*, the Court of Appeal for the Ninth Circuit upheld California's ban, characterizing conversion practices as conduct subject to the lowest level of protection.[51] The Court of Appeal for the Third Circuit in *King v Christie* instead chose to characterize New Jersey's ban as bearing on professional speech subject to an intermediate level of protection, upholding the law.[52] In *Otto v City of Boca Raton*, the majority of the Court of Appeal for the Eleventh Circuit struck down two cities' bans on conversion practices for failing to withstand strict scrutiny, which is the highest level of protection.[53] However, a dissenting judge would have upheld the bans even under the highest level of free speech protection, due to the sheer harmfulness of the conversion practices. Reflecting on these three cases, I am of the view that the approach in *Pickup* is the most philosophically convincing and that the majority in *Otto* misunderstood the nature and consequences of conversion practices.[54] The US Supreme Court has thus far declined to consider the constitutionality of bans on conversion practices. How future courts will reason remains to be seen.

In jurisdictions that apply a more flexible, proportionality-based approach to freedom of expression, such as Canada, bans on conversion practices should have little difficulty passing constitutional muster.[55] Nonetheless, proponents of conversion practices appeal to freedom of expression in excess of its legal plausibility. Freedom of expression claims are common in defence of all sorts of homoantagonistic and transantagonistic behaviours, but they do not necessarily reflect a genuine belief that freedom of expression protection is available or likely to be successful. Instead, they are often couched as political and natural rights claims. Parallels may be drawn between freedom of expression arguments against bans on conversion practices in Canada and the freedom of expression arguments that were levied against Bill C-16, *An Act to Amend the Canadian Human Rights Act and the Criminal Code*, which added gender identity and expression to the *Canadian Human Rights Act*.[56] In both cases, freedom of speech is mobilized as a politico-legal shield for psychopathologizing hostile and harmful attitudes towards trans people.[57] As University of Toronto law professor Brenda Cossman observes, freedom of expression is deceptively attractive as a "rhetorical and legal vehicle for ongoing resistance" to minority rights in the post-truth era.[58] The idea that freedom of expression protects all practices involving oral expression – no matter that they are demonstrably harmful, no matter that they have little to no expressive content, and no matter that they are often engaged in by individuals who have willingly subjected themselves to professional standards of conduct – has little politico-legal plausibility in Canada and, I would venture to guess, in most jurisdictions.

Overbreadth

The second critique levied against statutory bans on conversion practices is that, although prohibiting certain forms of conversion practices may be legitimate, the bans go too far, curtailing morally acceptable practices. This critique understates the moral case against conversion practices and fails to adequately recognize the state's interest in curtailing practices that are dangerous, unproven, contrary to scientific principles, and contrary to egalitarian values. The accusation of overbreadth has primarily been couched in political terms,[59] although overbreadth has a legal meaning in the United States and Canada.[60] Psychiatrist William Byne has cautioned against legislative bans because they might restrict legitimate practices. Supporting his point, he gives the example of the closure of the CAMH clinic in the wake of Ontario's Bill 77, the *Affirming Sexual Orientation and Gender Identity Act.*[61]

While it is true that the closure of the CAMH clinic left an unfortunate gap in services, this is not a reason to allow illegitimate and potentially harmful practices. Given that Byne acknowledged the negative judgments towards transitude implicit in the corrective approach that was used at the CAMH clinic,[62] it strikes me as inconsistent of him to then criticize bans as being overbroad on account that they prohibit that specific approach. He supports his claim that the prohibition is overbroad because no professional consensus exists over the treatment of prepubescent gender-creative youth, relying on an outdated 2011 report published by the American Psychiatric Association. Furthermore, even if the 2011 report reflected current expert opinion, we must distinguish consensus over which approach is best and consensus over whether a given approach is unacceptable. Although it could be argued that no consensus exists over which approaches fall within the range of competent therapeutic care, there is a clear consensus that conversion practices are illegitimate. The seventh version of the World Professional Association for Transgender Health's (WPATH) "Standards of Care," published in 2012, disavows the practice, and over fifty professional organizations currently oppose attempts to change individuals' gender identity.[63] While some organizations focus solely on change to gender identity, many expressly understand conversion practices to include attempts to change a person's gender expression, to repress or discourage their gender identity and/or expression, and to promote certain gender identities and/or expressions. For instance, the American Psychological Association defines conversion practices by reference to "the goal of changing gender identity, gender expression, or associated components of these to be in alignment with gender role behaviors that are stereotypically associated with sex assigned at birth."[64]

It should be emphasized that laws targeting dangerous practices do not become overbroad simply because some people are not harmed by the prohibited practice. Many, if not most, criminal offences include behaviours that will sometimes be harmless. Dangerous driving and driving under the influence are clear examples. People may be convicted of dangerous driving even if no one is present in the vicinity, and people may be convicted of driving under the influence even if they are exceptionally good at driving while drunk or high. Russian roulette does not become a good idea because players have a five out of six chance of surviving. The risk of harm from conversion practices is enough to justify the law, a harm that can be expressed by the 2.27 times higher odds of lifetime suicide attempts among trans people who have experienced conversion practices – a rate that climbs to 4.15 times higher odds for those who have experienced conversion practices before ten years of age.[65] For those who were harmed by conversion practices, the fact that harm was not guaranteed offers little solace.

Bans on conversion practices would be reasonable even if it could be established that no professional consensus exists that pre-adolescent conversion practices are harmful overall. Governments regularly regulate practices that are not proven to be harmful and practices that are harmless. Pseudoscientific practices are routinely prohibited despite often being harmless. As pointed out by the District Court in *Doe v Christie,* a case bearing on the same New Jersey law as *King v Christie* but brought by patients rather than therapists, "[s]urely it is undisputed that a state has the power to regulate not only medical and mental health treatments deemed harmful, but also those that are ineffective or that are based not on medical or scientific principles but, instead, on pseudo-science."[66] Professional freedom may be curtailed even if a minimum threshold of psychological harm is not yet proven.[67] Governments may legitimately prohibit practices that are ineffective or contrary to scientific principles. Practices can also be prohibited if they are antithetical to equality. As I will explain, each of these rationales applies to prepubertal conversion practices.

First, let us consider the matter of ineffectiveness. By ineffective therapies, I mean both therapies that are proven not to be effective as well as therapies whose effectiveness is unproven. Although the scope of the state's legitimate prohibition of untested medicine is contested – notably, through right-to-try laws – it remains relatively uncontroversial that governments may prohibit access to drugs and medication that have yet to be shown to be safe and effective.[68] In Canada, the Health Products and

Food Branch of Health Canada is charged with approving drugs whose safety and efficacy has been demonstrated through clinical trials. Drugs yet to be proven safe and effective are disallowed from the market. I am not arguing here that the government should prohibit all psychosocial interventions whose safety and effectiveness remain unproven, as it does with drugs. A blanket ban on unproven therapies would be prohibitive, to be sure. It is more difficult to assess both the safety and efficacy of psychosocial interventions than of pharmaceutical drugs because the testing environment can rarely be adequately controlled, because neither therapist nor patient can be reliably blinded to the approach applied to them, and because the assessment of clinical endpoints often relies on the subjects' perception. Because of those various difficulties, assessing the safety and efficacy of psychosocial interventions is challenging and at times more art than science. Tolerating unproven psychosocial interventions may be justified. Nevertheless, the uncontroversial fact that governments can prohibit unproven drug treatments demonstrates that the absence of proven harm is not an overriding consideration when considering whether something may be regulated. To the extent that prepubertal conversion practices are not proven to be either safe or effective, and insofar as we have reasons to prohibit them, the legislative bans are not demonstrably overbroad.

Second, even in the context of prepubertal youth, conversion practices are contrary to scientific principles. Being trans is recognized as a part of healthy human diversity and is not pathological. Some authors like Richard Green have argued that, on the contrary, trans conversion practices are aligned with scientific principles:

> Whereas homosexuality per se was dropped by the APA as a disorder in 1973, in 1980, gender identity disorder was added, addressing cross-gender identification and behaviors of children and adults. Although homosexuality is no longer categorized as a disorder, gender identity disorder, or transsexualism, or gender dysphoria remains in the current DSM (Fifth Edition) [*Diagnostic and Statistical Manual of Mental Disorders*]. Therefore, the argument against attempting to modify sexual orientation because it is not a disorder is not symmetrical with attempts to modify or treat gender dysphoria.[69]

The claim that gender identity disorder remains in the fifth edition of the *Diagnostic and Statistical Manual of Mental Disorders* (DSM) is misleading and arguably dishonest.[70] Gender Identity Disorder and Gender Dysphoria are not equivalent diagnoses. From 1980 to 2013, the *DSM* included the diagnosis of Gender Identity Disorder of Childhood.[71] In 2013, the diagnostic category was changed to Gender Dysphoria in Children.[72] This shift in language was far from meaningless, being motivated by the need to de-pathologize people whose gender identity does not correspond to the gender they were assigned at birth. The change had been recommended by WPATH and aligns with the organization's statement that "the expression of gender characteristics, including identities, that are not stereotypically associated with one's assigned sex at birth is a common and culturally diverse human phenomenon [that] should not be judged as inherently pathological or negative."[73] By abandoning the terminology of "Gender Identity Disorder" in favour of "Gender Dysphoria," the fifth edition of the *DSM* expresses the view that although trans people may experience clinically significant distress, their gender identity is not pathological but, rather, part of normal human diversity. The *DSM* specifies that the terminology of Gender Dysphoria "is more descriptive than the previous DSM-IV term *gender identity disorder* and focuses on dysphoria as the clinical problem, not identity per se."[74]

A similar linguistic shift operated between versions 10 and 11 of the *International Classification of Diseases* (ICD).[75] Under version 10 of the *ICD*, which was published in 1992, the Gender Identity Disorder of Childhood diagnosis fell under the section on Mental and Behavioural Disorders. Under the latest version, published in 2018, the diagnosis was renamed Gender Incongruence in Childhood and placed under Conditions Related to Sexual Health, outside of the section on Mental, Behavioural, or Neurodevelopmental Disorders. The shift was motivated by reasons similar to those that led to the diagnosis of Gender Dysphoria in the fifth edition of the *DSM*.[76] A survey of the members of WPATH found that only 7.5 percent of the members "had the view that it should be placed in the Mental and Behavioural Disorders chapter."[77]

Although diagnostic categories specific to trans people continue to exist in both the *DSM* and the *ICD*, neither text views being transgender as pathological. Given this disavowal, it is hard to take seriously Green's claim that we have reasons to treat conversion practices targeting sexual orientation and gender identity differently due to the existence of the Gender Dysphoria diagnosis. Neither the fifth edition of the *DSM*'s Gender Dysphoria in Childhood diagnosis nor the eleventh version of the *ICD*'s Gender Incongruence in Childhood category suggests that interventions can or should target gender identity for change in youth. On the contrary, conversion practices are contrary to the teachings of both of these texts. Attempting to change a person's gender identity is contrary to the settled view that being trans is a part of healthy human diversity. Under the principle of non-maleficence, practitioners should not attempt to "cure" healthy human diversity. Prohibiting practices that attempt to do so is justified.

Third, prepubertal conversion practices promote inequality, which is contrary to the values underpinning the Canadian constitutional order. As Byne points out in relation to the CAMH clinic's work, "a negative judgment of transsexuality is, nevertheless, implicit in the desire to prevent it."[78] Equality is a recognized value of Canada's constitutional order, entrenched in the deepest roots of the *Canadian Charter of Rights and Freedoms*.[79] It no longer needs defending that legislation can properly aim at promoting equality and repressing inequality. Practices that promote inequality – for example, by enacting a negative evaluation of transitude – would nevertheless be legitimate if the patient's best interests significantly outweighed the value of addressing inequality. This would be the case if, for example, patients of conversion practices were shown to fare significantly better than patients of the gender-affirmative approach. However, conversion practices demonstrate no significant benefits to patients over other approaches. On the contrary, as I detail later in this work, all evidence points towards the gender-affirmative approach leading to better adaptation and mental well-being. But even if no evidence existed as to the superiority of the gender-affirmative approach, the fact that prepubertal conversion practices are prejudicial to trans people suffices to resolve the uncertainty. Given the importance of equality, it is not sufficient to claim – even if it were true – that no consensus exists over the harmfulness of prepubertal conversion practices.

Under Canadian law, a law is overbroad if it restricts liberty more than is necessary to accomplish its purpose.[80] Bans on conversion practices have complex multifaceted purposes that include concern over harmfulness, dubious effectiveness, the psychopathologization of healthy human diversity, and expressive inequality. To establish that bans are overbroad in the face of each of these purposes is a daunting task. To do so, proponents of conversion practices would need to establish that there exists an identifiable subset of practices that do not run afoul any of these concerns. Only where the ban includes conduct that bears no relationship to the law's purposes will it be overbroad. Since it is not possible to determine with accuracy in advance who will not be harmed by conversion practices based on the current state of science, a blanket ban is not overbroad.[81] Similarly, concerns over ineffectiveness, psychopathologization, and promoting inequality recur across the entire spectrum of conversion practices. Further studies could perhaps lead to the identification of a subset of people for whom conversion practices are harmless and effective, though it strikes me as unlikely given current scientific knowledge and the prevalent belief that such studies would be unethical. Concerns over psychopathologization and expressive inequality are, however, less susceptible to change, and it is far less clear what sort of evidence would make bans on conversion practices overbroad on these two counts. To establish that bans on conversion practices are overbroad, critics would have to prove that an identifiable subset of practices is harmless, effective, does not psychopathologize healthy human diversity, and does not perpetuate negative views towards trans people. Given the current state of scientific knowledge, this is an insurmountable task. The claim that bans on conversion practices are overbroad is wholly unsupported.

Autonomy and Religious Freedom

A third critique of bans on conversion practices casts them as illegitimate incursions on the autonomy and religious freedom of patients and their parents. Like freedom of expression, these claims are typically subject to a two-step structure: first, how much autonomy and religious freedom are impaired and, second, whether the impairment is justified. Since I have already spelled out the evidence applicable to the second step of justification in the section on therapist freedom of expression, I will not rehash it now. Instead, I focus on the first step of whether bans on conversion practices impair autonomy and religious freedom to such a degree that they might be unconstitutional. According to this third argument, patients and/or their parents have a right to choose care that aligns with their values, especially religious values. They see queerness and/or transitude as being incompatible with their values and wish to pursue conversion practices as a result. Since bans on conversion practices prevent them from doing so, they infringe on their autonomy and religious freedom. In contrast to claims of freedom of expression and overbreadth, which have centred on the perspective of practitioners, the counterarguments based on autonomy and religious freedom centre on the perspectives of patients and their parents (or other legal guardians). Because most bans on conversion practices only protect minors, the rights of patients and parents have been merged in the various arguments, which notably presumes that children and parents share the same religious views and desire to live in accordance with the precepts.

The claim that bans on conversion practices violate autonomy and religious freedom has perhaps been made most clearly by Richard Green, a proponent of conversion practices working with trans patients. In an editorial, he suggested that parental rights could be used to overturn bans, suggesting that "[v]accination laws, education, and blood transfusion provide examples of limitations and strengths of parental authority."[82] Interweaving religious freedom with parental rights, he argues:

> Parental insistence on intervention to modify a child's gender behaviors on the grounds that it would diminish prospects of a life style that is anathema to their religious beliefs could have some traction, unless the consequences of intervention were substantial. Clearly, the consequences would not rise to the level of a parental demand, based on a religious tenet of Jehovah's Witnesses, to withhold a potentially life-saving blood transfusion. That is not allowed.[83]

Reading his argument charitably, I interpret Green as claiming that parents can choose interventions for their children unless those interventions are sufficiently harmful. While many jurisdictions have affirmed courts' rights to intervene when parents refuse blood transfusions, autonomy and religious rights are strong enough that the legal outcome is not a bygone conclusion even in life-or-death circumstances.[84] Unlike withholding blood transfusions, conversion practices are not typically life threatening in the short term, and causal links to future suicide attempts remain difficult to prove. On the contrary, Green believes that conversion practices may be beneficial, at least when it comes to trans people, since "it is a helluva lot easier negotiating life as a gay man or lesbian woman than as a transwoman or transman."[85]

As an aside, I would point out that such views cast trans lives in abjection and suggests that they are full of difficulties and suffering – a gross oversimplification. While being trans may be difficult, we must distinguish between easy lives and good lives. Difficult lives can be overwhelmingly happy and satisfying. Easy lives can be deeply unhappy and dissatisfying, especially for those who suppress core parts of themselves. But, either way, for Green, conversion practices are undeniably less harmful than withholding blood transfusions. Links to serious psychological harm and suicide are far less direct. Since conversion practices are much less harmful than the near certainty of death from withholding life-saving blood transfusions, we have good reason to believe that autonomy and religious freedom should triumph over the state's legitimate interest in prohibiting practices that it perceives as harmful. Hence, according to this argument, bans on conversion practices are likely unconstitutional.

The argument fundamentally conflates the right to refuse care with the right to determine care. Patients and parents do not have a general right to demand harmful interventions that are inimical to egalitarian values. Nor does religious freedom operate as a trump card to generally applicable laws that do not try to target religious conduct or suppress the exercise of religion.[86] While conversion practices are sometimes religiously motivated, they are not religious practices. Conversion practices are not targeted out of religious animus either but, rather, because they are harmful and embody discriminatory motives. If freedom of religion could so readily defeat legislative endeavours, then nearly every law would need exceptions – few behaviours cannot be depicted as a consequence of religious commitment. Bans on conversion practices are generally applicable laws that do not single out or especially burden the exercise of religion. As such, they do not run afoul of freedom of religion. If they did, they would still be justified given the harmfulness of conversion practices, as explained earlier. Arguments against bans rarely deploy freedom of religion as a standalone argument, however. Instead, they usually fold freedom of religion into the purported right to choose interventions based on religious values, which I will now examine in more detail.

The appellate court in *Pickup*, which considered the validity of California's ban on conversion practices, most cogently explained the problem with challenges based on autonomy and religious freedom:

> [W]e have held that "substantive due process rights do not extend to the choice of type of treatment or of a particular health care provider." Thus, we concluded that "there is no fundamental right to choose a mental health professional with specific training." The Seventh Circuit has also held that "a patient does not have a constitutional right to obtain a particular type of treatment or to obtain treatment from a particular provider if the government has reasonably prohibited that type of treatment or provider." ...
>
> [I]t would be odd if parents had a substantive due process right to choose specific treatments for their children – treatments that reasonably have been deemed harmful by the state – but not for themselves. It would be all the more anomalous because the Supreme Court has recognized that the state has greater power over children than over adults.[87]

Green's analogy between blood transfusions and conversion practices fundamentally fails insofar as the former involves refusing an intervention while the latter involves demanding it. These are not analogous in the eyes of the law. My right to bodily integrity might mean that I can refuse cardiopulmonary resuscitation, but it does not mean that I can order someone to stab me, even if the outcome is the same. From a legal standpoint (and an ethical standpoint, depending on your preferred moral framework), there is a significant difference between refusing beneficial treatment and undergoing detrimental or ineffective treatment because the latter involves the conscription of another person. That other person has a legal and ethical duty to refrain from harming me. The difference is most clearly illustrated in the context of surgical care: although, as an adult, I may refuse a life-saving surgery, I could not demand that a surgeon remove one of my healthy kidneys and throw it in the garbage.[88] Patient consent does not offer a defence against disciplinary complaints or malpractice lawsuits when professionals engage in practices that are out of line with the established standards of the profession. Nor does consent offer a defence against a whole slew of criminal charges, from sexual offences involving minors to non-sexual assault causing bodily harm.[89] Consent does not entail harmlessness – hence, the need for laws that apply regardless of consent. This point is crucial in the context of conversion practices since there is no evidence that they are substantially less harmful, let alone harmless, when consent is obtained. On the contrary, many survivors report serious harm despite having sought out the conversion practices and/or ostensibly consented.[90]

The idea that no one has a general right to demand a specific intervention applies to adults just as well as to children and their parents. The principle does not turn on children's lower capacity to consent. On the contrary, the judges in *Pickup* emphasized that "it would be odd if parents had a substantive due process right to choose specific treatments for their children – treatments that reasonably have been deemed harmful by the state – but not for themselves."[91] Governments' ability to regulate or ban unproven, ineffective, risky, and harmful treatment is well established. Without it, organizations like Health Canada or the US Food and Drug Administration could not exist in their current form. While autonomy entails a right to refuse treatment, it does not grant a right to demand a specific treatment regardless of age. This disjunction between the right to refuse care and the alleged right to demand a specific intervention is well recognized in healthcare ethics. Indeed, it lies at the very heart of the Hippocratic Oath: *primum non nocere* (first, do no harm). In bioethics, *primum non nocere* translates into the principle of non-maleficence, which offers a counterweight and constraint on unfettered autonomy. Non-maleficence is one of the four recognized principles of bioethics, alongside autonomy, beneficence, and justice.[92] Non-maleficence is a sturdy principle and must not bow as soon as autonomy rears its head. In cases where ineffective or detrimental interventions are requested, autonomy must typically capitulate to non-maleficence.

The law in many contexts distinguishes between acts done to oneself and acts done to us by a third party. No law prohibits self-harm, yet I cannot consent to assault causing bodily harm.[93] No law prohibits suicide, but I cannot typically consent to someone else causing my death. It is difficult to challenge the constitutionality of laws that prohibit third-party involvement in actions that, if done alone, would be legal. Medical assistance in dying offers a quintessential example. In Canada, aiding or abetting someone in dying by suicide was a criminal offence in all circumstances until the 2015 decision of the Supreme Court of Canada in *Carter v Canada*.[94] In that decision, the court declared the law unconstitutional because it forced individuals to go through intolerable suffering as a result of a grievous and irremediable condition. The judges found that the law was overbroad and grossly disproportionate because it forced people to go through inhumane and irremediable suffering even in situations where it was clear that the person was not being induced to suicide in a moment of weakness. The bar for invalidating laws is high. It cannot be reasonably suggested that being queer or trans is a grievous and irremediable condition nor that it causes intolerable suffering. And unlike medical aid in dying, there is no evidence that conversion practices can change gender identity or sexual orientation or that it is harmless to those who consent. Rather than imposing suffering, bans on conversion practices prevent it. Any constitutional challenge based on the principles enunciated in *Carter* would be doomed to fail.

When it comes to consenting adults, a helpful comparison can be made between conversion practices and doctor-patient sexual relationships.[95] A patient may genuinely desire a sexual and/or romantic relationship with their doctor and argue that bans on these relationships impede their autonomy. Yet, despite these arguments, laws and professional codes of conduct prohibiting doctor-patient relationships have been relatively uncontroversial.[96] Sex between doctors and patients poses significant risks of harm, raises doubts about the validity of consent due to a doctor's position of authority, and can interfere with the doctor's commitment to professional integrity.[97] However strong the patient's desire, however genuine and untainted their consent could be proven to be, sexual relationships between doctors and patients continue to be strictly prohibited by countless jurisdictions and professional bodies.

Like doctor-patient sexual relationships, conversion practices involve significant risks of harm and raise doubts as to the validity of consent given the prevalence of social and internalized homoantagonism and transantagonism.[98] Many trans people come into contact with conversion practices at a most vulnerable point of their lives. They may have experienced social or familial rejection. The practitioner might be the first person they have told of their gender identity or sexual orientation. They may believe themselves broken, not knowing that queer and trans lives can be full of joy, love, community, and happiness. Conversion practitioners, for their part, wield significant institutional and social power. Many trans people have anecdotally reported seeking out, or consenting to, conversion practices out of deep-seated self-hatred and fear, under a promise that they could medically transition if they persisted in their gender identity despite lengthy conversion practices or due to the practitioner's sheer influence in their social and religious communities. Others have been pressured or coerced by their family, while the practitioner dons the garb of ignorance.[99] Serious concerns over consent and the risk of harm regardless of consent are recognized as sufficient reasons to ban doctor-patient sexual contact. By analogy, they are also sufficient to justify banning conversion practices. Consent does not justify risky, harmful, and unethical acts, and no one has a right to enlist another in committing them.

I have repeated multiple times that no one has a general right to demand a specific intervention. I now turn my attention to the right-to-try movement, which has challenged this general principle and sought to carve out an exception to it. The narrow bounds of the suggested right to try strengthen my conclusions regarding conversion practices. According to the right-to-try movement, people whose life is threatened and who have exhausted all available treatment options should have a right to try experimental treatments that have yet to be proven safe or effective.[100] The right to try is predicated on the assumption that terminally ill patients have little to lose and everything to gain from experimental treatments. Under those conditions, the combination of autonomy and beneficence would outweigh the principle of non-maleficence and warrant access to treatment. The argument is controversial, and many scientists and bioethicists oppose the recognition of a right to try.[101]

It is also worth noting that no court, to my knowledge, has elevated the right to try into a constitutional requirement. It has only ever been recognized by statute. Even if such a right were to be recognized, however, it would not apply to conversion practices. Being queer or trans is not a life-threatening illness, let alone one that would justify dangerous interventions that have been shown to harm many of those individuals subjected to them. Given that the right to try is disanalogous to the purported right to receive conversion practices, and given that the right to try emanates from legislatures rather than from constitutional law, there is all the more reason to doubt the existence of a constitutional right to conversion practices. While precedent may always change at the whim of judges, it is not surprising that US appellate courts have so far rejected constitutional challenges based on autonomy and religious freedom.[102]

It is also crucial to recognize that equality considerations are at play in conversion practices. Unlike conversion practices, refusing blood transfusions is not underpinned by the view that certain forms of life are inherently undesirable, wicked, or wrong. No prejudice, no discriminatory animus can usually be found behind a refused blood transfusion. These considerations are not only relevant because they emphasize the moral objectionability of conversion practices but also because they shed doubt on the quality of consent and point to a risk of bias in parents' assessments of their child's best interest. Queer and trans people often display internalized homoantagonism and/or transantagonism, which are often reflected in desires to undergo conversion practices. Consent can also be motivated by pressures from prejudiced conversion practitioners, religious authorities, family members, peers, and members of the community. These biased influences cast aspersions on the quality of consent and on whether it reflects a genuine self-assessment of best interests. On the contrary, there is reason to believe that 2SLGBTQIA+ people will be harmed by conversion practices regardless and that many who express consent will later regret it.

A parent's prejudice towards queer and trans lives can bias their evaluation of the best interests of their child. Queer and trans children are meaningfully different from their cisgender and heterosexual parents, and we cannot assume they share the same religious views about queer and trans people or that they will continue to do so as they grow up.

Being queer and trans yourself offers a strong impetus to revise religious commitments that demean your existence, an impetus that cisgender heterosexual parents do not share or appreciate on an intimate level. Whereas it may be fair to attribute a parent's non-prejudiced beliefs to their children, the same cannot be said of a parent's beliefs that demonstrate prejudice towards core aspects of their child's self such as gender identity and sexual orientation.

This is not to say that religious beliefs should play no part in determining a child's best interests. Religious beliefs are a crucial consideration when assessing a child's best interest. However, so are gender identity and sexual orientation. The United Nations Committee on the Rights of the Child's *General Comment No. 14* confirms that gender identity and sexual orientation are components of the child's best interest.[103] The importance of gender identity and sexual orientation in the best interest of the child are increasingly enshrined in law. In Ontario, the two notions were added to considerations of a child's best interest under the *Child, Youth and Family Services Act, 2017*.[104] In jurisdictions that do not recognize gender identity and sexual orientation as a matter of statute, the considerations may nonetheless be part of the notion of sex or be judicially understood as independent relevant factors. Gender identity and sexual orientation are essential components of children's long-term well-being. Children are better served by parenting approaches that acknowledge the importance of religion, gender identity, and sexual orientation and that strive for harmony between them.[105] Parental demands for conversion practices underestimate the importance of respecting and fostering their children's gender identity and sexual orientation, subordinating them to prejudiced attitudes towards trans and queer lives. Given the conflict between parental values and children's best interests implicated by conversion practices, governments have good reason to prohibit the practices.

Bans on conversion practices pursue serious policy objectives. Bans prevent severe harm. They prevent depression, suicidal ideations, and suicide attempts. Additionally, they promote the equality of trans and queer communities, rejecting prejudiced and discriminatory practices that cast being queer or trans as undesirable, wrong, and pathological. The egalitarian function of bans is doubly important in the context of licensed professionals, whose authority is recognized and supported by the state. By disavowing practices that psychopathologize or devalue queer, trans, and gender-creative people, the government communicates that queer, trans, and gender-creative people are of equal worth, fulfilling its legitimate interest of promoting equality.[106] Though hardly a panacea for the problems created by cis heteronormativity, governments' disavowal of conversion practices positively impacts society and advances the mental health of queer, trans, and gender-creative people.[107] Whether under the heading of autonomy, parental authority, or religious freedom, there is no defence for conversion practices. No one has the right to demand harmful, unethical interventions.

∼

For all their noise, accusations of unconstitutionality levied against bans on trans conversion practices seem to be – in the words of William Shakespeare – "much ado about nothing." Practitioners, and especially licensed professionals, have no constitutional right to harm others. Neither individuals nor their parents have an unrestrained right to enlist practitioners in unethical and harmful conduct. Allegations of overbreadth are overstated. Conversion practices are dehumanizing and harmful, and no subgroup may be clearly identified that is not harmed by conversion practices. While not everyone is harmed by conversion practices, we cannot know ahead of time who will and who will not be, and the risks are far too great to accept.

The application of constitutional law is subject to the vagaries of judges. However philosophically compelling arguments may be, judges can always disagree. Though Canadian constitutional law is robust and very unlikely to condone trans conversion practices, there is a greater polarization of views within the US judiciary around the question of freedom of speech. Judges in the United States have shown themselves to be borderline absolutist at times, interpreting free speech broadly and demonstrating an inordinate reluctance to allow restrictions. Lawyers will have to come philosophically and scientifically ready for a fight. However, even in the most hostile of jurisdictions, the constitutionality of bans on trans conversion practices remains a strong position to take.

Analyzing the Benefits and Limitations of Bans

5

The closure of the Centre for Addiction and Mental Health (CAMH) Gender Identity Clinic for Children and Youth was perceived as a good thing by many members of trans communities. Although it closed in the wake of Ontario's ban on conversion practices, it was never authoritatively determined whether the corrective approach that it employed violated the law. Once it closed, its practitioners fanned out to other employments and into private practice, and many likely continued to employ the same approach to trans care. The ongoing uncertainty over whether the corrective approach violates the law gestures towards a major limit of bans. It took me an entire chapter to confirm that the Ontarian ban covers the corrective approach. How can we expect practitioners to obey the law and others to hold them accountable if they are uncertain what the law prohibits? Bans are broad. Bans are valid. But are bans good? How good? Our incursion into the legal regulation of trans conversion practices aims to answer those questions. Formal protections and legal prohibitions often fail to bring about substantial improvements to trans lives.[1] If we are genuinely committed to trans well-being, we cannot simply presume that existing bans have optimal or even good enough outcomes. Instead of taking the virtues of bans for granted, I use this chapter to analyze their benefits and limits, productively taking up the question of how desirable bans are from the standpoint of trans communities.

Existing bans have positively impacted professional practices and have undeniable symbolic reach. The closure of the CAMH clinic likely prevented many from undergoing trans conversion practices, and the Ontario law continues to be cited approvingly as evidence that trans lives are valuable. Yet bans also suffer from countless limitations. They are often restricted to minors and non-consensual forms of conversion practices. They lack clarity and detail, making self-regulation and mutual accountability difficult. They struggle to reach unregulated practitioners. They may generate professional resentment, making enforcement through disciplinary complaints more difficult. They often fail to provide compensation to survivors. They do not effectively restrict public funding of conversion practices. They are heavily dependent on legislative will, making them difficult to pass in conservative jurisdictions. And where the laws take on a criminal form as in Malta, they may make proof of conversion practices unduly difficult as well as contribute to the expansion of the carceral state. Taken together, these limitations highlight the need for not only better-drafted laws but also a multipronged approach to trans conversion practices that moves beyond exclusive reliance on bans.

Benefits

Changes in Professional Practices

Legislation can encourage changes in practices among professionals despite a reluctance on the part of regulatory bodies to curtail conversion practices using the tools available to them, such as disciplinary proceedings. Speaking before the Standing Committee on Justice Policy, Joyce Rowlands of the College of Registered Psychotherapists of Ontario deemed Bill 77, the *Affirming Sexual Orientation and Gender Identity Act,* unnecessary: "Our point, really, is that this matter can be dealt with by the regulatory colleges."[2] In her opinion, statutory prohibition was unnecessary because conversion practices were already denounced by the professional orders and would be appropriately subject to sanctions. Jake Pyne responded to her assertion that the law as it was sufficed to prohibit the practices: "I think it's mistaken to assert that the various colleges of the helping professions in this province have the power to address this issue adequately. If that were the case, we would not have had this problem for the past 40 years."[3] They may well have the power to punish conversion practices, as I have argued in a previous publication, but the fact of the matter is that they have not done so.[4] The positive impact of bans in discouraging conversion practices is clear from the role that Bill 77 played in the closure of the CAMH clinic, which continued to operate until the bill came into force despite decades of criticism. If its closure is positive, as many professionals and members of trans communities have perceived it, then legislative bans on trans conversion practices show considerable promise.

Although the law's chilling effect has mostly been mentioned negatively, such reactions also speak to the pedagogical role that legislation can play in shaping practices.[5] Even if trans conversion practices are contrary to professional malpractice and disciplinary law, as I believe them to be, an explicit ban informs practitioners of their professional obligations and may motivate disciplinary bodies to enforce their regulations. As Wake Forest University law professor Marie-Amelie George has noted, news coverage on conversion practices in California increased by roughly 789 percent after the practice was prohibited by law.[6] Although the content of this news coverage was not critically analyzed, it cannot be doubted that legislation prohibiting conversion practices can play a significant role in educating the public, practitioners, and institutions.

Symbolic Impact of Laws on Culture and Mental Health

Beyond their pedagogical and material effects, laws play a symbolic function that can precipitate cultural changes and improve the mental health of trans communities. Bans on trans conversion practices send the message that trans and gender-creative lives are equally valuable as lives that perform or conform to hegemonic gender configurations. As George explains,

> law can change the social meaning of an action. ... Even if individuals object to a policy choice, by conforming to the law, they create a cultural environment that supports the law's normative commitment. ... Thus, even if a law does not affect a specific individual's conduct, it still may have an expressive impact on that person.[7]

I do not believe that her description of bans as primarily expressive is accurate in the trans context. Nonetheless, it is undeniable, based on trans advocacy and the legislative history of Bill 77, that there are expressive elements to these laws. Expressive ends are a secondary goal, even if the primary goal is to discourage and sanction conversion practices.

This change to social meaning can have a positive impact on the mental health of trans communities. Research has found correlations between the legalization of same-sex marriage and significantly reduced suicidality among lesbian, gay, bisexual, and queer (LGBQ) students and between laws permitting denials of services to same-sex couples and significantly increased mental distress among LGBQ adults.[8] These studies support the thesis that laws bearing on 2SLGBTQIA+ people – including trans people – have an impact on mental health that exceeds their material effects. However, polarized media debates related to the contemplated legislative changes can harm mental health, suggesting a need for caution.[9]

While the symbolic effects of bans on trans conversion practices are likely positive, there is room to ask whether we might overvalue such effects to the detriment of more material changes. Writing in the context of hate crime laws, York University gender studies researcher Evan Vipond points out: "In passing laws that are reactionary rather than preventive, the government offers a band-aid solution under the guise of equality."[10] We must ask whether the law's message will lead to a tangible impact or become yet another forgotten law on the books. At least one individual whose work appears to have motivated Bill 77 expressed the belief that the law did not apply to him, which suggests that Bill 77 may fail to alter professional practices.[11] There is an opportunity cost to prioritizing legal reforms that are primarily symbolic and fail to address the lived conditions of trans people. The symbolic effects of laws become all the more questionable in light of the relationship that George establishes between symbolic ends and marriage equality: "For advocates, securing the right to marry – not just enjoy the benefits of marriage through civil unions – was essential because of the expressive function of the marriage label."[12] Indeed, the narrow focus on marriage in large-scale 2SLGBTQIA+ movements has been heavily criticized by activists and scholars for engaging in politics of respectability, legitimizing the distribution of social benefits around a specific vision of the family and failing to care for the most vulnerable members of these communities.[13] As Seattle University law professor Dean Spade suggests,

> [w]e must have a long-term view about how social change works or else we get short-sighted strategies. The struggle for same-sex marriage is a relevant example in this moment. That fight makes perfect sense from a lawyer's perspective – "These things are not equal under the law. I'm going to make them equal." It only stops making sense when you think a little more broadly about resource allocation in our movements, and about the broader context of the resistance to family and sexual regulation.[14]

Is the fight for the well-being of trans and gender-creative youth best done through laws that may or may not implicitly recognize the legitimacy of medical and professional authority over those same youth? The involvement of professionals in trans and gender-creative lives is controversial.[15] Leading scholars have opposed the existence of a diagnostic category for trans and gender-creative children in the *Diagnostic and Statistical Manual of Mental Disorders* and the *International Classification of Diseases*, arguing that the diagnosis is stigmatizing and that such children do not need medical care simply for being trans or gender creative, at least before puberty.[16]

Even as models of care grow more progressive, the implicit message remains that it is scientists and professionals who determine what amounts to ethical practice, not those who are most impacted by their work. Most statutes that prohibit conversion practices do so by entrusting disciplinary bodies with the task of enforcing the ban, legitimating their power at the same time that they seek to restrict professional practices. However, there is also reason to question whether symbolism is all bad. I have reflected on my own negativity towards symbolism in an invited contribution to the *University of Toronto Press Blog*, saying:

> Although I continue to believe that purely symbolic laws should be criticised, the underlying critique stays with me to this day. The symbolic is one of the most characteristic traits of human societies.

> We lead symbolic lives, and deal in symbols every day of our lives.
> What does it mean, as activists who aspire to a grounded approach,
> to demean symbolic change?[17]

Legislation may have positive impacts on mental health independently
from its immediate material impact. Marriage equality, for instance,
has been associated with reduced suicidality among queer adolescents,
even though they were not yet directly impacted by the (in)ability to
marry.[18] Passing laws prohibiting conversion practices may help trans
youth and adults feel more accepted in society and improve their mental
well-being. Hope remains that the laws will significantly impact practice
and thus will have tangible positive effects on people's lives. Although
symbolic impacts should not be overvalued or become the primary
guide to legislation purporting to improve trans and gender-creative
lives, and although we must remain critical of the disciplinary regimes
that underpin trans healthcare,[19] I believe that bans retain the potential
to precipitate or at least encourage cultural shifts as they communicate
approval of gender-affirmative practices to practitioners and the public.

Limitations

Age and Consent Restrictions
With the exception of Spanish regions and Malta, laws prohibiting
trans conversion practices thus far have been limited to minors. Some
places, like Malta, also protect some vulnerable adults. The rationale
for excluding adults from the application of the law is to pre-empt
legislative opposition on grounds that the law interferes with individual
autonomy.[20] Speaking before the Legislative Assembly of Ontario, Cheri
DiNovo explained Bill 77's restriction to minors by stating: "Adults
are free to do what adults will do."[21] Though many scholars, activists,
and politicians may wish to also prohibit trans conversion practices for
adults, passing laws that prohibit conversion practices directed at adults
may be politically difficult. Passing laws that only prohibit practices
targeting minors could impact how professional malpractice law and
disciplinary complaints by adults are treated due to the belief that if the
legislature wanted to prohibit trans conversion practices against adults

it would have done so. However, it could also be argued that the laws do not demonstrate legislative intent to exclude adult trans conversion practices from legal regulation but, rather, seeks to guarantee that trans conversion practices on minors are prohibited independently of the state of scientific consensus and knowledge. How these age-based restrictions will feature in lawsuits is therefore uncertain.

Conversion practices on adults are common. In a 2019 international survey, 63.1 percent of those who experienced conversion practices were adults at the time.[22] In Canada, 48.8 percent of those who experienced conversion practices first did so in adulthood – a proportion that appears to be larger among trans people.[23] Before the Canadian federal legislature, Erika Muse and Peter Gajdics reported experiencing conversion practices as young adults and having ostensibly consented.[24] Both successfully exhorted the federal government to extend their proposed ban on conversion practices to all ages and regardless of consent, arguing that valid consent cannot be given to fraudulent and harmful practices. There is little evidence that such conversion practices are any less harmful for adults. As I pointed out previously, adults are not free to demand harmful treatment despite being otherwise free to consent to, or refuse, proposed treatment. Jack Drescher and colleagues have cogently argued against this point in the context of sexual orientation:

> Conversion therapists have at times defended their actions by claiming their clients should be able to choose to take part in these therapies. We disagree and suggest that a parallel proscribed behavior that regulatory bodies can consider while assessing how to respond to these complaints is sexual contact between therapists and patients. Sexual contact, even when consensual, has been shown to be very detrimental to the patient and has no place in the clinical setting.[25]

Adults who are trans or are questioning their gender are particularly vulnerable. Stigma against trans people is profoundly anchored in our culture, leading many individuals to internalize negative attitudes towards trans lives. Lack of information about therapeutic practices and the difficulty of finding alternative practitioners in given locales also create a risk of less than fully informed consent being given to conversion practices.[26] This is especially true for intellectually disabled adults. Though most trans adults are capable of free and enlightened consent – we must be wary of narratives that infantilize them – there is reason to doubt the autonomy-based arguments in favour of allowing conversion practices for adults. Autonomy is more complex than giving or withholding consent and does not trump the duty of practitioners to provide competent, beneficial care.[27]

Insufficiently Detailed Wording
Laws prohibiting conversion practices rarely include detailed explanations of what they cover. Practitioners and institutional actors who read the law without being aware of the legislative history, social context of the statute, and link between the statute and the *Report of the American Psychological Association Task Force on Appropriate Therapeutic Responses to Sexual Orientation* may find themselves unable to realize its scope.[28] Multiple practitioners whose practices are routinely characterized as conversion practices reject both the label and the characterization of their work as attempting to change gender identity even though they implicitly or explicitly maintain the prevention of adult trans outcomes as a clinical goal.

The difficulties posed by insufficiently detailed wording are particularly severe in jurisdictions whose laws are framed around the intention to "change gender identity" rather than "change or direct gender identity" or "change, repress and, or eliminate," which are wordings that can respectively be found in the original version of Ontario's Bill 77 and in the Maltese law.[29] In a recent Canadian study, only half of the participants felt that the then newly proposed federal law's language encompassed their experience with conversion practices.[30] The federal law defined conversion practices as any "practice, treatment or service designed to change a person's sexual orientation to heterosexual or gender identity to cisgender, or to repress or reduce non-heterosexual attraction or sexual behaviour," despite the language already being more expansive than the wording of bans that focused solely on attempts to change gender identity and sexual orientation. Although careful interpretation of the statute clarifies its meaning and scope, the impact on practice will be limited by its ability to communicate effectively which practices are prohibited and which are not. Adopting more detailed wording may be particularly helpful to well-meaning practitioners who hold subtler cisnormative or transantagonistic attitudes. I discuss the psychological aspects of insufficiently detailed bans at greater length in Chapter 6.

Criminal Laws

Some jurisdictions have opted for criminal bans of conversion practices. Malta's law is criminal in nature, and recent Canadian efforts have revolved around adding conversion practices to the *Criminal Code*.[31] Although criminal penalties may discourage practices more readily than disciplinary sanctions, the previously mentioned lack of details in the statute's prohibition creates additional challenges in the criminal context. Interpretation of penal provisions is subject to a narrower rule of interpretation. In the words of then Chief Justice Antonio Lamer of the Supreme Court of Canada, writing for the majority in *R. v McIntosh*: "It is a principle of statutory interpretation that where two interpretations of a provision which affects the liberty of a subject are available, one of which is more favourable to an accused, then the court should adopt this favourable interpretation."[32] The rule that interpretations favourable to the accused should be favoured is limited to instances of genuine ambiguity.[33] The applicability of this rule has been eroded over time insofar as a careful, contextual interpretation can lead courts to hold that no genuine ambiguity exists.[34] Nevertheless, judges may be more reluctant to interpret provisions broadly when a professional is faced with the risk of jail time, even if it means limiting the state's ability to sanction conversion practices.[35] Should bans be interpreted narrowly, it may negatively impact the deterrent effect of the law as well as constrain the future interpretation of non-criminal laws prohibiting conversion practices.

Criminal bans also create evidentiary difficulties. Defendants cannot be compelled to testify in a criminal trial, making it more difficult to establish the required *mens rea*. Proof beyond a reasonable doubt is an exacting standard that will be difficult to meet, especially without the defendant's testimony. The civil standard of balance of probabilities is, by contrast, much easier to meet, especially since the defendant may be forced to testify. In jurisdictions that grant a right against self-incrimination, the presence of a criminal prohibition may also mean that the defendant can decline to testify in civil suits, making it more difficult for survivors of conversion practices to prevail.

The adoption of a criminal approach additionally raises concerns regarding the expansion of the carceral state. The law has a long and shameful history of tolerating and often encouraging discrimination and violence against marginalized populations. From the overt criminalization of same-sex intimacy until 1969, through the 1980s Toronto bathhouse raids and the 1990 Montreal Sex Garage raid, to the ongoing criminal-ization of people living with human immunodeficiency virus (HIV), we share painful memories of the criminal law's targeting of 2SLGBTQIA+ communities. Even when the law appears neutral on its face, it has been and continues to be deployed disproportionately against marginalized groups, leading to police violence and the over-incarceration of Black and Indigenous populations in Canada. Prisons are sites of untold violence, and recourse to carceral solutions are antithetical to critical trans politics.[36] Approaches that decentre prison as a response to social problems should be favoured wherever possible. Placing discretion over enforcement in the hands of police and prosecutors is a fraught exercise, especially given the fraught relationship between trans communities, the police, and legal institutions. The rigid and punishment-centric nature of criminal processes may be inimical to the mental health of survivors of conversion practices, giving them little control over the process or outcome and re-traumatizing them in the course of the trial. Prosecutors may force survivors to testify against their will, which may be a great risk of re-traumatization. They may lay charges against family members or survivors who subsequently took part in offering conversion practi-ces, regardless of the will of the complainant. By contrast, non-carceral approaches may offer more flexibility and sensibility, centring on the needs of survivors and impacted communities.

Unregulated Practitioners

In jurisdictions that do not prohibit the unlicensed practice of psycho-therapy, the prohibition of trans conversion practices may fail to include a wide range of harmful practices, notably when done in a religious context. However, this limitation should be contextualized. In Canada, the unlicensed practice of psychotherapy is often prohibited, and, in the United States, constitutional protections of religious freedom might make it impossible to prohibit conversion practices by members of the clergy or other unlicensed individuals.[37] Where real concerns exist over the constitutionality of prohibiting conversion practices by unlicensed individuals, bans should be drafted carefully to ensure severability and to avoid the entire ban being invalidated as a result. Extending bans to cover non-professionals may be partly unnecessary or undesirable in some jurisdictions. Where regulating unlicensed practice would be constitutional but has not been done, prohibiting conversion practices by anyone would plausibly be allowed. The prohibition of harmful psychotherapeutic practices by unlicensed practitioners is a narrower operationalization of the same legitimate legislative interest of preventing risks of harm. If unlicensed practices and harmful licensed practices can be banned, it stands to reason that harmful unlicensed practice may generally also be banned.

Prohibiting conversion practices by non-professionals is nevertheless a broader and, consequently, more desirable ban than simply prohibiting conversion practices by licensed clinicians as well as the unlicensed practice of psychotherapy. Unsystematic transantagonistic behaviours that fall short of conversion practices are extremely unlikely to ever amount to the illegal practice of psychotherapy, whereas many practices that fall short of the illegal practice of psychotherapy will nevertheless be sufficiently systematic to amount to conversion practices. Although it is preferable for bans to include non-professionals if the goal is to discourage all forms of conversion practices, it should be remembered that licensure and a practice's degree of systematicity are loosely proportional to responsiveness to legal regulation. Unlicensed faith-based conversion practices have shown themselves to be resistant to legal disincentives and may be best addressed through non-legal means.

Professional Resentment and Adjudicator Reluctance

Professionals may resent legislative interference in their work. Approaches to care are traditionally left to self-regulating professions. Legislation may create opposition and resentment within professional associations and discourage adjudicators from sanctioning professionals faced with disciplinary complaints. Joyce Rowland's comments before the Ontario Standing Committee on Justice Policy raises the concern of resentment on the part of professional associations.[38] Professional bodies are tasked with licensing practitioners and maintaining the standards of the profession through disciplinary procedures. These bodies, such as the College of Registered Psychotherapists, operate as a form of professional self-regulation. Whereas governments grant privileges and benefits – notably, monopolies – to professionals who are licensed by regulatory bodies, the structure of licensure privileges self-regulation under the presumption that professionals are best positioned to judge each other's practices given the in-depth knowledge typically required to evaluate the quality of the interventions.

Laws such as Bill 77 are incursions on a terrain traditionally left to professionals, raising concerns of legislative interference with the proper functioning of the profession. Professional resentment risks manifesting itself by a lack of policy-level engagement with conversion practices, a hostility to developing clear guidelines opposing conversion practices, and a reluctance on the part of adjudicators to impose disciplinary sanctions on fellow professionals for practices. Adjudicators may also be led to believe that laws such as Bill 77 would not have been passed if conversion practices were already contrary to the duty of professionals to provide competent care, and they may be reluctant to sanction professionals who they believe to be respecting this duty.[39] Professional resentment and adjudicator reluctance suggest that bans may have a more limited impact than assumed. The limitation highlights the need to supplement bans with other measures targeting the behaviour and culture of licensed professionals. Professional resentment and adjudicator reluctance may be possible to mitigate by involving professionals and professional associations in the drafting of bans.

Lack of Compensation for Survivors
Most bans on conversion practices do not provide compensation, even though it is crucial to the well-being of those harmed by conversion practices. Connecticut's law is the only one to expressly provide for compensation to patients subjected to conversion practices. It does so by declaring that conversion practices are an "unfair or deceptive

trade practice" within the meaning of the state's consumer protection laws, which grants individuals the right to sue for damages.[40] Whether compensation can be sought for violations of the prohibition on trans conversion practices in other jurisdictions is less clear and will largely vary from jurisdiction to jurisdiction. In Canada, violations of codes of ethics, while they do not automatically constitute professional malpractice, may give rise to a civil claim where the violated provision establishes "elementary standards of care."[41] Nevertheless, it will not be sufficient to demonstrate a violation of disciplinary law: further legal arguments will be necessary to establish that this violation falls short of the requirements of professional malpractice law – arguments that will not be detailed in this book.

Continued Funding of Conversion Practices

Many bans prohibit public funding of conversion practices. However, they typically do not contain inquiry and enforcement mechanisms to identify practitioners seeking funding for conversion practices without identifying their practices as such. The misconception that disallowing billing for conversion practices precludes the disbursement of public funds to cover them is found among some legislators. BC legislator Spencer Chandra Herbert exemplifies this misconception:

> I've been assured by the Ministry of Health, specifically, that there is no way, currently, that somebody could bill to accept money to do a practice like conversion therapy.
>
> Now, that's different from Ontario. Ontario, I understand, introduced legislation to make it clear to actually ban that billing category from existing in their health legislation. In B.C., there is no such category. So for a number of years, that hasn't been possible. I'm really happy to hear that.[42]

However, Ontario did not provide a specific billing code for conversion practices. Conversion practices would instead be billed under other codes – notably, those for depression, anxiety, Gender Dysphoria, transsexualism, transvestic disorder, and so on. The lack of a specific billing code for conversion practices does not mean that it cannot be funded by public insurance. Since alternative billing codes are used to fund conversion practices, the lack of inquiry and enforcement mechanisms limits the impact of bans on the public funding of conversion practices. Bans on the public funding of conversion practices also fail to encompass private insurance coverage. Given the prevalence of private insurance and out-of-pocket payments for psychotherapists due to the dearth of available, publicly funded mental healthcare, the impact of prohibiting public coverage of conversion practices, in all probability, will be paltry at most.

Unwillingness to Legislate

The last and perhaps biggest challenge to laws as a means of curtailing trans conversion practices is that many jurisdictions seem unwilling to adopt a ban. Only three provinces in Canada have passed acts prohibiting conversion practices as of July 2020, though a few more have expressed the interest or intent to follow suit. Nonetheless, most provinces and territories remain without laws against conversion practices on the books. In the United States, eighteen states, Puerto Rico, and the District of Columbia have prohibited trans conversion practices, leaving thirty-two states without a ban. Very few historically conservative states have banned conversion practices, with Utah standing out as a clear exception. Utah became the first conservative state to ban conversion practices after the Church of Jesus Christ of Latter-Day Saints, also known as the Mormon Church, endorsed the ban. Close to 90 percent of the legislators are members of this church.[43]

Jurisdictions in which conversion practices are less common may be more likely to introduce legislation. Using the prevalence data reported by Jack Turban and colleagues, it appears that US jurisdictions that ended up adopting bans on conversion practices saw substantially fewer conversion practices on average before the bans were adopted.[44] In states that have not yet banned the practices, 6.03 percent of adults reported recent exposure to conversion practices versus 4.50 percent in states that did, which is a reduction of 25.37 percent. Of note, only two of the states that now prohibit conversion practices – California and New Jersey – enacted their bans during the period under study (2010–15), both in 2013. Both show an above-average prevalence of conversion practices. All other bills were enacted after 2015; the lower prevalence in these states cannot be attributed to their respective bans. Since only adults were included in the study, recent exposure excludes children and, as a result, may underestimate exposure. Insofar as conversion practices are more common in jurisdictions that are yet unwilling to prohibit them, legislative means of curtailing conversion practices may be least effective in areas that could benefit the most from them. Nonetheless, the prevalence of conversion practices in jurisdictions that have enacted bans remains considerable. Bans are hardly useless in those jurisdictions, notwithstanding the lower prevalence of conversion practices.

Some policy-makers have suggested that it would be better to focus on supporting access to transition-related and gender-affirmative care rather than on penalizing conversion practices, especially in light of the legislative unwillingness to ban these practices.[45] Conversion practices and poor access to care, while related, are nevertheless distinct problems. Professionals engaging in conversion practices may promote public funding of transition-related care for those they deem worthy, for instance. Lack of insurance coverage and long wait times are some of the biggest problems in access to transition-related care and do not directly concern professional practices.[46] Mandating gender-affirmative care in a manner that effectively undermines conversion practices poses substantial challenges. Laws are blunt instruments that may lack the flexibility required to account for individualized care and the evolution of best clinical practices. Conversely, retaining flexibility may well fail to adequately discourage trans conversion practices, which take on diverse and nuanced shapes. Supporting access to transition-related and gender-affirmative care is not a replacement for prohibiting conversion practices. The policy angles are not mutually exclusive, as shown by the Spanish laws that grant rights to transition-related and gender-affirmative care alongside their bans on conversion practices. Both are required to meet the health needs of trans communities.

The election of conservative governments across North America makes it increasingly unlikely that legislation prohibiting trans conversion practices will sweep across Canada and the United States. Divisions along political lines will likely continue to define the legislative landscape for years to come. Given the limits of legislative approaches to trans conversion practices, how can we more effectively discourage them?

~

At the beginning of this chapter, I asked how good bans are. The answer seems to be: fairly good ... but not as good as they could be. Existing bans on trans conversion practices are not fatally flawed, though they are flawed nonetheless. An abolitionist argument could be made that criminal bans are fatally flawed insofar as they contribute to the expansion of the carceral state. It is a compelling argument but one that goes beyond the scope of this book. I do not need to answer once and for all whether criminal bans are acceptable. It suffices that I favour non-criminal approaches and stay away from carceral sanctions in the model law of Chapter 7.

Some of the limits of bans can be addressed through astute drafting, which is what I attempt to do with the model law. Other limits inhere to legislative approaches to complex social problems like trans conversion practices. It will not surprise anyone that some governments' unwillingness to legislate cannot be legislated away. Legal scholars should investigate whether there are other avenues of legal recourse in jurisdictions where a ban is not forthcoming. I have previously argued that trans conversion practices violate disciplinary standards and professional malpractice laws, for instance.[47] And, in the United States, consumer fraud law has successfully been used to close an organization offering conversion practices.[48] However, law alone will not spell the end of trans conversion practices. Grassroots, community-driven movements and pressures by healthcare professionals and organizations are vital tools for challenging legislative inertia and supplementing bans.

Developing an Affirmative Professional Culture

6

The closure of the Centre for Addiction and Mental Health (CAMH) Gender Identity Clinic for Children and Youth showed the potential of extralegal action in curtailing conversion practices. Although the Ontario ban seemingly played a role in motivating the external review of the clinic's practices and its subsequent closure, it is significant that the ban was never directly enforced. It was the combination of peer opprobrium and CAMH's decision-making structures that led to the closure of the clinic. So long as those in positions of professional authority believed the clinic's practices to be wrong, they could effect a change. How can we build on the power and potential of professional opprobrium to supplement legislative bans?

Trans conversion practices by licensed practitioners are foremost a problem of professional culture. While legislation may plant the seed of a culture shift, more is often needed to supersede past attitudes and eliminate harmful practices from the professional landscape. If we wish to fully eradicate trans conversion practices, we must supplement bans with initiatives that intervene in professional culture. If practitioners are to be discouraged from trans conversion practices, they must be informed of the practices they must refrain from and be sufficiently motivated not to engage in them. Motivation to refrain from practices can be internal (desiring to act in accordance with one's own ethical standards or self-identity) or external (desiring to avoid the potential negative consequences of acting against prescribed norms of behaviour).

I draw on the sociology of professions and moral psychology literature to respond to the limitations of bans identified in the previous chapter and propose a means of discouraging trans conversion practices through professional measures targeting knowledge and motivation. Issues such as insufficiently detailed wording, professional resentment, and adjudicator reluctance may be allayed through detailed professional guidelines that clearly identify the prohibited behaviours, through educational measures that instill an understanding of the importance of gender-affirming care and the unacceptability of trans conversion practices at a crucial point in professional identity formation, and through the creation of accountability structures that ensure visible oversight and enforcement of professional standards regarding trans conversion practices. The three poles of policy-making, education, and accountability are mutually reinforcing and offer promising ways of supplementing bans.

Clear Professional Guidelines

Discouraging conversion practices effectively requires clear professional guidelines. The scope of trans conversion practices bans is not immediately evident from reading the law. Without an in-depth knowledge of the history of these bans and of approaches to trans healthcare, it is difficult for practitioners to know which behaviours and interventions are prohibited and which are not. Similarly, practitioners without extensive knowledge of conversion practices are unlikely to appreciate which behaviours and interventions fall under the notion of conversion practices and are at odds with professional principles to which they are bound such as competency, non-discrimination, and respect for dignity.[1]

Some professional associations have already developed detailed practice guidelines in parallel with their opposition to trans conversion practices. The Ordre des travailleurs sociaux et des thérapeutes conjugaux et familiaux du Québec (Order of Social Workers, Family, and Marriage Therapists of Québec [OTSTCFQ]) has developed a dossier titled *Pratiques anti-oppressives auprès des jeunes trans* (*Anti-oppressive practices with trans youth*) that provides strong support for the gender-affirmative approach to trans youth care.[2] Shortly after, the OTSTCFQ endorsed the Joint

Statement on the Affirmation of Gender Diverse Children and Youth of the Canadian Association for Social Work Education and the Canadian Association of Social Workers, which declared that any "attempt to alter the gender identity or expression of a young person to align with social norms is considered unethical and an abuse of power and authority."[3] The OTSTCFQ positioned its endorsement as part of a broader range of efforts to guide trans youth care that included the dossier. Professional guidance respects the spirit of professional orders, which have as a main purpose the protection of the public.[4]

Moral psychology research demonstrates that the malleability of ethical norms allows unethical actors to preserve their moral self-image. Individuals internalize social norms and values and then compare their behaviour to them.[5] Compliance with norms and values is psychologically satisfying, whereas failing to comply with those norms forces moral agents to negatively update their self-image.[6] However, when ethical norms are unclear, ambiguous, or malleable, people will seek to avoid negatively updating their self-image by reinterpreting the behaviour as morally acceptable in a self-serving manner.[7] The rejection of the conversion practices label by practitioners of the corrective approach may be an example of self-concept maintenance through norm malleability. This self-serving psychological process is limited by the ethical context, including the specificity of the ethical norm. The more the norm is malleable, the more people will engage in norm-violating behaviour and preserve their self-image as a good person.[8] Greater norm specificity forces people to either act more ethically or accept that they willingly act unethically, which is psychologically undesirable.

The lack of specificity of prohibitions on trans conversion practices allows professionals who engage in conversion practices to preserve their self-image as moral individuals despite their engagement in those practices. As we have seen, some professionals who adopt the corrective approach deny that they are acting contrary to Bill 77, the *Affirming Sexual Orientation and Gender Identity Act*,[9] despite a detailed interpretation of the law revealing that they run afoul of the ban. Clear professional guidelines would preclude this moral self-image preservation and confront professionals engaging in conversion practices with the immorality of their actions. The presence of clear guidelines also facilitates mutual enforcement of norms against trans conversion practices. Mutual enforcement through peer shaming and peer pressure plays a significant role in defining the contours of professional practice.[10] Because of the small size of trans populations, most clinicians do not have significant clinical experience with trans people or with the academic literature on therapeutic approaches to trans people. Those who engage in trans conversion practices regularly often boast a specialization in trans care. This difference in authority over trans care makes it difficult for most clinicians to confront and challenge practitioners of conversion practices, despite the presence of laws that prohibit conversion practices. Concept malleability applies not only to the evaluation of one's own behaviour but also to the evaluation of others' behaviour. The presence of clear professional guidelines offers an authoritative point of reference for clinicians not specialized in trans health in confronting practitioners of trans conversion practices, as these guidelines would be sufficiently specific to label such practices unethical authoritatively.

Disciplinary decision-makers are not always familiar with trans healthcare and may be unwilling to sanction practitioners that are more specialized and knowledgeable than them. Clear professional guidelines can enhance the disciplinary process by providing an authoritative point of reference for adjudicators akin to the Ontario Human Rights Commission's policies, which do not have the force of law and yet have been undeniably influential on human rights jurisprudence in Ontario.[11] The guidelines should be developed by a committee constituted by representatives from trans communities as well as by trans and cis professionals. The inclusion of professionals and members of trans communities is essential to create a sense of in-group consensus over trans therapeutics as well as to foster a culture of trust that contributes to discouraging unethical practices.

As highlighted earlier, one of the factors limiting the efficacy of bans on trans conversion practices is professional resentment. Professional orders are quintessentially defined as self-regulated, and legislatively imposed prohibitions risk being perceived as undue interference in professional self-regulation. The classification of behaviour and norms as in-group instead of out-group leads professionals to more readily adopt them.[12] In their work on ethical contagion, Francesca Gino, Shahar Ayal, and Dan Ariely observed that unethical behaviour by in-group members makes clinicians more likely to replicate the unethical behaviour, whereas unethical behaviour by out-group members leads them to avoid that unethical behaviour even more.[13] The reason is that professionals share a social identity with other professionals and thus see themselves as being subject to the same social norms. Because legislatures are perceived as out-group members, clinicians are less likely to internalize legal bans on trans conversion practices, and conversion practices by clinicians will have an outsized impact on the perceived acceptability of conversion practices despite the law.[14] To adopt Gino, Ayal, and Ariely's metaphor, a bad apple spoils the barrel – thus, the importance of crafting barrels that inhibit mould growth and do not trap ethylene.

Clear professional guidelines established by professionals – in-group members – can help remedy this situation. Gino, Ayal, and Ariely conclude that the impact of bad apples can be minimized through institutional techniques that stigmatize them and reclassify them as out-group members.[15] Not only do clear guidelines promoted by professionals provide a normative counterweight to professionals who engage in conversion practices, but they also serve to disavow those practitioners and classify them as other. This phenomenon parallels one we have already observed in trans health professional spheres in North America, in which practitioners of the corrective approach are increasingly unwelcome at some academic conferences and subject to protests.[16] Based on this reasoning, it may be preferable for professionals to be involved in legislative drafting. However, the nature of legislation and the political aspects of legislative processes might undermine the perception of legislated bans as reflecting in-group norms regardless of professional involvement in the process.

Members of trans communities should also be included in the drafting of professional guidelines, which should be inspired by the model law presented in Chapter 7. The guidelines should make clear how conversion practices relate to, and violate, existing professional obligations of competence, dignity, non-discrimination, and so on. While codes of ethics and standards are essential to discouraging unethical behaviour, developing a culture of trust within the profession and between professionals and service users is crucial to maintaining an effective ethical culture within professions.[17] A culture of trust is cultivated by "trusting others, being trusted and seeking to be trusted" and ensures greater compliance with legal and ethical norms of behaviour.[18] To the extent that including trans communities in institutional, professional norm setting leads to greater trust from trans communities, their inclusion will contribute to the effectiveness of bans.

Education

The second component of my proposal is the integration of education on the importance of gender-affirmative care and the dangers of trans conversion practices in both university courses and continuing professional education. Education contributes to greater knowledge of ethical norms in professional practice and plays a crucial role in the internalization of norms and values among professionals. The formation of a strong professional identity has been linked with the ability to resist institutional and social pressures, of which transantagonism is an example.[19] Professional identity refers to the internalization of values, knowledge, practices, and so on that are constitutive of a profession.[20] It is an internal sense of being in harmony with what it means to be a social worker, physician, psychologist, and so on. Those who have a strong sense of professional identity are likelier to respect the ethical norms of the profession.[21] Professional socialization has been shown to be a stronger determinant of behaviour than pre-socialization biographical details.[22]

Education, both in the university and in the continuing education context, contributes to discouraging conversion practices in multiple ways. Apart from teaching professionals not to engage in conversion practices through direct learning, education also contributes to peer pressure, presents model practitioners for students and young professionals, and diminishes the impression that professional consensus does not exist over trans care. However, it is important to note that the presence of accountability structures is essential for training to be effective.[23] Institutions that assign responsibility for ensuring compliance with ethical norms in a clear manner see a greater positive effect from education. Peer pressure directly discourages conversion practices through injunctions not to engage in conversion practices and social sanctions such as facing exclusion for violating professional norms.[24] Pressures of this kind are closely related to mutual enforcement of disciplinary measures, such as when professionals make official complaints to their order in the name of trans communities or service users. Because of the status derived from being a member of a profession, professionals who do not work in trans healthcare have both moral and pragmatic motives to pressure others not to engage in unethical behaviour since other professionals' unethical behaviour reflects poorly on the profession, undermining the culture of trust that lies at its roots.[25] University professors and presenters in continuing education courses play the role of authority figures on whom students and early career professionals model themselves. As London Business School professor Herminia Ibarra points out, "[i]dentification with role models infuses behavior with meaning, goals, and purposes, ... providing a motive for people to change their own behavior."[26] Because professors and presenters are already individuals whom professionals imitate, having professors and presenters express a commitment to affirmative practices and a strong opposition to conversion practices will influence practice across the profession.[27]

Education can also promote a sense of consensus within the profession, which mitigates the influence of practitioners of conversion practices on the rest of the profession. By teaching gender-affirmative therapy as the accepted best practice and establishing the consensus against trans conversion practices, students are invited to categorize practitioners of conversion practices as exceptions who do not truly belong within the profession.[28] Further evidence shows that behaviour and moral judgments among professionals are determined by whether these behaviours are perceived as being shared or not.[29] The appearance of consensus matters more than the presence of consensus. It is insufficient for there to be a consensus: professionals must also know that a consensus exists on the matter. University education is the first medium through which professional identity is formed and is the first point of contact for professionals with the values of their profession.[30] Because professional identity is most malleable early in people's careers, university education is a promising locus of intervention in discouraging trans conversion practices.[31] The centralized nature of university education, in contrast to the multiplicity of contexts of clinical practice, makes it easier to successfully intervene. Studies have shown that university education on transgender issues correlates with greater knowledge of trans health and increased comfort with trans patients.[32] Short follow-up periods make it difficult to estimate whether knowledge and comfort are retained over the long term. Since trans health is in constant evolution, refreshers will be necessary regardless. Furthermore, scientific knowledge and self-reported comfort may not translate into greater-quality care from the perspective of patients. Much remains unknown about how effective specific educational measures are on quality clinical care for trans and gender-creative people. Combining university education with continuing professional development is essential due to the long-term limitations of university education and since all current professionals have already graduated from university.

Developing content for university courses and continuing professional development can be done through professional committees, with integration into the curriculum being either suggested or mandated by the profession pursuant to its role in accrediting university programs and continuing professional development courses. The content should include teaching on best practices with trans clients, including the importance of respecting their gender identity and desires regarding social and medical transition.[33] Crucially, pedagogical content should include training on how to support the healing of survivors of conversion practices.[34] Professional bodies can require universities to teach trans health as a condition for licensure.[35] The existence of clear professional guidelines facilitates the integration of trans health into teaching since these guidelines can serve as a point of reference for teachers and educators and as a resource for professionals. These guidelines will also give new course content an allure of legitimacy and authoritativeness since it will have been created by a committee of their professional order. Because continuing professional development presentations are accredited on a per-event basis, greater oversight and monitoring strategies of content and teaching quality are possible.[36] Selected providers who are known for high quality, gender-affirmative content and who include trans voices in their presentations could be incentivized with money from a specially constituted fund or a greater number of accredited hours. Similarly, attending continuing education events on trans health could be incentivized by offering 1.5 times or 2 times the accreditation hours up to a certain number of hours.

Accountability Structures

The third component of my proposal involves creating accountability structures that are tasked with ensuring that professionals do not engage in conversion practices. Besides the previously mentioned tasks of overseeing educational initiatives, this body would produce reports on the employment of trans conversion practices among professionals and play an active role in supporting the enforcement of the prohibition against conversion practices by lodging disciplinary complaints or recommending investigations into professionals they have identified through their work. Visible enforcement and credible threats of sanctions act as a deterrent and punishment for unethical professional behaviour. Psychological models suggest that professionals contemplating acting unethically are in part motivated or discouraged from doing so based on their estimated likelihood of being caught.[37] Whereas unpunished practitioners of trans conversion practices have an outsized effect in authorizing others' conversion practices, punishment helps stigmatize these practitioners and position them as out-group members, which has the opposite effect: it discourages trans conversion practices.[38]

The enforcement function of specialized committees can be structured in different ways depending on the jurisdiction and whether legislative changes to the distribution of power within legislative bodies are plausible. In Québec, disciplinary complaints to professional associations are not limited to service users, and a committee would be able to lodge complaints against professionals engaging in trans conversion practices.[39] The committee could also request an inquiry from the syndic of the order. In Ontario, disciplinary complaints could also be lodged by the committee.[40] The committee could also recommend that the registrar appoint an investigator with the approval of the Inquiries, Complaints and Reports Committee.[41] Because the appointment of an investigator depends on two entities other than the trans conversion practices committee, it may be insufficiently effective as an enforcement mechanism. The Ontario *Health Professions Procedural Code* could be amended to grant the specialized committee tasked with discouraging conversion practices the power to appoint investigators and/or to grant the specialized committee the ability to refer allegations of misconduct to the Discipline Committee, which adjudicates complaints under section 36 of the code.[42]

The impact of enforcement structures also plays out in terms of professional identity. As was previously noted, professional identity is constituted in part through the imitation of people in leadership and authority positions.[43] Official committees of professional associations hold a position of authority that is conducive to imitation and integration in professional identity. Seeing the committee act teaches professionals that opposing conversion practices is at the core of the profession's ethos. Producing reports on the state of trans conversion practices within the profession helps foster a sense of surveillance among professionals, who may see the threat of sanctions as being more credible because of it. Furthermore, reports showing a high incidence of conversion practices are likely to be perceived as failures on the part of the profession and subject it to negative press and judgment from trans communities, generating professional resentment towards practitioners engaging in conversion practices for giving the profession a bad name. As shown in the research of organizational studies professors Alexandra Kalev, Frank Dobbin, and Erin Kelly, establishing responsibility and public accountability for enforcing norms is correlated with compliance.[44] Such reports could be used to enhance the attribution of responsibility to the committee and disciplinary instances by holding them to account for their failure to extinguish trans conversion practices.

Constituting a committee tasked with elaborating clear professional guidelines, establishing educational initiatives that promote gender-affirmative care and inform professionals of the harms of trans conversion practices, and supporting the enforcement of trans conversion practices bans through accountability structures are essential if we want to discourage these harmful practices more effectively and, eventually, eradicate them. The main limitation of my proposal is that it relies on the willingness of professional associations and/or legislators. For professional culture to change, professionals must be willing to act. Nevertheless, many professional associations have shown themselves willing to take a stance against trans conversion therapies and may be amenable to the proposed scheme. This proposal is not meant to replace legislative bans but, rather, to supplement them. What I have proposed here interacts with and supports the model law presented in the next chapter, which notably includes a provision that would alter the mandate of professional licensing and certifying bodies to include discouraging conversion practices and educating members about their dangers. The model law also offers a strong template on which to craft clear professional guidelines adapted to the reality of each profession.

Annotated Model Law for Prohibiting **7**
Conversion Practices

I am reminded of a conversation I had with a friend a few years ago, the first time I turned to study conversion practices. As I told her of my subject of research, she responded: "Torture isn't therapy. There you go." The comparison to torture mirrors the indignity of conversion practices.[1] Among Two-Spirit, lesbian, gay, bisexual, transgender, queer, intersex, asexual, and so on (2SLGBTQIA+) communities, these practices are experienced as deeply hurtful: after all, what is more deservedly human than being oneself? This chapter synthesizes the information found throughout the previous chapters into a model law for prohibiting conversion practices, providing lengthy annotations that explain the purpose and rationale behind every one of its provisions. Because the chapter may be used as a standalone resource, it provides a cursory overview of the science and ethics of conversion practices.

It is a most unfortunate reality that conversion practices, known under various names including conversion and reparative therapy, remain practised to this day. Roughly put, these practices seek to alter or repress people's gender identities or sexual orientation to make them cisgender and/or heterosexual. While the frequency of conversion practices is difficult to know with certainty, it remains common. In the United States, 13.5 percent of trans adults reported being subjected to conversion practices, a number that climbed to 18 percent among those who discussed their gender identity with a professional.[2] Recent Canadian studies found that around 11–12 percent of trans people had experienced conversion practices.[3] The Williams Institute estimates that 698,000 adults in the United States have been subjected to conversion practices and that 77,000 youth will be subjected to them before reaching the age of majority.[4] Among UK cisgender lesbian, gay, and bisexual people, 2 percent were subjected to conversion practices and another 5 percent were offered them.[5] These numbers respectively rise to 4.3 percent and 8.3 percent for transgender people.[6] Since many respondents were uncertain of whether they underwent or were offered conversion practices, these statistics likely underestimate the incidence of these practices.

Many first-person accounts of individuals harmed by conversion practices have been published.[7] In his doctoral dissertation, Dr. Sé Sullivan, a survivor of conversion practices, recounts: "The psychological 'treatment' I had as a child did not have my best interests at heart. It was child abuse. … Self-loathing and shame guided all of my decisions and suicide became a frequent thought."[8] Reflecting on his own experiences, sociologist Karl Bryant explains: "The study and the therapy that I received made me feel that I was wrong, that something about me at my core was bad, and instilled in me a sense of shame that stayed with me for a long time afterward."[9] Their words reverberate in my mind. Despite a dearth of sound scientific studies, the existing scientific and anecdotal evidence suggests that conversion practices are harmful.[10] Individuals who undergo conversion practices report higher psychological distress, suicidality, and homelessness than those who did not.[11] Trans people who have experienced trans conversion practices are 2.27 times more likely to have attempted suicide, and they are 4.15 times more likely to have attempted suicide if they experienced trans conversion practices before the age of ten.[12] Another study found that LGBTQ respondents who experienced conversion practices were 1.76 times more likely to seriously consider suicide, 2.23 times more likely to attempt suicide, and 2.54 times more likely to attempt suicide multiple times.[13] The same study found that experiencing conversion practices had a greater negative impact on suicidality than physical violence and threats thereof. Support and acceptance of gender identity and access to social and medical transition are strongly correlated with better mental health and lower suicidality among transgender people.[14] Unsurprisingly, countless prominent professional organizations oppose the practices.[15]

Little evidence exists as to the effectiveness of conversion practices. Research purporting to demonstrate the possibility of changing sexual orientation and gender identity fails to distinguish between genuine change and being forced back in the closet.[16] Evidence suggests that changing these core traits is rarely if ever possible in the long term.[17] Given the evidence of their harm, conversion practices are contrary to competent and ethical practice. Even if gender identity and sexual orientation could be harmlessly changed, conversion practices would still be unethical insofar as they are contrary to the equality and dignity of 2SLGBTQIA+ people. Conversion practices are unethical because they imply that 2SLGBTQIA+ lives are less valuable, less desirable, or less worth living. When presented with two clinical approaches that are otherwise morally equal except for one of them being demeaning, practitioners should always choose the one that is not demeaning.[18] Unlike conversion practices, 2SLGBTQIA+ affirmative practices do not demean or devalue 2SLGBTQIA+ lives.

In the hopes of eliminating – or at the very least abating – conversion practices, many jurisdictions in the last decade have introduced legislation purporting to prohibit them,[19] responding to the call of the *Yogyakarta Principles*.[20] More recently, the United Nations Independent Expert on Sexual Orientation and Gender Identity has called on governments to ban conversion practices and undertake a wide range of legislative and non-legislative measures aimed at discouraging conversion practices and supporting survivors.[21] The laws that have been adopted thus far are an important step towards eradicating conversion practices, and other governments should follow in their footsteps. However, many of the existing laws suffer from flaws that impede their ability to effectively discourage conversion practices. To fulfill their goal, laws must be drafted with sufficient precision and clarity for practitioners and patients to know, upon reading the text of the law, whether specific approaches are prohibited. A pedagogical ethos must guide law-making around conversion practices.

Currently, confusion reigns. Though the laws may be interpreted to assess with relative certainty whether an approach is illegal, this exercise requires a thorough familiarity with the standards of interpretation, the legislative history, and the relevant healthcare literature. Because such a convergence of knowledge is rare, conflicts of opinion abound, and at least some practitioners who openly seek to discourage youth from growing up trans have claimed that laws prohibiting conversion practices do not apply to them.[22] Bans on conversion practices are a legitimate means for protecting the public and promoting equality. While they restrict individual liberties, they do not do so any more than the regulation of medication, which is subject to a rigorous approval process in most countries. The power of legislatures to regulate professionals and individuals who offer similar services for the benefit of the public is well recognized. While the right to autonomy is central to healthcare, it should not be distorted into a right to demand harmful or ineffective interventions such as conversion practices.

This model law is intended to assist legislators and policy-makers who wish to prohibit conversion practices in their jurisdiction. It may also be of use to lawyers and judges faced with a lawsuit relating to conversion practices. Its greatest benefits over previous bans on conversion practices are twofold. First, it adopts a pedagogical mindset in defining conversion practices, seeking to define conversion practices in as clear and detailed a manner as possible to ensure that professionals and the public alike can readily ascertain whether a given practice is prohibited. A prohibition is of limited help if it is not understood by the people who engage in conversion practices; by the people who experience them; or by the healthcare professionals, lawyers, judges, and government employees who come into contact with conversion practitioners. At the heart of the model law's philosophy is that anyone should be able to ascertain without extensive legal training whether a delineated practice violates the ban. Second, it targets a wide range of practices that go beyond offering and advertising conversion practices. The model law notably prohibits taking a person outside their jurisdiction to have them undergo conversion practices, offers a means of dissolving a corporation in the conversion practices business, and prohibits various forms of financial benefits to organizations that facilitate or engage in conversion practices. It also extends legal aid coverage to survivors of conversion practices to help them pursue legal recourse. Given the difficulty of enforcing prohibitions on conversion practices, these provisions are crucial to effectively discouraging them.

While extensive, the model law does not exhaust the legal changes necessary to eradicate conversion practices. For instance, it does not attempt to adapt child protection law to the realities of conversion practices or integrate enforcement mechanisms in human rights commissions.[23] Because of the complex and jurisdiction-specific nature of these institutions, including measures targeting them in the model law is impracticable. Where I had to choose a specific wording, I centred expressions found at common law. This language will be most familiar to individuals in Australia, Canada, the United Kingdom, the United States, and other common law countries. However, its language can be easily adapted to the language of other legal systems, and the explanatory notes occasionally contain suggestions as to how the language may be adapted for such purposes. The model law should be adapted to the law of the jurisdiction as well as to the realities of the 2SLGBTQIA+ communities within it. Different jurisdictions apply different constitutional doctrines under different judicial contexts when evaluating the validity of a law. For instance, the vagueness doctrine in US criminal law could favour excluding the definitions provided in subsections 1(4)–1(10). Moreover, conversion practices take varied forms and are underpinned by philosophies that vary across cultures. While I have sought to draft the model law as expansively as possible, I am nevertheless constrained by my positionality as a Canadian scholar who is less familiar with practices outside of the Global North. Accordingly, some conversion practices found in other cultural contexts might not be cleanly captured by the model law's wording. Laws should be drafted in collaboration with concerned communities to ensure that the law benefits from their broad expertise and creativity and is well adapted to the experiences of conversion practices in their jurisdiction. The model law is best viewed as a starting point for any jurisdiction contemplating a ban on conversion practices.

Model Law

1. (1) Conversion practices are any treatment, practice, or sustained effort that aims to change, discourage, or repress a

person's sexual orientation, gender identity, gender expression, or any behaviour associated with a gender other than the person's sex assigned at birth or that aims to alter an intersex trait without adequate justification.

(2) Conversion practices include:

a. Treatments, practices, and sustained efforts that proceed from the assumption that certain sexual orientations, gender identities, gender modalities, or gender expressions are pathological or less desirable than others;

b. Treatments, practices, and sustained efforts that seek to reduce cross-gender identification or intimate or sexual relations with people of a given gender identity or sex assigned at birth;

c. Treatments, practices, and sustained efforts that have as a primary aim the identification of factors that may have caused the person's sexual orientation, gender identity, gender expression, or behaviours associated with a gender other than the person's sex assigned at birth, except in the context of research that has been approved by an institutional review board;

d. Treatments, practices, and sustained efforts that direct parents or tutors to set limits on their dependents' gender non-conforming behaviour, impose peers of the same sex assigned at birth, or otherwise intervene in the naturalistic environment with the aim of changing, discouraging, or repressing the dependent's sexual orientation, gender identity, gender expression, or any behaviour associated with a gender other than the person's sex assigned at birth;

e. Treatments, practices, and sustained efforts that proceed from the assumption that social or medical transition is undesirable or less desirable;

f. Treatments, practices, and sustained efforts that delay or impede a person's desired social or medical transition without reasonable and non-judgmental clinical justification;

g. Surgical or hormonal interventions relating to an intersex trait unless

(i)   the person requests it and provides free and informed consent or assent, or

(ii) it is strictly necessary and urgent to protect the life or physical health of the person, excluding from consideration social factors such as psychosocial development, atypical appearance, capacity for future penetrative sexual or procreative activity, or ability to urinate standing up; and the conditions referred to in subparagraph (g)(i) or (g)(ii) were duly documented at the time of the intervention;

h. Treatments, practices, and sustained efforts that persistently and knowingly use names, pronouns, gendered terms, and sexual orientation terms other than those chosen or accepted by the person, except as required by law.

(3) Unless otherwise provided under subsection 1(2), conversion practices do not include:

a. Necessary or desired assessments and diagnoses of gender dysphoria or another comparable diagnostic category under the latest version of the *Diagnostic and Statistical Manual of Mental Disorders* or the *International Classification of Diseases*;

b. Treatments, practices, or sustained efforts that provide non-judgmental acceptance and support of the person's expressed sexual orientation, gender identity, gender expression, or behaviours associated with a gender other than the person's sex assigned at birth;

c. Treatments, practices, or sustained efforts that teach individuals coping strategies to help resolve, endure, or diminish stressful life experiences while taking reasonable steps to avoid repressing, discouraging, or changing the person's sexual orientation, gender identity, gender expression, or any behaviour associated with a gender other than the person's sex assigned at birth;

    d.   Treatments, practices, or sustained efforts that aim at the development of an integrated personal identity by facilitating the exploration and self-assessment of components of personal identity while taking reasonable steps to avoid repressing, discouraging, or changing the person's sexual orientation, gender identity, gender expression, or any behaviour associated with a gender other than the person's sex assigned at birth; or

    e.   The expression of a political, religious, or ideological thought, belief, or opinion unless it aims to change a person's sexual orientation, gender identity, gender expression, or any behaviour associated with a gender other than the person's sex assigned at birth.

(4)   "Sexual orientation" refers to a person's capacity for profound emotional, affectional and sexual attraction to, and intimate and sexual relations with, individuals of the same gender, of a different gender, or of more than one gender. Sexual orientation is typically expressed with terms such as queer, straight, pansexual, lesbian, gay, bisexual, and asexual. Terms and understandings of sexual orientation vary by culture.

(5)   "Gender identity" refers to a person's deeply felt internal and individual experience of gender including the personal sense of the body. Gender identity is typically expressed with terms such as female, genderqueer, male, man, non-binary, or woman. Terms and understandings of gender identity vary by culture.

(6)   "Sex assigned at birth" refers to the classification of a person as female, male, or another gender based on their anatomy, karyotyping, or other biological traits present at birth. It is typically the gender on the person's declaration of birth or original birth certificate.

(7)   "Intersex trait" refers to biological characteristics, including genitals, gonads, and chromosome patterns, that do not fit typical binary notions of female or male bodies, including

differences in sex development resulting from androgen insensitivity syndrome, congenital adrenal hyperplasia, and hypospadias.

(8) "Gender expression" refers to a person's desired external appearance as it relates to social expectations, understandings, and norms of femininity and masculinity. Gender expression may include a person's behaviour, name, pronouns, clothing, haircut, voice, tattoos, piercings, and anatomical features.

(9) "Social transition" refers to the voluntary alteration of a person's gender expression to align it with their gender identity that differs from the one they were assigned at birth, other than through medical interventions. Social transition is personal and may not reflect others' understanding of which gender expressions correspond to a given gender identity.

(10) "Medical transition" refers to the voluntary alteration of a person's gender expression to align it with their gender identity that differs from the one they were assigned at birth, through medical interventions such as puberty blockers, hormone replacement therapy, voice therapy, facial hair removal, and surgical procedures. Medical transition is personal and may not reflect others' understanding of which gender expressions correspond to a given gender identity.

(11) Sexual orientation, gender identity, gender expression, and behaviours associated with a gender other than the person's sex assigned at birth may be proved by self-report.

2. Anyone who engages in conversion practices or knowingly refers an individual to someone who engages in conversion practices has committed an act of negligence and discrimination.

3. Anyone who does anything for the purpose of removing from the jurisdiction a person who is ordinarily resident in the jurisdiction with the intention that this person undergo conversion practices has committed an act of negligence and discrimination.

4. Anyone who advertises or receives compensation in exchange for engaging in or teaching conversion practices has engaged in unfair or deceptive trade practices.

5. Any licensed or certified professional who engages in, teaches, or advertises conversion practices has engaged in unprofessional conduct and shall be subject to discipline by their licensing or certifying board.

6. It is illegal and constitutes an act of negligence and discrimination for any organization or governmental entity to:

   a. Engage in or knowingly refer an individual to practitioners of conversion practices;

   b. Knowingly provide insurance coverage for conversion practices;

   c. Knowingly provide preferential tax treatment, including non-profit or charitable status, to any entity that facilitates engaging in, advertising, or referring an individual to practitioners of conversion practices;

   d. Knowingly provide a grant or contract to any entity that engages in or refers individuals to practitioners of conversion practices; or

   e. Refuse to provide a grant or contract to any entity for refusing to engage in, teach, or advertise conversion practices.

   Organizations and governmental entities shall take reasonable steps to ensure compliance with paragraphs (a) to (e).

7. Any person who suffers harm or losses due to a breach of section 2, 3, 4, or 6 may bring a private action against the perpetrator under this act to enjoin further breaches, or to recover special and general damages, or both.

8. The court shall award reasonable attorney's fees and costs to a prevailing plaintiff upon a finding by the court or trier of fact that the defendant engaged in conversion practices.

9. The court may award nominal, aggravated, and punitive damages upon a finding by the court or trier of fact that the defendant engaged in conversion practices.

10. The court may, on the application of an interested person or the government, make an order for the dissolution of a corporation carrying on the business of engaging in, advertising, or referring individuals to practitioners of conversion practices.

11. Legal aid shall be granted, to the extent determined by law, to the plaintiff in any action brought under section 7 or section 10.

12. The mandate of professional licensing and certifying bodies includes discouraging conversion practices and educating members about the dangers of conversion practices.
13. Proceedings brought pursuant to section 7 must be filed within ten years of the latter of:
    a. The day of the breach of a provision of this act;
    b. In the case of multiple breaches, the day of the last breach of a provision of this act;
    c. The day on which the claimant turned eighteen years old; or
    d. The day on which a reasonable person with the abilities and in the circumstances of the person subjected to conversion practices would have realised that they suffered harm or losses caused by a breach of a provision of this act.
14. If any provision or application of a provision of this act is found to be unconstitutional, invalid, or of no force or effect, the remaining provisions and applications of provisions shall continue in force as law.

Explanatory Notes

Section 1: Defining Conversion Practices

Subsection 1(1): Basic Definition
Subsection 1(1) provides a definition of conversion practices, defining them as "any treatment, practice, or sustained effort that aims to change, discourage, or repress a person's sexual orientation, gender identity, gender expression, intersex traits, or any behaviour associated with a gender other than the person's sex assigned at birth or that aims to alter an intersex trait without adequate justification."

CONVERSION PRACTICES
Terms that have been used to refer to conversion practices include conversion therapy, reparative therapy, corrective therapy, the corrective approach, the (psycho)therapeutic approach, ex-gay therapy, reorientation therapy, gay cure therapy, sexual attraction fluidity exploration in therapy, the pathological response approach, intersex surgeries and/or interventions, intersex genital mutilation, surgeries or interventions

on disorders of sex development, genital normalizing surgeries and/or interventions, and sexual orientation (and/or gender identity) change efforts.[24] The model law opts for the terminology of conversion practices for reasons of recognizability, intelligibility, and coherence and to avoid the positive connotations associated with therapy (and other terms such as "reparative"), which are inappropriate in the context of unethical and harmful practices. The label "therapy" for these clinical practices has been criticized by clinicians along such lines and may falsely communicate legitimacy.[25] Therapy may also suggest that these practices only occur within a therapeutic relationship, whereas faith-based conversion practices often occur in non-therapeutic relationships. The terminology of "practices" in lieu of "therapy" avoids these undesirable connotations. The expression "conversion practices" can be found in the Maltese ban.[26]

The term "conversion" is readily recognizable and identified with the practices targeted by the model law. It captures the underlying animus of the practices – namely, converting patients into sexually and gender-normative subjects. In the conversion practices literature, being 2SLGBTQIA+ is often recast as a failure of masculinity/femininity or a "gender role" problem.[27] Clinicians using conversion practices often claim that their patients' targeted characteristics do not reflect an underlying true, fixed identity or disposition but, rather, a pathological confusion about their true gender or sexual orientation.[28] In the context of trans and gender-creative youth, the presence of the subjective experience of gender dysphoria[29] or its diagnostic codification under the *Diagnostic and Statistical Manual of Mental Disorders* (DSM)[30] is seen as evidence that trans people's gender identity constitutes a mental illness that must be cured or repaired.[31]

Interventions that aim at altering an intersex trait without adequate justification are properly understood as conversion practices insofar as they seek to produce gender-normative subjects regardless of the individual's will. Historically, clinicians believed that intersex traits led to same-sex desires, even though – or perhaps because – these traits made them uncertain about what constituted same-sex intimacy.[32] Surgical means ensured conformity to the social ideals of heterosexual marriage. Intersex communities in the jurisdiction should be consulted before including protections for intersex people under a ban on conversion practices, as they may favour a comprehensive approach to intersex protections, as exemplified in Argentina's Proyecto de Ley Sobre Proteccion Integral de Las Caracteristicas Sexuales.[33] Interventions relating to intersex people are discussed in greater length under paragraph 1(2)(g).

The definition applies to people of all ages and regardless of consent. While youth are most vulnerable to conversion practices, adults are also at risk of being harmed by them. Individuals may be motivated to seek out or accept conversion practices due to social pressures, internalized negative attitudes towards their target characteristic(s), lack of knowledge of available options and best practices, and ignorance of the fact that the practitioner engages in conversion practices. In some jurisdictions, prohibiting conversion practices for ostensibly consenting adults may be politically unfeasible, despite their harm. While extending the ban to adults regardless of consent is strongly recommended, especially given evidentiary difficulties surrounding consent, a provision excluding inappropriately obtained consent may offer a politically viable alternative while reducing the risks and harm associated with allowing conversion practices for ostensibly consenting adults. While reiterating that a ban should extend to all conversion practices regardless of consent, Canadian scholars and activists have suggested adopting a provision explaining circumstances in which consent would not be obtained. For the purposes of the model law, I would propose the following:

(1) Consent must be present at the time the conversion practice in question takes place.

(2) For the purposes of this law, no consent is obtained if:

   (a) the agreement is expressed by the words or conduct of a person other than the one who underwent conversion practices;

   (b) the person is incapable of consenting for any reason;

   (c) the defendant did not adequately inform the person that the treatment, practice, or sustained effort constitutes a conversion practice;

   (d) the defendant did not adequately inform the person of the inefficacy and risks of conversion practices;

   (e) the defendant induces the person to consent by abusing a position of trust, power, or authority;

(f)   the person is vulnerable to coercion, manipulation, or social pressure taking into consideration their age, maturity, physical and mental health, psychological and emotional state, and any other relevant condition including any situation of dependence;

(g)   the person consents as a prerequisite to social or medical transitioning;

(h)   the person expresses, by words or conduct, a lack of agreement to undergo conversion practices; or

(i)   the person, having consented, expresses, by words or conduct, a lack of agreement to continue undergoing conversion practices.

(3)   Nothing in subsection (2) shall be construed as limiting the circumstances in which no consent is obtained.[34]

The text is inspired by the sexual consent provisions of the Canadian *Criminal Code* and the Maltese law's provisions on vulnerable adults.[35] Circumscribing consent rather than banning all conversion practices will make recourse difficult, if not impossible, for many adults harmed by them because it fails to account for the social, clinical, and interpersonal pressures that lead people to express consent to conversion practices. It is an acutely substandard option and should only be resorted to if a wholesale ban is not within the realm of possibility.

TREATMENT, PRACTICE, OR SUSTAINED EFFORT THAT AIMS TO REPRESS, DISCOURAGE, OR CHANGE TARGETED CHARACTERISTICS

Conversion practices may include any "treatment, practice, or sustained effort." The three notions connote a degree of systematicity to distinguish conversion practices from isolated actions on the part of family members or strangers while remaining sufficiently broad to capture conversion practices adopted by individuals who are not licensed professionals and do not have a clinical or therapeutic relationship to the person. Since conversion practices are often undertaken by members of religious organizations, including practices that are not predicated on a professional-patient relationship is necessary to capture all conversion practices.[36]

Conversion practices aim to "repress, discourage, or change" the targeted characteristics. This language is broader than the narrow focus on change found in many existing laws and better depicts the goals and theoretical assumptions of conversion practices. As previously mentioned, claims of gender identity ("I am a girl") or sexual orientation ("I am gay") are understood by some clinicians as a form of cognitive confusion that may not reflect an underlying "true" gender identity or sexual orientation.[37] In the case of gender-creative youth, practitioners may deny any attempt at changing gender identity, instead couching their goals as seeking to prevent a child whose gender identity is not yet established from growing up to be transgender. The addition of "discourage, or repress" broadens the prohibition to accommodate different theoretical views of conversion practices and the psychology of sexual orientation, gender identity, gender expression, and gendered behaviour.

GENDER EXPRESSION OR ANY BEHAVIOUR ASSOCIATED WITH A GENDER OTHER THAN THE PERSON'S SEX ASSIGNED AT BIRTH

Practices that target gender expression or behaviours associated with a gender other than the person's sex assigned at birth fall within the scope of conversion practices. Historically, conversion practices have targeted gender-creative children not only because they may grow up to be transgender or gay but also because their gender non-conformity is seen as indicative or constitutive of psychological disorder.[38] The defunct University of California Los Angeles (UCLA) Gender Identity Research Clinic, which is now associated with conversion practices, focused its work on feminine youth assigned male at birth, whom clinicians of the clinic described in terms of "deviant sex-role behaviours" or "Sissy Boy Syndrome."[39] George Alan Rekers, of the UCLA clinic, justified his approach as an attempt to discourage rigid adherence to sex roles, deeming gender-creative children's behaviours narrow and obsessive.[40] Clinical approaches that seek to discourage youth from growing up trans have continued to target gender expression and gendered behaviours for intervention, despite a shift in clinical focus from classical behavioural therapy to mixed approaches that, according to these practitioners, can "fully alter internal gender schemas."[41]

Subsection 1(2): Disallowed Practices

Subsection 1(2) provides a list of practices that are non-exhaustively included in the notion of conversion practices.

PSYCHOPATHOLOGIZING PRACTICES: PARAGRAPH 1(2)(A)

Conversion practices include treatments, practices, and sustained efforts "that proceed from the assumption that certain" targeted characteristics "are pathological or less desirable than others." Conversion practices are typically underpinned by the view that being lesbian, gay, bisexual, or transgender is a mental illness, a mental disorder, or otherwise undesirable. In the case of transgender and gender-creative people, practitioners may engage in conversion practices even if the person does not demonstrate discomfort, distress, or impaired functioning due to their gender.[42] In some cases, distress is argued to be present insofar as the fact of being trans is a valid marker of distress or impairment or insofar as the distress caused by misrecognition and social marginalization is sufficient for trans people to be considered inherently mentally ill.[43] The "extremeness" of medical transition is often used to justify the claim that being trans is a marker of distress or impairment in and of itself.[44]

In the case of sexual orientation, conversion practices may be justified by the belief that ego-dystonic sexual orientation is a mental illness or condition. It may also be justified under the belief that same-gender sexual urges or behaviour deemed reckless or unsafe by practitioners or patients are a form of impaired functioning. Sexual acts between men are disproportionately labelled reckless or unsafe, compared to similar sexual acts in other gender configurations, hinting at homoantagonistic prejudice. Ego-dystonic sexual orientation refers to sexual orientation that is not desired by the patient and causes them clinically significant distress. Oftentimes, this distress is due to internalized homoantagonism or external factors such as a fear of the human immunodeficiency virus (HIV).[45] While homosexuality was removed from the third edition of the *DSM* in 1973, this edition retained Ego-dystonic Homosexuality as a diagnosis.[46] Ego-dystonic Homosexuality was replaced in the third revised edition and in the fourth edition of the *DSM* by the diagnosis of Sexual Disorder Not Otherwise Specified for "persistent and marked distress about sexual orientation," legitimating continued conversion practices.[47] Conversion practices were presented as one of two choices for patients presenting with ego-dystonic homosexuality, with the other choice being interventions aimed at self-acceptance. However, patients with high levels of internalized homoantagonism are unlikely to opt for interventions aimed at self-acceptance despite their clinical indicability.[48] A similar problem also arises with trans patients with high levels of internalized transantagonism.

REDUCTION OF CROSS-GENDER IDENTIFICATION AND SAME-SEX INTIMACY:
PARAGRAPH 1(2)(B)

Conversion practices include treatments, practices, and sustained efforts "that seek to reduce cross-gender identification or intimate or sexual relations with people of a given gender identity or sex assigned at birth." The notion of cross-gender identification accommodates theoretical disagreements over the nature of gender identity and how it ought to be conceptualized. "Cross-gender identification" is a common term in the scholarly literature[49] and was mentioned in the text of the Gender Identity in Childhood Diagnosis in the fourth edition and revised fourth edition of the *DSM*.[50] The term bears a broader connotation than gender identity insofar as it does not imply the presence of an underlying gender identity, referring to the fact of psychologically identifying with another (binary) gender rather than the fact of having a certain gender identity. The term is most common in the literature on trans and gender-creative youth, whose expressions of gender identification may be interpreted as evidence of gender confusion rather than as an expression of gender identity by practitioners engaging in conversion practices.[51]

Conversion practices include attempts to reduce romantic and sexual involvement with people of a given gender identity or sex assigned at birth.[52] A common form of conversion practice involves counselling abstention from romantic and sexual relationships with people of the same gender, regardless of, and sometimes despite, one's continuing sexual attraction to them. In recent years, these efforts have increased as part of a rebranding by conversion organizations, following the motto of "hate the sin, not the sinner."[53] These understandings are muddied when the target of the conversion practices is a trans individual, and abstention might be counselled towards either or both people of the same gender and of different genders. For instance, people who engage in conversion practices may oppose intimacy between trans women and men because they believe trans women are men and that it constitutes same-gender intimacy; they may oppose intimacy between trans women and women because, as women, it is inappropriate for them to pursue same-gender intimacy; or they may oppose all intimacy for trans women due to their perceived gender deviance. These scenarios all manifest conversion practices. The American Psychological Association recommends against promoting celibacy even among patients who wish to resolve tensions between their religious commitments and sexual orientation through sexual abstinence.[54] Both gender identity and sex assigned at birth are mentioned in paragraph 1(2)(b) due to the different understandings of gender than those engaging in conversion practices may have.

ETIOLOGICAL LENS: PARAGRAPH 1(2)(C)

Conversion practices include treatments, practices, and sustained efforts "that have as a primary aim the identification of factors that may have caused the person's" targeted characteristics "except in the context of research that has been approved by an institutional review board." The identification of factors that have led to targeted characteristics in clinical settings serves no legitimate purpose other than to select interventions to repress, discourage, or change the targeted characteristics and is predicated on the view that the targeted characteristics are abnormalities that are caused, in part or in whole, by external factors.[55] Posited causes include family encouragement or lack of discouragement of gender non-conformity, the level of cognitive development, belief that being a certain gender is advantageous, family functioning, trauma, unresolved conflict, and psychopathology.[56] Some practitioners have also suggested that "limited cognitive abilities and immaturity may make [a child assigned male at birth] no match for other boys," leading them to play with girls and feminine-coded toys.[57] Oftentimes and increasingly, conversion practices are defended under the pretext that the person's gender identity reflects internalized misogyny, internalized homoantagonism, unwanted sexual attention, and/or sexual trauma.[58]

The etiological lens, which seeks to identify causes for the targeted characteristics, is closely connected to psychopathologizing views of sexual and gender minorities.[59] As psychotherapists Robert Wallace and Hershel Russell explain, "if gender variant behavior is pathological, then we must inquire into its etiology and do what can be done to prevent and to treat it."[60] Inquiries into etiology are symptomatic of psycho-pathologizing practices. The paragraph does not preclude therapeutic interventions addressing low self-esteem, internalized oppression, and/or sexual trauma outside of attempts to identify the cause(s) of the targeted characteristics. Etiological inquiries undertaken under ethically approved scientific research are not conversion practices. However, institutional review boards should be mindful of the possibility that research into the etiology of targeted characteristics could be used for eugenic or otherwise detrimental purposes and that the integration of research and clinical teams may undermine the validity of informed consent due to patients' belief that refusing to participate in research could jeopardize their access to desired healthcare services.[61]

INTERVENTIONS IN THE NATURALISTIC ENVIRONMENT: PARAGRAPH 1(2)(D)

Conversion practices include treatments, practices, and sustained efforts "that direct parents or tutors to set limits on their dependents' gender non-conforming behaviour, impose peers of the same sex assigned at birth, or otherwise intervene in the naturalistic environment" for the listed purposes. The explicit inclusion of such interventions in the law is crucial since they are carried out by parents or tutors at the direction of practitioners rather than by the practitioners themselves. Parents or tutors are frequently enlisted in conversion practices in the belief that interventions set in every-day life play an important role in discouraging, repressing, or changing the targeted characteristics.[62] These interventions are known as "interventions in the naturalistic environment" and proceed from the assumption that targeted characteristics may be caused by a failure to identify with models and peers of the same sex assigned at birth and by parental encouragement or failure to discourage non-conforming behaviour.[63] Interventions in the naturalistic environment include directing parents to prevent or set limits on their child's gender non-conforming behaviours, make their child participate in differently gendered activities and/or with peers of a different gender, or otherwise alter their everyday environment in the hope that they will cease to display the targeted characteristic.

PRESUMING THE UNDESIRABILITY OF TRANSITION: PARAGRAPH 1(2)(E)

Conversion practices include treatments, practices, and sustained efforts that "proceed from the assumption that social or medical transition is undesirable or less desirable." Instead of being directly motivated by a negative view of transitude – the fact of being transgender – conversion practices may instead be motivated by the view that social or medical transition is undesirable or less desirable than not transitioning. The focus of negativity is often placed on medical transition,[64] and the language of "mutilation" is sometimes used to describe gender-affirming interventions.[65] The assumption that transition is undesirable may also relate to specific bodily configurations, such as when desired medical interventions would lead to bodies that "fall outside of the [rigidly binary] cisnormative view of the body"[66] or when people desire to medically transition without socially transitioning.[67] Conversion practices may also be motivated by negative judgments of social transition, frequently due to the belief that social transition inevitably leads to medical transition or an otherwise more difficult life.[68] This view is notably contrary to emerging evidence that prepubertal trans youth who socially transition have a quality of mental health comparable to the general population.[69] The view of trans people as mentally ill may flow from a view of transition as being "drastic" or as "simply too radical" for transitude to reflect normal human diversity.[70]

UNDULY DELAYING OR IMPEDING TRANSITION: PARAGRAPH 1(2)(F)

Conversion practices include treatments, practices, and sustained efforts "that delay or impede a person's desired social or medical transition without reasonable and non-judgmental clinical justification." Impediments or delays to transition may be used to discourage individuals from transitioning and thus minimize the number of people who transition.[71] Undue impediments and delays to transition may be deployed alone – a sort of conversion practice by attrition – or in conjunction with other conversion practices. Because older adolescents and adults cannot as readily be forced to attend clinical sessions motivated by conversion goals, the promise of medical transition under the condition of respecting impediments and delays can serve to keep patients in a clinical relationship with conversion practitioners. Expressions of doubts or observations that do not match the provider's understanding of transitude are then used to justify further impediments and delays. Imposing undue barriers or delays unreasonably subjects patients to ongoing gender dysphoria, poses risks of significant psychological harm, and can pressure patients back into the closet.[72]

Such undue impediments and delays may be rationalized by the belief that a longer assessment period is needed to ascertain whether the person is "truly" transgender or "truly" gender dysphoric, despite evidence that regret is rare for all age groups.[73] Some practitioners seek to justify delaying or impeding transition by arguing that youth are being pushed into transitioning to avoid being gay or lesbian and that allowing transition may even be a form of conversion practice.[74] However, these arguments do not accord with empirical and theoretical reality since transantagonism is more pervasive and intense on average than homoantagonism and since few trans people are straight after transition.[75] It is also worth noting that these arguments often mistake the label used by the person for their sexual orientation ("gay," "lesbian," "bisexual," and so on) for the sexual orientation itself (to whom they are romantically and sexually attracted). These arguments weaponize sentiments in favour of lesbian, gay, bisexual, and queer people in an attempt to legitimate conversion practices towards trans people.

Not all impediments or delays to transition are tantamount to conversion practices. Impediments and delays that are both reasonable and non-judgmental in nature are acceptable. Reasonability is a common concept in the law of negligence and civil liability. The reasonable person test may be used to evaluate whether a delay or impediment is reasonable. The test asks that decision-makers imagine how a reasonable person would have acted in the context at hand.[76] Impediments and delays must be non-judgmental, reflecting the view that the reasonable person should not hold homoantagonistic or transantagonistic beliefs.[77] Non-judgmental care in the context of 2SLGBTQIA+ populations is predicated on the view that practitioners should avoid making value or moral judgments regarding the targeted characteristics of patients.[78] This approach to care entails that their practices must not be predicated on heteronormative or cisnormative prejudice.[79] Non-judgment is added as an explicit requirement because not all legal systems incorporate such a criterion in their equivalent of the reasonable person test.

Reasonable and non-judgmental impediments and delays may arise for various reasons. Requiring blood testing before prescribing hormone replacement therapy is legitimate despite the added delay. Requiring an assessment of gender dysphoria pursuant to the latest edition of the World Professional Association for Transgender Health's "Standards of Care" is not a conversion practice unless the breadth or chronology of the assessment process is excessive.[80] Delays that are not due to clinical practice but, rather, are a by-product of resource scarcity in the healthcare system cannot be attributed to the practitioner as unreasonable or judgmental, although it could be discriminatory on the part of the government or healthcare institution.[81] As a matter of good practice, professionals should account for, and adapt to, systemic realities so as to minimize delays for their patients. Impediments such as further testing required due to serious physical health concerns may also be reasonable and non-judgmental. The requirement that impediments and delays be reasonable and non-judgmental shifts the burden of justification onto providers, who must be able to provide rationales for their practices. Such a requirement fosters greater thoughtfulness and introspection in clinical work and alleviates the evidentiary burden on complainants by recognizing that practitioners have greater access to relevant facts relating to their work.[82] Healthcare institutions should consider adopting formal policies and review mechanisms aimed at ensuring the absence of undue impediments or delays to transition.

NON-CONSENSUAL INTERVENTIONS RELATING TO INTERSEX
TRAITS: PARAGRAPH 1(2)(G)

Conversion practices include "surgical or hormonal interventions relating to an intersex trait unless (i) the person requests it and provides free and informed consent or assent, or (ii) it is strictly necessary and urgent to protect the life or physical health of the person, excluding from consideration social factors such as psychosocial development, atypical appearance, capacity for future penetrative sexual or procreative activity, or ability to urinate standing up; and the conditions referred to in subparagraph (g)(i) or (g)(ii) were duly documented at the time of the intervention." Intersex communities in the jurisdiction should be consulted before including protections for intersex people under a ban on conversion practices, as they may favour a comprehensive approach to intersex protections.[83]

This definition is inspired by the Lambda Legal and InterACT document *Providing Ethical and Compassionate Health Care to Intersex Patients: Intersex-Affirming Hospital Policies* and by Argentina's Proyecto de Ley Sobre Proteccion Integral de Las Caracteristicas Sexuales.[84] The practices are properly understood as conversion practices insofar as they seek to produce sexually and gender-normative subjects regardless of the individual's will. Historically, clinicians believed that intersex genitals led to same-sex desires, even though – or perhaps because – these traits made them uncertain about what constituted same-sex intimacy.[85] Surgical means ensured conformity to social ideals of heterosexual marriage. Under more recent medical models, the justification focusing on heterosexuality has shifted towards securing gender-normative futures more broadly and normalizing intersex bodies, which are seen as inherently undesirable by practitioners.[86]

Non-consensual surgeries and hormonal interventions on intersex youth are harmful and may lead to negative outcomes such as loss of reproductive function and genital sensation as well as psychological trauma.[87] These outcomes are ethically unacceptable in the absence of proper consent. Interventions such as excess genital examinations, masturbation of external genitals, and dilations of internal genitals performed by doctors and parents – some parents are asked to regularly insert dilators in their child's genital canal (frequently called a vagina, though many intersex people use other terms) despite their protesting and/or fighting back – are frequently experienced as a form of sexual assault by intersex youth.[88] Non-urgent surgeries and hormonal interventions are often practised on newborns and young children despite the possibility of delaying them until they can make an informed choice as to whether they wish to undergo interventions.[89] Such non-consensual practices are condemned by intersex communities as well as by various medical and policy bodies.[90] They are notably prohibited in the public healthcare systems of the Spanish regions of Andalucía, Madrid, and Murcia.[91] Interventions that are strictly necessary and urgent, such as when the life of the person is directly and immediately threatened, do not fall within the scope of this prohibition.

The capacity to provide free and enlightened consent or assent must be assessed carefully when applying this provision. Some doctors pressure parents and youth to consent or assent to the procedures.[92] The perspective of intersex individuals is often disregarded or devalued by practitioners.[93] The requirement that the procedure was requested helps ensure that it genuinely emanates from the youth whose bodily and sexual integrity is implicated and not from doctors or parents. Failing to obtain fully free and enlightened consent or assent from the individual undergoing surgery would fall within the prohibition set out in this paragraph. Where possible, the law should require an independent assessment that the youth satisfies these conditions by a child advocate or equivalent office. The reasons for the intervention must be duly documented. Practitioners must clearly articulate the reasons that justify the intervention. The requirement of documentation seeks to avoid after-the-fact justifications, at a time when providing contrary evidence may be more difficult. This condition helps address the disparity in knowledge between patients and practitioners, the latter being uniquely positioned to ascertain the strict urgency and necessity of interventions. This requirement may have the further benefit of encouraging greater reflection on the part of practitioners.

MISGENDERING AND MISATTRIBUTING ORIENTATION: PARAGRAPH 1(2)(H)

Conversion practices include treatments, practices, and sustained efforts "that persistently and knowingly use names, pronouns, gendered terms, and sexual orientation terms other than those chosen or accepted by the person, except as required by law." Respect for a person's chosen or accepted name, pronouns, and gendered terminology communicates acceptance and respect for their gender identity. Gendered terms include gender labels such as "girl," "boy," and "non-binary," which may be denied through questions and affirmations such as: "But you know you're really a boy, right?" Gendered terms may also include words like "pretty" or "handsome," the grammatical gender of nouns, adjectives, and so on in many languages,[94] and gender markers on documents and records.[95] Sexual orientation terms should also be respected, and imposing terminology inconsistent with a patient's self-understanding (such as "you're gay, not bisexual" or "you can't say you're a lesbian if you are non-binary") is inappropriate.

Miscategorizing a person's gender is known as misgendering.[96] Misgendering is integral to conversion practices and serves to communicate

that the person's gender identity should not be taken seriously or is
not a true reflection of who they are. Being misgendering is associated
with substantially poorer mental health.[97] However, misgendering may
sometimes be required by law. For example, a person's legal name and
gender marker may be required on documents used for insurance coverage.[98] Legal requirements should not be overstated. Gender markers are
not a reliable identity-verification measure, and "shadow files" – files
containing the person's legal name and gender marker that are only available to designated individuals – may be used in cases where the person's
legal name and gender marker must be used for some purposes but not
others.[99] To count as conversion practices, misgendering and misattributing orientation terms must be done persistently and knowingly, and
must count as treatments, practices, or sustained efforts. Acts will not
meet these conditions if they are occasional and accidental or if they are
due to the innocent ignorance of the person's chosen or accepted name,
pronouns, gendered terms, and sexual orientation terms. The degree of
systematicity implied in the terms "treatments, practices, or sustained
efforts" also excludes misgendering and misattributing orientation terms
in everyday settings, as these would not amount to treatments, practices,
or sustained efforts. Misgendering and misattributing orientation terms
may nevertheless be contrary to human rights protections against harassment based on the protected characteristics.[100]

Subsection 1(3): Permitted Practices

Subsection 1(3) provides a list of practices that are non-exhaustively
excluded from the notion of conversion practices. The subsection provides that they are not included in the notion of conversion practices
unless otherwise included under subsection 1(2). In other words, practices
falling under subsection 1(3) cannot become conversion practices by the
sole operation of the general definition under subsection 1(1) and only
become conversion practices if subsection 1(2) is applicable.

DIAGNOSIS AND ASSESSMENT: PARAGRAPH 1(3)(A)

Conversion practices do not include "necessary or desired assessments
and diagnoses of gender dysphoria or another comparable diagnostic
category under the latest version of the *Diagnostic and Statistical Manual*

of Mental Disorder or *International Classification of Diseases.*" Assessments and diagnoses of gender dysphoria or gender incongruence are often required to access trans healthcare services or insurance coverage, or to change legal gender markers.[101] These requirements vary across jurisdictions, service providers, and insurance providers. Mandatory assessments and diagnoses are opposed by a large subset of trans healthcare professionals and trans communities and may be considered dehumanizing or psychopathologizing.[102] However, including these assessments and diagnoses under the definition of conversion practices even when necessary and/or desired by the patient could severely impede access to healthcare in trans communities.

The exclusion of assessments and diagnoses of gender dysphoria or comparable diagnostic categories does not reflect the belief that these diagnostic categories should continue to exist or that it is legitimate to require assessments or diagnoses for access to healthcare, insurance, or legal gender marker changes. The exclusion of assessment and diagnoses from the definition of conversion practices does not preclude a finding that the practitioner was otherwise engaging in conversion practices and will notably constitute conversion practices if the assessments or diagnoses lead to unreasonable delays in social or medical transition. In jurisdictions that use a modified or older version of the *DSM* or the *International Classification of Diseases*, the words "latest version" should be substituted for the appropriate reference.

ACCEPTANCE AND SUPPORT: PARAGRAPH 1(3)(B)

Conversion practices do not include treatments, practices, or sustained efforts "that provide non-judgmental acceptance and support of the person's expressed" targeted characteristics. Accepting and supporting the person's expressed target characteristics is not included in the notion of conversion practices.[103] Acceptance and support are grounded in a client-centred approach to therapeutic care and are practised through "unconditional positive regard for and congruence and empathy with the client," "openness to the client's perspective as a means of understanding their concerns," and "encouragement of the client's positive self-concept."[104] This approach may involve addressing factors impeding the patient's psychosocial adaptation, such as drug addiction. In the context of patients who wish to alter their targeted characteristics, acceptance and support aim at reducing distress brought on by stigma, isolation, and internalized shame, which may involve exploring why the patient wishes to change their targeted characteristics without negatively judging them for struggling with self-acceptance.

Specifying the expressed nature of characteristics clarifies the temporal nature of conversion practices and complements the proof of targeted characteristics by self-reporting set out in section 1(10). Acceptance and support will not amount to conversion practices even if the practitioner believes in good faith that the patient is misrepresenting these characteristics. For instance, practitioners who believe for good reasons that a patient of theirs is a trans woman but continues to represent themselves as a cis man would not be committing a wrong by continuing to refer to them using masculine terminology, even if they were to later self-identify as a woman. Non-judgmental and unconditional acceptance and support of a person is appropriate and would not be tantamount to conversion practices regardless of the outcome of this exploration process, even if the patient retrospectively expresses always having known. The requirement that acceptance and support be non-judgmental – without preference about targeted characteristics – indicates that foreclosing future identity development may nevertheless fall under the umbrella of conversion practices. Suggesting that one is accepted and supported as is but would not be accepted or supported if their targeted characteristics were different (for example, "I accept you as long as you're straight") would not fall under the notion of acceptance and support since it would be judgmental.

COPING STRATEGIES: PARAGRAPH 1(3)(C)

Conversion practices do not include treatments, practices, or sustained efforts "that teach individuals coping strategies to help resolve, endure, or diminish stressful life experiences while taking reasonable steps to avoid repressing, discouraging, or changing the person's" targeted characteristics. Empowering patients by teaching them coping strategies in dealing with negative experiences, notably linked with gender- or sexuality-related marginalization, can be an appropriate therapeutic practice.[105] These strategies may include common therapeutic interventions such as psychoeducation, cognitive-behavioural therapy, mindfulness-based therapy, and narrative therapy. The motivational underpinning and context of practices are crucial to distinguishing between conversion practices and legitimate therapeutic practices. For instance, reading religious texts is often associated with faith-based conversion practices but may also be used to reduce "the salience of negative messages about homosexuality and increasing self-authority or understanding" over religious texts through active engagement.[106] Helping patients navigate strategic reductions in gender non-conforming behaviour in severely hostile and dangerous environments should also be properly contextualized since it may reflect a coping strategy motivated by reasonable self-preservation rather than a disavowal of gender non-conformity amounting to a conversion practice.

However, some professionals engaging in conversion practices seek to justify their work by framing them as merely teaching helpful coping strategies to patients who wish to avoid transitioning or engaging in sexual acts with people of a certain gender.[107] Oftentimes, the desire to avoid transitioning or engaging in sexual acts with people of a certain gender is underwritten by internalized transantagonism and/or homoantagonism and outsized fears of ostracization and rejection (for example, "I should not transition because being trans is unnatural and wrong" or "if I come out everyone will reject me and I will never be loved or happy"). Conversion practices agree with and reinforce these feelings instead of addressing, disrupting, and undermining them. Proposed treatments of ego-dystonic sexual orientation, mentioned in the explanatory notes to paragraph 1(2)(a), are often framed as teaching coping strategies. Appropriate therapeutic practices towards such patients involve helping them work through their internalized transantagonism and/or homoantagonism and fears while respecting and supporting the patient's targeted characteristics. It can be appropriate to teach coping strategies to patients who do not wish to transition or refrain from sexual activities with others. However, practitioners should ensure that the decision is well considered and that internalized transantagonism and/or homoantagonism have been worked through.

Given the dangers of practitioners seeking to justify conversion practices under this paragraph, the model law specifies that practitioners must take reasonable steps to avoid repressing, discouraging, or changing targeted characteristics. Reasonability may be evaluated using the reasonable person test, which is common in law. The type of precautions to be taken is left open-ended to avoid further restricting practices where flexibility and sensitivity to context are needed. The steps that should be taken must be evaluated on a case-by-case basis based on the person's vulnerability, perspectives, and relationship to the practitioner. Patients should benefit from a clear understanding that coping strategies are not about delaying or avoiding transitioning or engaging in same-sex acts but, rather, about managing in a healthy and sustainable manner the social, emotional, and psychological difficulties associated with stigma and marginalization. Research on conversion practices shows that denying or downplaying one's sexual desire or desire to transition is neither healthy nor sustainable.

INTEGRATED PERSONAL IDENTITY: PARAGRAPH 1(3)(D)

Conversion practices do not include treatments, practices, or sustained efforts "that aim at the development of an integrated personal identity by facilitating the exploration and self-assessment of components of personal identity while taking reasonable steps to avoid repressing, discouraging, or changing the person's" targeted characteristics. Enabling identity exploration and development is predicated on the idea that "conflicts among disparate elements of identity appear to play a major role in the distress of those seeking" conversion practices.[108] People whose religion or culture are hostile to their targeted characteristics, in particular, may struggle to integrate and harmonize the various elements of their personal identity. Personal identity is understood holistically, comprising "a coherent sense of one's needs, beliefs, values, and roles, including those aspects of oneself that are the bases of social stigma, such as age, gender, race, ethnicity, disability, national origin, socioeconomic status, religion, spirituality, and sexuality."[109] Identity development refers to the active exploration and self-assessments of personal identity and its various components to attain an integrated personal identity that is free from major tension or conflict between components.[110]

Conversion practitioners have oftentimes sought to justify repressing or discouraging targeted characteristics by claiming that their goal is to reduce the tension between the person's religious commitments and these characteristics.[111] Those practices, however, place religious commitment in a hierarchy above the targeted characteristic instead of attempting to make both of them compatible for the individual. As such, it is not truly aiming at the development of an integrated personal identity. In this context, as elsewhere, practitioners must always consider target characteristics "to be absolutely as valid and legitimate an outcome as any other identity or practice."[112] Given the dangers of practitioners seeking to justify conversion practices under this paragraph, it specifies that practitioners must take reasonable steps to avoid repressing, discouraging, or changing targeted characteristics. Patients should clearly understand that free exploration is about improving one's self-understanding and reducing tensions within one's personal identity by reconciling aspects of it, not about denying aspects of one's identity or conforming to societal or religious expectations. The reference to reasonability here again invokes the reasonable person test. The question is: what steps would a reasonable practitioner take in the same circumstances to avoid, intentionally or unintentionally, repressing, discouraging, or changing the person's targeted characteristics? The type of precautions to be taken is left open-ended in the model law to avoid further restricting practices where flexibility and sensitivity to context is needed, but it may involve establishing therapeutic strategies that highlight the compatibility of a religion and its associated texts with the targeted characteristics.[113] The development of an integrated personal identity is predicated on retaining both the religious commitment and the targeted characteristic of a person and bringing them into harmony.

MERE SPEECH: PARAGRAPH 1(3)(E)

Conversion practices do not include "the expression of a political, religious or ideological thought, belief or opinion" without the aim of repressing, discouraging, or changing the person's targeted characteristics.

This paragraph makes explicit that merely expressing a belief about gender or sexuality without attempting to repress, discourage, or change a person's targeted characteristics does not amount to a conversion practice. It is included in the model law to address directly the concern that bans might prohibit family members and religious leaders who express a religious or personal belief about gender or sexuality, without engaging in systematic attempts to repress, discourage, or change the person's targeted characteristics. Beyond its clarificatory function, the provision may play a supplemental role in the event of a legal or constitutional challenge based on freedom of expression. The paragraph is inspired by the proposed New Zealand ban on conversion practices.[114] Its language is based on the terrorism provisions of the Canadian Criminal Code.

Subsections 1(4)–1(10): Definitions

SEXUAL ORIENTATION: SUBSECTION 1(4)

Sexual orientation is defined as "a person's capacity for profound emotional, affectional and sexual attraction to, and intimate and sexual relations with, individuals of the same gender, of a different gender, or of more than one gender. Sexual orientation is typically expressed with terms such as queer, straight, pansexual, lesbian, gay, bisexual, and asexual." The definition further acknowledges that "[t]erms and understandings of sexual orientation vary by culture." In Canada, for instance, some Two-Spirit people may identify their sexual orientation as Two-Spirit or use more specific terms under the Two-Spirit umbrella. This definition of sexual orientation is inspired by the one provided in the *Yogyakarta Principles*.[115] I have updated the definition to acknowledge the importance of self-labelling and the culturally specific nature of terms and understandings of sexual orientation.[116] Judging whether a practitioner is engaging in conversion practices requires cultural sensitivity, and it would be inappropriate for a practitioner to impose a Western understanding of sexuality and sexual orientation onto their patients. The proposed definition acknowledges that terms used to express sexual orientation are often gender specific, but it does not define sexual orientation by reference to the person's own gender.[117]

The choice to define sexual orientation solely by reference to the targets of attraction seeks to avoid the potential interpretive difficulties arising when transgender people change their self-elected gender labels. In the past, the claim that a shift in self-elected gender labels (for instance, from "butch lesbian" to "straight man") entails a change in sexual orientation was used to falsely accuse gender-affirmative practices of being conversion practices based on sexual orientation, despite the targets of attraction not having changed.[118]

Gender identity is defined as "a person's deeply felt internal and individual experience of gender including the personal sense of the body. Gender identity is typically expressed with terms such as female, genderqueer, male, man, non-binary, or woman." The definition further acknowledges that "[t]erms and understandings of gender identity vary by culture." In Canada, for instance, some Two-Spirit people may identify their gender identity as Two-Spirit or use more specific terms under the Two-Spirit umbrella such as *iskwêhkân, napêhkân* (Nehiyawewin), *asegi udanto* (Tsalagi Gawonihisdi), *niizh manidowaag* (Ojibwe), *sts'iyóye smestíyexw slhá:li* (Halq'eméylem), or *onón:wat* (Kanien'kéha).[119] As with sexual orientation, this definition substantively builds upon the definition provided in the *Yogyakarta Principles*.[120] The definition explicitly recognizes gender identities that lie outside of the male/female binary such as "non-binary" and "genderqueer." This recognition closes a potential gap in the law and precludes attempts to justify conversion practices by arguing that non-binary identities are not validly included in the notion of gender identity. Accessing transition-related care remains difficult for non-binary individuals, and some countries do not offer them any medical transition services. As with sexual orientation, the definition was supplemented by an understanding of the importance of self-labelling and cultural sensitivity.[121] The definition of gender identity in the *Yogyakarta Principles* includes components corresponding to gender expression. These were not included, as gender expression bears its own definition under the model law. The merging of gender identity and gender expression under the *Yogyakarta Principles* reflects the historical context of the document. The 2017 *Yogyakarta Principles plus 10* provided separate definitions for gender identity and gender expression.[122]

Sex assigned at birth is defined as "the classification of a person as female, male, or another gender based on their anatomy, karyotyping, or other biological traits present at birth. It is typically the gender listed on the person's declaration of birth or original birth certificate." Sex assigned at birth is most commonly based on the presence or absence of a penis at birth. However, the assignment of gender at birth is often based on a more complicated process when it comes to intersex people, who do not correspond to the binary socio-medical conceptions of female or male bodies. Original declarations of birth and birth certificates typically reflect this classification; however, errors of notation may occur, and the documents of intersex youth drafted shortly after their birth do not always reflect the process of gender assignment imposed upon them. While sex assigned at birth may not be female or male, it is extremely rare for it to be classified otherwise on declarations of birth and birth certificates.

INTERSEX TRAITS: SUBSECTION 1(7)

Intersex traits are defined as "biological characteristics, including genitals, gonads, and chromosome patterns, that do not fit typical binary notions of female or male bodies, including differences in sex development resulting from androgen insensitivity syndrome, congenital adrenal hyperplasia, and hypospadias." The definition is based on the one found in California Senate Bill 201, which prohibits non-consensual surgeries on intersex minors.[123] Intersex traits are sometimes known as disorders of sex development (DSDs), though this terminology is rejected as pathologizing by many intersex individuals.[124] Medical examples are included in the definition for greater clarity.

GENDER EXPRESSION: SUBSECTION 1(8)

Gender expression is defined as "a person's desired external appearance as it relates to social expectations, understandings, and norms of femininity and masculinity. Gender expression may include a person's behaviour, name, pronouns, clothing, haircut, voice, tattoos, piercings, and anatomical features." This definition is offered *de novo* for the model law and does not substantively reflect definitions such as the one provided in the *Yogyakarta Principles plus 10*.[125] Gender expression is defined by reference to gendered social expectations, understandings, and norms, must be desired, and includes anatomical features. References to gendered social expectations, understandings, and norms serve to exclude minor or non-gendered changes to external appearances from the scope of conversion practices; though such changes may be unethical, they do not form conversion practices. Framing the gendered nature of gender expression by reference to gendered social expectations, understandings, and norms avoids implying that appearances are inherently gendered. External appearance must be desired. To define gender expression without reference to desire might prevent practitioners from encouraging patients to adopt desired appearances, which they are hesitant to embrace. Lastly, gender expression includes anatomical features. The inclusion of anatomical features in the definition of gender expression facilitates labelling practices that seek to discourage desired anatomical changes as conversion practices.

Gender expression is occasionally defined as how a person chooses to express their gender. In the context of the model law, this definition would be inadequate. Components of external appearance that are socially perceived as masculine or feminine may not reflect a choice to express gender and may instead reflect non-gender-related desires. For instance, many people find clothing coded as masculine more comfortable. Discouraging gender non-conformity may be a conversion practice independently of whether the patient's external appearance is desired for gender-related reasons.

SOCIAL AND MEDICAL TRANSITION: SUBSECTIONS 1(9) AND 1(10)

Social transition is defined as "the voluntary alteration of a person's gender expression to align it with their gender identity that differs from the one they were assigned at birth, other than through medical interventions." Medical transition is defined as voluntary alterations of the same kind, but for operating "through medical interventions such as puberty blockers, hormone replacement therapy, voice therapy, facial hair removal, and surgical procedures." The definitions acknowledge that social and medical transition are "personal and may not reflect others' understanding of which gender expressions correspond to a given gender identity." Social and medical transition may include changes to behaviour, name, pronouns, clothing, haircut, voice, tattoos, piercings, and anatomical features.

Social and medical transition must be voluntary. Involuntary alterations of gender expression are not social transition, as they do not emanate from the person's free choice. This terminology precludes an understanding of medical transition as including surgical procedures on intersex newborns and children who have not personally provided free and enlightened consent or assent. These procedures are harmful and unethical and are not comparable to medical transition for transgender people, which are beneficial and ethical.[126] Surgeries and interventions relating to intersex traits fall under the notion of medical transition for the purposes of the model law if they emanate from the person's free choice. As provided by paragraph 1(2)(g), free and enlightened consent or assent must be present. These surgeries and interventions may or may not be understood as falling under the concept of medical transition by intersex individuals.

Social and medical transitions are personal, individual processes. The person's chosen social and/or medical transition may not reflect conventional understandings of the traits associated with womanhood, manhood, or other genders. For instance, it is frequently assumed that women do not have penises and that, therefore, medical transition for trans women should, must, or always includes vaginoplasty. A person's social and/or medical transition may even be directly contrary to lay expectations. For instance, a non-binary person assigned female at birth but whose given name is unisex may wish to change their name to a typically feminine name as part of their social transition. To discourage uncommon or unconventional social and/or medical transitions would be included within the prohibition set out in paragraph 1(2)(f) as the adequacy of social and/or medical alterations is based on the individual's desire rather than on conformity to an external norm.

Voluntary alterations of gender expression solely motivated by reasons other than the person's gender identity or by a gender identity aligned with their sex assigned at birth are not included within the notions of social and medical transition. This reference to underlying motives reflects the common understanding that gender non-conformity alone does not constitute social and/or medical transition. Although this definitional feature restricts the application of paragraph 1(2)(f), seeking to repress, discourage, or change gender expression is prohibited under section 1(1). Practices targeting voluntary alterations of gender expression for non-gender-identity-related reasons may also fall within the scope of paragraph 1(2)(e), which prohibits treatments, practices, and sustained efforts that "proceed from the assumption that social or medical transition is undesirable or less desirable." It is unnecessary to define the term "medical interventions" since social and medical transition covers the entire field of transition: all interventions are either medical or non-medical. By the law of the excluded middle, statements of the form (A ∨ ¬A) are always true. Common transition-related medical interventions are nevertheless provided in the definition for greater clarity.

Subsection 1(11): Proof by Self-Report
Sexual orientation, gender identity, gender expression, and behaviours associated with a gender other than the person's sex assigned at birth "may be proved by self-report." Allowing proof of targeted characteristics by testimony significantly curtails evidentiary difficulties involved in proving that someone has engaged in conversion practices since evidence of the targeted characteristic at the time of the practices may be difficult to prove later. This difficulty is lessened by allowing people to self-report the targeted characteristic they had at the time of the offence, including by testimony at trial. This subsection limits practitioners' capacity to raise as a defence the fact that the patient's self-reported targeted characteristic did not represent their true targeted characteristic but, rather, was a lie or false consciousness. Since conversion practices often label self-reported gender identities and sexual orientations as mere confusion, proof by testimony is essential to effectively prohibit conversion practices.

Sections 2–6: Prohibited Acts
Different acts are prohibited based on the entity that engaged in conversion practices and on the type of proceeding. Conversion practices and related actions may constitute individual negligence, discrimination, unfair or deceptive trade practices, professional misconduct, and organizational or governmental misconduct. Lawmakers should be mindful of the relationship between the type of proceeding and legal validity or constitutionality. For instance, some authors have suggested that in the United States, prohibiting conversion practices as unfair or deceptive trade practices is more likely to withstand a constitutional challenge than laws framing them as negligence, discrimination, or professional misconduct.[127]

Under section 2, it constitutes individual negligence and discrimination to "engage in conversion practices or knowingly refer an individual to someone who engages in conversion practices." Negligence is a tort under common law, and jurisdictions that do not recognize the tort of negligence should replace the term by its functional analog in their legal system, such as delict, quasi-delict, or civil liability. It applies to anyone, rather than merely to licensed professionals, because not everyone who engages in conversion practices is licensed, and many jurisdictions do not prohibit individuals without a licence from engaging in psychotherapy or other similar acts. This broad scope is necessary to effectively outlaw conversion practices and falls within the range of legitimate legislative action aimed at protecting the public. Despite applying to anyone, the terms "any treatment, practice, or sustained effort" under subsection 1(1) restrict this prohibition to acts evidencing a threshold degree of systematicity and would not typically apply to parents of gender-creative youth. Referring someone to a practitioner of conversion practices also constitutes negligence if it is done with the knowledge that the person will engage in conversion practices. Due to the requirement of knowledge, those who innocently refer individuals to practitioners of conversion practices, not knowing that their approach is conversion in nature, will not be in contravention of section 2. Conversion practices also constitute discrimination under section 2, opening the door to human rights complaints. Human rights bodies often have the power to conduct inquiries and may provide legal representation, which can improve access to justice. The language of section 2 should be tailored to the jurisdiction's human rights laws, for instance by referring to a specific anti-discrimination provision.

Under section 3, it constitutes negligence and discrimination to do "anything for the purpose of removing from the jurisdiction a person who is ordinarily resident in the jurisdiction with the intention that this person undergo conversion practices." The section aims at preventing people from circumventing bans on conversion practices by simply taking the person across jurisdictional lines to a place where conversion practices are legal or tolerated. Because conversion practitioners are not equally prevalent in every area, it is common for people to undergo conversion practices in another jurisdiction.

Under section 4, it constitutes an unfair or deceptive trade practice to "advertise or receive compensation in exchange for engaging in or teaching conversion practices." It is in the nature of trade practices that compensation be involved, giving rise to the requirement. Prohibiting the advertisement of harmful or ineffective services is within the usual scope of consumer protection laws. Unfair and deceptive trade practices are subject to sanctions in many jurisdictions and aid in curtailing conversion practices insofar as these laws grant extensive powers of inquiry to state agents in addition to creating independent sanction mechanisms.[128] In jurisdictions where psychotherapy and counselling are not reserved acts, the ability to investigate and impose sanctions under consumer protection laws is imperative since their professional bodies cannot investigate and punish conversion practices by unlicensed or unregulated professionals.

Under section 5, it constitutes unprofessional conduct subject to discipline by professional licensing or certifying boards to engage in, teach, or advertise conversion practices. This provision ensures that conversion practices can be sanctioned by professional orders, which have significant power of inquiry and may suspend or revoke the licences of professionals in addition to imposing fines. Advertising and teaching conversion practices are not included under the individual negligence provision of section 2 because tortious liability requires individuals to suffer identifiable harms or losses flowing from the actions. By contrast, unprofessional conduct may be sanctioned regardless of the resulting quantifiable harm or losses to identifiable individuals. The terminology of "licensing or certifying board" should be adapted to the language used in the jurisdiction, as terminology for such bodies is not standard. The prohibition against teaching risks running afoul of constitutional protections of freedom of speech in some jurisdictions. It should only be included after careful legal analysis.

Under section 6, any organization, including corporations and governmental entities, is committing an act of negligence and discrimination if they "engage in or knowingly refer an individual to practitioners of conversion practices," "knowingly provide insurance coverage for conversion practices," "knowingly provide preferential tax treatment, including non-profit or charitable status, to any entity that facilitates engaging in, advertising, or referring an individual to practitioners of conversion practices," "knowingly provide a grant or contract to any entity that engages in or refers individuals to practitioners of conversion practices," or "refuse to provide a grant or contract to any entity for refusing to engage in, teach, or advertise conversion practices." Furthermore, "organizations and governmental entities shall take reasonable steps to ensure compliance with" these prohibitions. The section ensures the prohibition of conversion practices for legal persons other than natural persons as organizations may be involved in the provision of conversion practices, especially in the context of unlicensed, faith-based practices. It also prohibits acts that are specific to organizations, such as providing insurance coverage. The prohibition of financial support for conversion practices is a common legislative feature and seeks to limit the ability of individuals to engage in such practices.[129] "Governmental entities" is a broad term that includes governments, the subdivision of governments, and entities that exercise governmental functions.

Sections 2–6 share prohibited acts, which may facilitate proceedings if a prior decision by a juridical or administrative body can be invoked. For instance, the decision of a licensing board sanctioning a psychologist for engaging in conversion under section 5 could be entered into evidence during a proceeding under section 2.

Sections 7–11: Cause of Action, Damages, and Legal Aid
Under section 7, any person "who suffers harm or losses due to a breach of sections 2, 3, 4, or 6 may bring a private action against the perpetrator under this act to enjoin further breaches, or to recover special and general damages, or both." This section grants a civil cause of action to those who were subjected to conversion practices and enables them to seek an injunction and/or recover damages. While sections 2, 3, 4, and 6 may suffice to enable private suits due to the language of negligence and of unfair or deceptive trade practices, this section provides additional certainty and precludes a finding that the sections do not give rise to a right to sue for survivors. At common law, special damages refer to harms and losses that may be quantified in monetary terms, such as loss of earnings and medical expenses. General damages are also included, which would encompass pain, mental distress, loss of enjoyment of life, and harm to dignity, which are common consequences of conversion practices. Since

the harms of conversion practices may be difficult to quantify and go beyond monetary losses, it is crucial to enable the recovery of general damages. The categorization of damages varies by jurisdiction and should be adapted to reflect the legal system in which the model law is adopted. The expression "under this act" may or may not be adapted to the structure of the legislation. If the model law is legislated as a chapter of a code, for instance, "under this chapter" may be more appropriate.

Under section 8, judges "shall award reasonable attorney's fees and costs to a prevailing plaintiff upon a finding by the court or trier of fact that the defendant engaged in conversion practices" in private suits. Given widespread poverty in 2SLGBTQIA+ communities,[130] providing for attorneys' fees and costs is an essential component of access to justice. The provision of fees may encourage attorneys to represent survivors of conversion practices on a contingent or conditional fee agreement, which provides for payment of attorneys if the suit is successful or leads to a settlement and typically pays a percentage of the recovered damages.

Under section 9, courts "may award nominal, aggravated, and punitive damages" if the defendant is found to have engaged in conversion practices. Nominal damages refer to token amounts that may be awarded even when the plaintiff is unable to prove that they suffered harm as a result of conversion practices. They aim at discouraging the practices despite evidentiary difficulties. Aggravated damages aim at compensating for the aggravation of the injury due to the egregiousness of the defendant's act. In Canada, aggravated damages are sometimes described as a part of general damages and sometimes as a separate head of damages.[131] To ensure that aggravating factors can be properly considered, the model law names aggravated damages separately. Punitive damages aim at deterring behaviours rather than compensating for losses. Allowing judges to award punitive damages recognizes the gravity of conversion practices, which are antithetical to the dignity of 2SLGBTQIA+ people and may be used to further discourage them. Because the aim of laws prohibiting conversion practices is not only to enable compensation but also to discourage conversion practices, allowing and encouraging awards of punitive damages is legitimate.

Under section 10, courts "may, on the application of an interested person or the government, make an order for the dissolution of a corporation carrying on the business of engaging in, advertising, or referring individuals to practitioners of conversion practices." This section aims to prevent further conversion practices by providing an avenue for dissolving organizations whose business centres or partially centres on conversion practices. The provision is inspired by the New Jersey Superior Court's decision in *Ferguson v JONAH*, which ordered the dissolution of the conversion practices organization JONAH after finding that its practices constituted consumer fraud.[132] The order does not need to be made within the context of a lawsuit contemplated by sections 6–8 and can be initiated independently by the application of an interested person to the court. Interested persons notably include individuals who have a claim against the corporation as a result of a violation of sections 2, 3, 4, or 6. The words "the government" should be replaced by the specific governmental body charged with enforcing this section of the law, which could notably be the attorney general or the entity that oversees the incorporation of businesses.

Under section 11, legal aid "shall be granted, to the extent determined by law, to the plaintiff in any action brought under section 7 or 10." The provision extends the subject matters regarding which legal aid is provided, but individuals remain subject to financial eligibility rules and other conditions set by law. This provision is essential due to widespread poverty in 2SLGBTQIA+ communities, which can be further aggravated by conversion practices due to its impact on mental health and, thus, financial stability.[133] In addition to the preceding, lawmakers may wish to consider creating a governmental body tasked with investigating complaints related to conversion practices, proposing and accepting legal undertakings relating to conversion practices, levying fines against those who violate the law, and/or representing complainants or the government in proceedings initiated under the law. Alternatively, an existing body could be attributed this mandate, as the Australian state of Victoria did with its Equal Opportunity and Human Rights Commission.[134] These bodies can also serve pedagogical and research functions.

Section 12: Licensing Boards

The mandate of professional licensing and certifying bodies is amended to include "discouraging conversion practices and educating members about the dangers of conversion practices." Enlisting professional associations in the contestation of conversion practices is essential to weed out such practices among licensed professionals. Altering the mandate of associations rather than creating a fully fledged regulatory framework enables individual bodies to shape their course of action to the realities of their particular profession. Because it emphasizes the self-regulation of professions, it also limits professional resentment towards legislative interference in professional self-regulation, which could impede efforts against conversion practices.

Adding to the bodies' mandate encourages them to take concrete action to eradicate conversion practices within their respective memberships. Creating a trans-affirming professional culture, fostering knowledge of conversion practices, and encouraging mutual enforcement of bans by professionals are three core components of effectively discouraging conversion practices in professions. Bodies should consider integrating education on conversion practices in university and professional development curriculum, drafting clear and thorough guidelines on providing care to individuals marginalized because of their sexual orientation, gender modality, or gender expression, and creating a committee tasked with holding professionals accountable for breaching conversion practices bans.

Section 13: Limitation Period

The limitation period for proceedings relating to conversion practices under the model law is ten years. This period runs from the day of the last conversion practice, the day on which the person turns eighteen years old, or "the day on which a reasonable person with the abilities and in the circumstances of the person subjected to conversion practices would have realized that they suffered harm or losses" from the conversion practices – whichever is the latest date. Limitation periods vary by jurisdiction, and the chosen period should be consistent with other limitation periods within the jurisdiction. In some jurisdictions, a different length of time may be adequate. Some jurisdictions may even want to remove all limitation periods, allowing lawsuits against conversion practitioners regardless of how much time has passed. Because conversion practices occur in therapeutic relationships or simulations thereof, it is appropriate to adopt a longer limitation period than the usual limitation period for civil claims. This longer limitation period better reflects the fiduciary or pseudo-fiduciary nature of the relationship.

Different dates are provided for the start of the limitation period. It can take a long time for individuals to work through their trauma and mental health problems and realize that they are linked to conversion practices. This section ensures that actions are not prescribed because the practices occurred early in childhood or because the person needed substantial psychological support to realize that they were harmed by them. Alternative periods for calculating whether claims are prescribed are common in suits relating to psychological harm and childhood sexual assault. The expression "under this act" may or may not be adapted to the structure of the legislation. If the model law is legislated as a chapter of a code, for instance, "under this chapter" may be more appropriate.

Section 14: Severability
The model law provides for severability, and if "any provision or application of a provision of this act is found to be unconstitutional, invalid, or of no force or effect, the remaining provisions and applications of provisions shall continue in force as law." This section ensures that the prohibition on conversion practices provided for in the model law remain in force if only a portion of it was found to be unconstitutional, invalid, or of no force or effect. It is a boilerplate inclusion. The language of "unconstitutional, invalid, or of no force or effect" should be modified to reflect the language used in the jurisdiction. The expression "under this act" may or may not be adapted to the structure of the legislation. If the model law is legislated as a chapter of a code, for instance, "under this chapter" may be more appropriate.

~

As legislators consider banning conversion practices, it is crucial for them to promote legislation that would have the greatest impact in curtailing these harmful and unethical practices. Generating momentum for modifying poorly written bans can be much more difficult than generating momentum to pass a well-drafted ban in the first place. This model law provides a clear and detailed template that accurately defines which acts fall under the notion of conversion practices and that provides for different avenues of enforcement, recognizing that multiple angles of approach are necessary to eliminate conversion practices. While I hope that this model law will contribute to the fight against conversion practices through legislation, completely eradicating them will require a deeper cultural shift that cannot be legislated. Dedicating resources to education on the realities of marginalized groups and to community organizations serving these groups remain crucial components in the fight for equality, as are actions undertaken by professional associations.[135] All levels of civil society must take part in the fight against conversion practices. Banning them is only the first step.

Conclusion

How many vivid, radiant lives were lost to conversion practices? How many ruined by them? The fight against trans conversion practices is not a theoretical one for trans communities. It is a fight against suffering, against dehumanization. It's a fight for survival, for happiness. I was inspired to write this book by my friends and partners who underwent trans conversion practices. They gave me the strength to research this difficult topic. Many of them are still struggling with the aftermath of being taught that they were broken. Survivors deserve love and acceptance. I can only hope it finds them, if it hasn't already. I dedicate my book to you and hope it did your experiences justice.

My book has sought to answer a few pressing questions about bans on trans conversion practices at this pivotal time in history. More and more jurisdictions are considering prohibiting conversion practices, and policy-makers and advocates must know what is being prohibited and what should be. In the introduction, I asked a few organizing questions: What does a standard ban look like and what is its scope? What are the different variants that these laws take? Do these laws stand up to constitutional scrutiny? What are the advantages and disadvantages of legislative approaches to trans conversion practices? How may we improve on them? We've unearthed answers to each of those questions. Bans are broad and include a wide range of practices that are predicated on a view of being trans as undesirable or pathological. Although bans vary in shape and form across jurisdictions, they share common features that gesture towards a similar scope. Constitutional and pseudo-constitutional arguments against the bans hold very little plausibility under dominant understandings of free speech and legitimate legislative interest. We were able to identify both benefits and limitations to bans on trans conversion practices and proposed improvements in the form of measures toward developing an affirmative professional culture and a comprehensive annotated model law.

While the topic is far from exhausted, I hope that these answers will provide a useful starting point for ongoing discussions on eliminating trans conversion practices. Academic scholarship, especially in law, has tended to focus on sexual orientation to the exclusion of gender. There is a dire need for more scholarship and especially legal scholarship on the matter. Trans conversion practices have their own history, theorizations, socio-professional context, and interventions. We cannot simply substitute sexual orientation for gender identity and call it a day.

The closure of the Centre for Addiction and Mental Health (CAMH) Gender Identity Clinic for Children and Youth shows that legislative action combined with grassroots advocacy can concretely alter practices. Legislative action alone cannot suffice. Limits inhere to the choice of political vehicle. Legislation can help change culture, but it is not itself a culture change. Legislative endeavours are also mediated by political will and, in jurisdictions where politicians show an unwillingness to regulate conversion practices, other legal approaches will have to be considered.

Since people and institutions' relationship to the law is variable, bans impact practice unequally across the social field. Large institutions like CAMH, which are composed of many people with diverse agendas and is concerned with maintaining its reputation both in the professional community and the local one, are more likely to be impacted by laws than are individual practitioners whose practices already meet the disapproval of colleagues and still fail to change. Though the law may prohibit these practices, individuals might continue to engage in them with impunity if peer disapproval does not threaten their interests and the laws are not enforced against them.

Future legal research should explore professional malpractice and disciplinary law as a potential means of sanctioning conversion practices in jurisdictions that do not have laws prohibiting conversion practices.[1] Since trans conversion practices do not respect the current professional consensus on competent care even in jurisdictions that do not have statutory bans on conversion practices, former and current patients may have recourse despite the absence of legislation. Professional malpractice and disciplinary law may also prove useful in jurisdictions that do have legislative bans on trans conversion practices since they are not similarly restricted by political willingness on matters such as age. Other avenues like consumer fraud laws are also worth exploring.[2] What we need are creative, multifaceted strategies that draw on the full spectrum of legal and non-legal tools.

Writing this book has strengthened my belief that we cannot assume that the mere existence of a law translates into effectiveness. If we want to bring an end to trans conversion practices, we must improve bans and improve *upon* bans. The conversation of how to combat trans conversion practices cannot end once bans come into force. Ultimately, only a thorough change in culture will ensure the extinction of these harmful and degrading practices. I look forward to it.

Appendix: Professional Organizations Opposing Trans Conversion Practices

The following organizations oppose trans conversion practices. In the case of joint statements, I only included a reference under one of the organizations' name. I have incorporated excerpts from select documents.

International

Federation of International Nurses in Endocrinology. "Endocrine Nurses Society Position Statement on Transgender and Gender Diverse Care" (2021) Journal of the Endocrine Society, online: <perma.cc/ EW9Z-4X3D>.

International Federation of Social Workers. "Global Social Work Statement of Ethical Principles" (July 2, 2018), online: <perma. cc/3X9C-H4D9>.

Society for Adolescent Health and Medicine. "Recommendations for Promoting the Health and Well-Being of Lesbian, Gay, Bisexual, and Transgender Adolescents: A Position Paper of the Society for Adolescent Health and Medicine" (2013) 52:4 Journal of Adolescent Health 506.

World Professional Association for Transgender Health. Eli Coleman et al, "Standards of Care for the Health of Transsexual, Transgender, and Gender-Nonconforming People, Version 7" (2012) 13:4 International Journal of Transgenderism 165 at 175 (references omitted):

Treatment aimed at trying to change a person's gender identity and expression to become more congruent with sex assigned at birth has been attempted in the past without success particularly in the long term. Such treatment is no longer considered ethical.

Australia and New Zealand

Australian and New Zealand Professional Association for Transgender Health. Michelle M Telfer et al, *Australian Standards of Care and Treatment Guidelines for Trans and Gender Diverse Children and Adolescents*, Version 1.1 (Melbourne: Royal Children's Hospital, 2018) at 5:

Withholding of gender affirming treatment is not considered a neutral option, and may exacerbate distress in a number of ways including increasing depression, anxiety and suicidality, social withdrawal, as well as possibly increasing chances of young people illegally accessing medications.

In the past, psychological practices attempting to change a person's gender identity to be more aligned with their sex assigned at birth were used. Such practices, typically known as conversion or reparative therapies, lack efficacy, are considered unethical and may cause lasting damage to a child or adolescent's social and emotional health and wellbeing.

Australian Professional Association for Transgender Health. AusPATH Board of Directors, "Position Statement on 'Rapid-Onset Gender Dysphoria (ROGD)'" (September 30, 2019), online: <perma.cc/FGG9-9PP9>.

Endocrine Nurses' Society of Australasia. See Federation of International Nurses in Endocrinology.

Royal Children's Hospital Gender Service. See Australian and New Zealand Professional Association for Transgender Health.

Canada

Alberta College of Social Workers. "Practice Statement on Reparative or Conversion Therapy" (February 21, 2020), online: <perma.cc/U5EK-2FDZ>. See also the documents "Reparative or Conversion Therapy Background Document," online: <perma.cc/F3ZC-5W33> and "Frequently Asked Questions: Reparative or Conversion Therapy," online: <perma.cc/FX7G-V6T6>, which are published along with it.

Canadian Association for Social Work Education. See Canadian Association of Social Workers

Canadian Association of Social Workers. "Joint Statement on the Affirmation of Gender Diverse Children and Youth" (January 9, 2015), online: <perma.cc/VQ5R-UU9G>.

Canadian Professional Association for Transgender Health. Nicole Nussbaum, "Submission to the Standing Committee on Justice Policy Re: Bill 77, Affirming Sexual Orientation and Gender Identity Act, 2015," online: <perma.cc/LR35-NBR9>.

Canadian Psychiatric Association. Albina Veltman & Gary Chaimowitz, "Mental Health Care for People Who Identify as Lesbian, Gay, Bisexual, Transgender, and (or) Queer" (2014) 59:11 Canadian Journal of Psychiatry 1.

Canadian Psychological Association. Kristopher Wells, *Conversion Therapy in Canada: A Guide for Legislative Action*, rev ed (Edmonton: MacEwan University, 2020), online: <perma.cc/NRH9-ZFFX>.

College of Alberta Psychologists. "Standards of Practice" (October 2019), online: <perma.cc/3A7F-3ZHD>.

College of Registered Psychotherapists of Ontario. *Professional Practice Standards for Registered Psychotherapists* (Toronto: College of Registered Psychotherapists of Ontario, 2016), online: <perma.cc/RS5G-HUJK>.

Manitoba College of Social Workers. "'Conversion Therapy' Position Statement" (May 2020), online: <perma.cc/VN8J-XAKK>.

Ordre des travailleurs sociaux et thérapeutes conjugaux et familiaux du Québec. "L'Ordre appuie la déclaration de la CASWE-ACFTS et l'ACTS" (January 10, 2019), online: <perma.cc/8JBK-GKJN>.

Ordre professionnel des sexologues du Québec. Denise Medico, Joanie Heppell & Martin Blais, "Avis au public concernant les effets nocifs des thérapies dites de conversion ou thérapies réparatrices pour l'orientation sexuelle et le genre" (May 17, 2018), online: <perma.cc/5T3D-JXL7>.

United Kingdom

Association of Christian Counsellors. See British Psychological Society.

Association of LGBT Doctors and Dentists (GLADD). See British Psychological Society.

British Association for Counselling and Psychotherapy. See British Psychological Society.

British Association of Behavioural and Cognitive Psychotherapies. See British Psychological Society.

British Psychoanalytic Council. See British Psychological Society.

British Psychological Society. "Memorandum of Understanding on Conversion Therapy in the UK, Version 2" (October 2017) at 2, online: <perma.cc/M23Y-9SAP>:

> For the purposes of this document "conversion therapy" is an umbrella term for a therapeutic approach, or any model or individual viewpoint that demonstrates an assumption that any sexual orientation or gender identity is inherently preferable to any other, and which attempts to bring about a change of sexual orientation or gender identity, or seeks to supress an individual's expression of sexual orientation or gender identity on that basis.

~

> Signatory organisations agree that the practice of conversion therapy, whether in relation to sexual orientation or gender identity, is unethical and potentially harmful.

> Signatory organisations agree that neither sexual orientation nor gender identity in themselves are indicators of a mental disorder.

College of Sex and Relationship Therapists. See British Psychological Society.

National Counselling Society. See British Psychological Society.

National Health Services England. See British Psychological Society.

National Health Services Scotland. See British Psychological Society.

Pink Therapy. See British Psychological Society.

Royal College of General Practitioners. See British Psychological Society.

Royal College of Psychiatrists. *Supporting Transgender and Gender-Diverse People: Position Statement No PS02/18* (London: Royal College of Psychiatrists, 2018), online: <perma.cc/S8HB-HK3U>.

UK Council for Psychotherapy. See British Psychological Society.

United States

American Academy of Child and Adolescent Psychiatry. "Conversion Therapy: Policy Statement" (February 2018), online: <perma.cc/35PU-HKA9?type=image>.

American Academy of Family Physicians. Jim Walker & Guy Albert, "U.S. Joint Statement on Conversion Therapy (Draft 2.1)" (October 18, 2017), online: <perma.cc/8P2N-3M3Q>. Note that the statement is a draft, and the partner organizations have not yet finalized their endorsement.

American Academy of Nursing. See American Academy of Family Physicians.

American Academy of Pediatrics. Jason Rafferty, "Ensuring Comprehensive Care and Support for Transgender and Gender-Diverse Children and Adolescents" (2018) 142:4 Pediatrics e20182162.

American Association of Sexuality Educators, Counselors and Therapists. "Position on Reparative Therapy" (February 9, 2017), online: <perma.cc/ASC5-XSGG>. See also American Academy of Family Physicians.

American College of Physicians. Hilary Daniel & Renee Butkus, "Lesbian, Gay, Bisexual, and Transgender Health Disparities: Executive Summary of a Policy Position Paper from the American College of Physicians" (2015) 163:2 Annals of Internal Medicine 135.

American Counselling Association. See American Academy of Family Physicians.

American Group Psychotherapy Association. See American Mental Health Counselors Association.

American Medical Association. *Health Care Needs of Lesbian, Gay, Bisexual, Transgender and Queer Populations H-160.991* (2018), online: <perma.cc/BXU9-G3GT?type=image>:

> Our AMA: (a) believes that the physician's nonjudgmental recognition of patients' sexual orientations, sexual behaviors, and gender identities enhances the ability to render optimal patient care in health as well as in illness ... and (c) opposes, the use of "reparative" or "conversion" therapy for sexual orientation or gender identity.

See also American Academy of Family Physicians.

American Medical Student Association. See American Academy of Family Physicians.

American Mental Health Counselors Association. "Open Letter from Mental Health Organizations" (June 2014), online: <perma.cc/E92F-2VSW>.

American Psychoanalytic Association. "Position Statement on Attempts to Change Sexual Orientation, Gender Identity, or Gender

Expression" (2012), online: <perma.cc/3ZTB-7L8F>. See also American Academy of Family Physicians.

American Psychological Association. "Resolution on Gender and Sexual Orientation Diversity in Children and Adolescents in Schools" (February 2015), online: <perma.cc/97KS-DKVL>; "Resolution on Gender Identity Change Efforts" (February 2021), online: <perma.cc/EC55-2PKR>:

> Gender identity change efforts (GICE) refer to a range of techniques used by mental health professionals and nonprofessionals with the goal of changing gender identity, gender expression, or associated components of these to be in alignment with gender role behaviors that are stereotypically associated with sex assigned at birth.

> ∼

> [T]he APA affirms that scientific evidence and clinical experience indicate that GICE put individuals at significant risk of harm;
> [T]he APA opposes GICE because such efforts put individuals at significant risk of harm and encourages individuals, families, health professionals, and organizations to avoid GICE.

American School Counsellor Association. "The School Counselor and LGBTQ Youth: Position Statement" (2016), online: <perma.cc/D9EW-Y4R5>.

Association of Lesbian, Gay, Bisexual, Transgender Addiction Professionals and Their Allies. See American Academy of Family Physicians

Association of Lesbian, Gay, Bisexual, Transgender Issues in Counseling. See American Academy of Family Physicians.

Association of LGBTQ Psychiatrists. See American Academy of Family Physicians.

Clinical Social Work Association. See American Academy of Family Physicians.

Endocrine Nurses Society. See Federation of International Nurses in Endocrinology.

Gay and Lesbian Medical Association. See American Academy of Family Physicians and American Mental Health Counselors Association.

National Association for Children's Behavioral Health. See American Mental Health Counselors Association

National Association of School Psychologists. See American Mental Health Counselors Association and American Psychological Association, first citation.

National Association of Social Workers. *Sexual Orientation Change Efforts (SOCE) and Conversion Therapy with Lesbians, Gay Men, Bisexuals, and Transgender Persons: Position Statement* (Washington, DC: National Association of Social Workers, 2015), online: <perma.cc/QN9D-Q8FD>.

National Coalition for Mental Health Recovery. See American Mental Health Counselors Association.

Pediatric Endocrinology Nursing Society. See Federation of International Nurses in Endocrinology.

Glossary

Centre for Addiction and Mental Health (CAMH): In Toronto; its defunct Gender Identity Clinic for Children and Youth has long been associated with the corrective approach.

cisgender: Of persons whose gender identity corresponds to the gender they were assigned at birth. Antonym of transgender.

cisheteronormative: Of actions, attitudes, beliefs, and ideological systems that are both cisnormative and heteronormative.

cisnormative: Of actions, attitudes, beliefs, and ideological systems that treat cisgender people as the norm and erase, marginalize, denigrate, and/or pathologize transgender people.

conversion practices: Sustained efforts to change, discourage, or repress someone's actual or perceived identity or behaviours as Two-Spirit, lesbian, gay, bisexual, transgender, queer, intersex, asexual, and so on (2SLGBTQIA+). Similar prejudicial practices targeting intersex and autistic people are sometimes also called conversion practices. A legal definition is offered in Chapter 6. Conversion practices are also known as conversion or reparative therapy, but the words "therapy" and "reparative" are frequently criticized as misleading since such practices are neither healing nor therapeutic.

corrective approach: A form of conversion practice that seeks to prevent or discourage gender creative youth, and especially prepubertal youth, from growing up transgender.

Diagnostic and Statistical Manual of Mental Disorders (DSM): Published by the American Psychiatric Association. Considered the bible of psychiatry, its fifth edition was published in 2013 and contains the diagnostic category of Gender Dysphoria. The third edition was published in 1980 and first added the objectionable diagnoses of Transsexualism and Gender Identity Disorder of Childhood.

gender: See gender identity.

gender-affirmative approach: An approach to care for trans and gender-creative youth that considers transitude and gender non-conformity to be healthy parts of human diversity and encourages respect for youths' gender regardless of age, with the understanding that they are best positioned to know their own gender. The gender-affirmative approach facilitates social transition at any age, including prior to puberty, and supports desired, age-appropriate medical interventions (for example, puberty blockers and/or hormone replacement therapy upon reaching puberty).

gender-affirming care: Healthcare interventions that are part of a person's medical transition, such as puberty blockers, hormone replacement therapy, and transition-related surgeries. The term is also used to refer more broadly to healthcare that is responsive to the needs and realities of trans people.

gender creative: Of youths, especially young children, who exhibit strong, ongoing behaviour patterns associated with a gender other than the one they were assigned at birth, regardless of whether they are trans and/or will grow up to be. Also known as gender independent, gender variant, gender expansive, and gender diverse.

gender dysphoria: A form of discomfort or distress caused by the lack of correspondence between a person's gendered self-image and their bodily traits, gender expression, and/or gender categorization by others. Gender dysphoria towards one's bodily traits or gender expression may be triggered by perceptions of oneself by actual or potential others. Gender Dysphoria may also refer to a diagnostic category applied to trans people, found in the fifth edition of the *DSM*. Capitalization is used to distinguish the two meanings throughout the book.

gender expression: External appearance as it relates to social expectations, understandings, and norms of femininity and masculinity. Gender expression may include a person's behaviour, name, pronouns, clothing, haircut, voice, tattoos, piercings, and anatomical features.

gender identity: A deeply felt internal and individual experience of gender including the personal sense of the body. Common gender identities include man, woman, non-binary, and Two-Spirit.

Gender Identity Disorder: Obsolete diagnostic category applied to trans and gender non-conforming people. Replaced by Gender Dysphoria in the fifth edition of the *DSM*.

gender modality: Refers to how a person's gender identity stands in relation to their sex assigned at birth. Being trans or cis are gender modalities.

gender non-conforming: Of persons whose gender expression does not accord with society's expectations. Also used to describe behaviours and appearances that transgress gender norms. Also known as gender variant.

gender transition: The voluntary alignment of a person's gender expression, role, or gendered body with their gender identity, which does not correspond to the one they were assigned at birth. Gender transition may involve social, medical, and/or legal aspects. Also known as transition.

genital reconfiguration surgery: A surgery on external genitals as part of a person's medical transition, such as vaginoplasty, vulvaplasty, metoidioplasty, and phalloplasty. Not typically used to refer to orchiectomy or hysterectomy. The terms sex reassignment surgery, gender reassignment surgery, gender-affirmation surgery, and gender-confirmation surgery are no longer considered appropriate.

heteronormative: Attitudes, practices, and ideological systems that treat straight people as the norm and denigrate, marginalize, and/or pathologize queer people.

homoantagonistic: Of actions, attitudes, beliefs, and ideological systems that are intolerant, prejudiced, hostile, or discriminatory towards lesbian, gay, bisexual, and queer people. The term homoantagonism is used instead of homophobia because the latter inaccurately suggests a relationship to phobias. The term further connotes fear and irrationality, contrary to some theorists' suggestion that homoantagonistic ideology is organized into a logical system and rarely involves fear.

homophobic: See homoantagonistic.

International Classification of Diseases (ICD):   Published by the World Health Organization. Its latest revision – the eleventh version of the *ICD* – was adopted in 2019 and includes the non-mental health diagnosis of Gender Incongruence. Its prior revision instead used the language of Transsexualism, placed in the chapter on mental and behavioural disorders.

LGBQ, LGBTQ, LGBTI, and 2SLGBTQIA+:   Initialisms used to refer to some or all of lesbian, gay, bisexual, trans, queer, intersex, asexual, and Two-Spirit people. When used, the + indicates the open-ended and non-exhaustive nature of the initialism. The appropriate acronym depends on context and intention. Using an acronym without intending to refer to each included group is improper.

misgendering: Miscategorizing a person's gender, whether verbally or not. To misgender someone using their pre-transition name is known as dead naming.

non-binary: Of a person or gender whose gender identity is not completely male or completely female. Non-binary is often used as an umbrella term that includes more specific genders like agender, bigender, genderfluid, and genderqueer. Genderqueer is sometimes used as an umbrella term with the same or similar meaning.

puberty blockers: Medication used to inhibit endogenous puberty by suppressing the production of sex hormones. Puberty blockers are considered reversible and reasonably safe. Also known as gonadotropin-releasing hormone agonists (GnRHa).

queer: Of a person whose sexual orientation is not straight. Also used as a specific sexual orientation label. See also LGBQ.

reparative therapy: Commonly used synonym for conversion practices. The term is also strongly associated with Joseph Nicolosi and the National Association for Research and Therapy of Homosexuality. See conversion practices.

sex: See gender identity.

sex assigned at birth: Classification as male, female, intersex, or another gender or sex based on their anatomy, karyotyping, or other biological traits present at birth. It is typically the gender listed on the person's declaration of birth or original birth certificate. Also known as gender assigned at birth.

sex reassignment surgery: See genital reconfiguration surgery and transition-related surgeries.

trans: Of a person, whose gender identity does not correspond to the gender they were assigned at birth. Trans* with the asterisk has fallen out of fashion, though some consider it very 1990s Boolean retro. The term transsexual, which is associated with the exclusion of non-binary people and the rigid medicalization of gender transition, is considered outdated and offensive when applied as an umbrella term or to people who do not self-identify as transsexual. Also known as transgender.

trans*: See trans.

transantagonistic: Of actions, attitudes, beliefs, and ideological systems that are intolerant, prejudiced, hostile, or discriminatory towards trans people. Psychopathologization and denials of gender are core forms of transantagonism. The term transantagonism is used instead of transphobia because the latter inaccurately suggests a relationship to phobias. The term further connotes fear and irrationality, contrary to some theorists' suggestion that transantagonistic ideology is organized into a logical system and rarely involves fear.

transgender: See trans.

transition: See gender transition.

transition-related surgeries: Surgeries, on any body part, that are or may be part of a person's medical transition. The terms sex reassignment surgeries and gender reassignment surgeries are no longer considered appropriate. The terms gender affirmation surgeries and gender confirmation surgeries are considered inappropriate by some trans people.

transitude: The state or quality of being trans. Also known as transness.

transphobic: See transantagonistic.

transsexual: See trans.

transsexualism: An obsolete diagnostic category applied to trans people. Replaced by Gender Incongruence in the eleventh version of the *ICD*. Also used as a synonym for transitude, but such usage is considered offensive.

Two-Spirit: Of a person; a cultural and spiritual identity for Indigenous persons whose spirit(s) have multiple gendered aspects, community roles and responsibilities, and/or ways of being. Two-Spirit is an umbrella term with multiple, complex meanings that includes more specific identities such as *iskwêhkân, napêhkân* (Nehiyawewin), *asegi udanto* (Tsalagi Gawonihisdi), *niizh manidowaag* (Ojibwe), *sts'iyóye smestíyexw slhá:li* (Halq'eméylem), and *onón:wat* (Kanien'kéha). Two-Spirit identities were historically recognized and respected in many Indigenous Nations and held a defined social and spiritual role within them. Because Indigenous world views differ from settler world views, Two-Spirit identity cannot readily be described as either sexual orientation or gender identity, but many Two-Spirit people understand "Two-Spirit" as their gender identity and/or sexual orientation. The term was coined in 1990 at the third Annual Intertribal Native American/First Nations Gay and Lesbian Conference in Winnipeg.

World Professional Association for Transgender Health (WPATH):   The association publishes the *Standards of Care for the Health of Transsexual, Transgender, and Gender-Nonconforming People* a leading guideline in transgender health. Version 7 was published in 2011, and version 8 is expected in 2022.

Notes

Introduction

1 See e.g. Simon D Pickstone-Taylor, "Children with Gender Nonconformity" (2003) 42:3 J American Academy Child & Adolescent Psychiatry 266.

2 Bill 77, *Affirming Sexual Orientation and Gender Identity Act, 2015*, SO 2015, c 18 [Bill 77].

3 Jake Pyne, "Discredited Treatment of Trans Kids at CAMH Shouldn't Shock Us," *Toronto Star* (December 17, 2015), online: <perma.cc/2RUW-GTKK>; William Byne, "Regulations Restrict Practice of Conversion Therapy" (2016) 3:2 LGBT Health 97 at 98.

4 Keith Leslie, "Ontario Eases Process for Sex Change Surgery," *The Star* (November 6, 2015), online: <perma.cc/D5RD-AGT2>.

5 Tey Meadow, *Trans Kids: Being Gendered in the Twenty-First Century* (Oakland: University of California Press, 2018) at 81.

6 *Ibid.*

7 Suzanne Zinck & Antonio Pignatiello, *External Review of the Gender Identity Clinic of the Child, Youth and Family Services in the Underserved Populations Program at the Centre for Addiction and Mental Health* (Toronto: Centre for Addiction and Mental Health, 2015) at 20.

8 Kenneth J Zucker & Susan J Bradley, *Gender Identity Disorder and Psychosexual Problems in Children and Adolescents* (New York: Guilford Press, 1995). Compare e.g. Kenneth J Zucker et al, "A Developmental, Biopsychosocial Model for the Treatment of Children with Gender Identity Disorder" (2012) 59:3 J Homosexuality 369.

9 Zinck & Pignatiello, *supra* note 7 at 1; Diana Kuhl, *Death of the Clinic: Trans-Informing the Clinical Gaze to Counter Epistemic Violence* (PhD dissertation, University of Western Ontario, 2019) at 25 [unpublished].

10 Zinck & Pignatiello, *supra* note 7 at 19, 20.
11 *Ibid* at 14.
12 *Ibid* at 20.
13 Zucker et al, *supra* note 8.
14 Zinck & Pignatiello, *supra* note 7 at 13.
15 *Ibid* at 22.
16 *Ibid* at 21.
17 *Ibid* at 22.
18 *Ibid*.
19 *Ibid* at 21.
20 *Ibid* at 25.
21 Byne, *supra* note 3 at 98; Zinck & Pignatiello, *supra* note 7 at 25.
22 Barbara Kay, "Scandal at CAMH – One Entirely of Its Own Making," *National Post* (February 3, 2016), online: <perma.cc/K3ZP-CQ6S>.
23 Jesse Singal, "How the Fight over Transgender Kids Got a Leading Sex Researcher Fired," *The Cut* (February 7, 2016), online: <perma.cc/S4V4-3PJN>; John Bancroft et al, "Open Letter to the Board of Trustees of CAMH," *iPetitions* (January 11, 2016), online: <perma.cc/FZK7-7KT9>; Sheryl Ubelacker, "CAMH Youth Gender Identity Clinic Closure Earns International Ire," *The Star* (January 23, 2016), online: <perma.cc/7E7N-WW8H>.
24 Ubelacker, *supra* note 23.
25 "CAMH Apology," *Centre for Addiction and Mental Health* (October 2018), online: <web.archive.org/web/20181008012114/www.camh.ca/en/camh-news-and-stories/camh-apology>. Zucker was awarded $400,000 in general damages.
26 Canadian Press, "CAMH Reaches Settlement with Former Head of Gender Identity Clinic," *CBC News* (October 7, 2018), online: <perma.cc/KXZ6-GEKQ>.
27 *Wallace v United Grain Growers Ltd*, [1997] 3 SCR 701, 152 DLR (4th) 1 [*Wallace*]; *Honda Canada Inc v Keays*, 2008 SCC 39.
28 *Wallace*, *supra* note 27 at para 98.
29 Meadow, *supra* note 5 at 56.
30 Pyne, *supra* note 3; Pickstone-Taylor, *supra* note 1; Susan J Langer & James I Martin, "How Dresses Can Make You Mentally Ill: Examining Gender Identity Disorder in Children" (2004) 21:1 Child & Adolescent Social Work J 5 at 18.
31 Legislative Assembly of Ontario, Standing Committee on Justice Policy, *Affirming Sexual Orientation and Gender Identity Act, 2015*, 41-1 (June 3, 2015) at JP-65 (Jake Pyne). Jake Pyne's criticism of the Centre for Addiction and Mental Health clinic was subject to a lawsuit that has now been settled. Pyne, *supra* note 3. For support of the gender-affirmative approach, see Michelle M Telfer et al, *Australian Standards of Care and Treatment Guidelines for Trans and Gender Diverse Children and Adolescents*, version 1.1 (Melbourne: Royal Children's Hospital, 2018); Ximena Lopez et al, "Statement on Gender-Affirmative Approach to Care from the Pediatric Endocrine Society Special Interest Group on Transgender Health" (2017) 29:4

Current Opinion in Pediatrics 475; Jason Rafferty, "Ensuring Comprehensive Care and Support for Transgender and Gender-Diverse Children and Adolescents" (2018) 142:4 Pediatrics e20182162; Jeannie Oliphant et al, *Guidelines for Gender Affirming Healthcare for Gender Diverse and Transgender Children, Young People and Adults in Aotearoa, New Zealand* (Hamilton, NZ: Transgender Health Research Lab, University of Waikato, 2018); Gabe Murchison, *Supporting and Caring for Transgender Children* (Washington: Human Rights Campaign, American Academic of Pediatrics, and American College of Osteopathic Pediatricians, 2016); *The Lancet*, "Gender-Affirming Care Needed for Transgender Children" (2018) 391:10140 Lancet 2576.

32 Pyne, *supra* note 3; Jemma Tosh, "'Zuck Off'! A Commentary on the Protest against Ken Zucker and His 'Treatment' of Childhood Gender Identity Disorder" (2011) 13:1 Psychology of Women Section Rev 10 [Tosh, "Zuck Off"]; Julia Serano, "Psychology, Sexualization and Trans-Invalidations" (Keynote lecture delivered at the 8th Annual Philadelphia Trans-Health Conference, 12 June 2009) [Serano, *Psychology*], online: <perma.cc/J7KQ-7YGH>.

33 Julia Temple Newhook et al, "A Critical Commentary on Follow-Up Studies and 'Desistance' Theories about Transgender and Gender-Nonconforming Children" (2018) 19:2 Intl J Transgenderism 212; Jake Pyne, "Health and Well-Being among Gender-Independent Children and Their Families: A Review of the Literature" in Elizabeth J Meyer and Annie Pullen-Sansfaçon, eds, *Supporting Transgender and Gender Creative Youth: Schools, Families and Communities in Action* (New York: Peter Lang, 2014) 27; Greta R Bauer et al, "Intervenable Factors Associated with Suicide Risk in Transgender Persons: A Respondent Driven Sampling Study in Ontario, Canada" (2015) 15:1 BMC Public Health art 525; Jake Pyne, "The Governance of Gender Non-conforming Children: A Dangerous Enclosure" (2014) 11 Annual Rev Critical Psychology 79; Jake Pyne, "Gender Independent Kids: A Paradigm Shift in Approaches to Gender Non-conforming Children" (2014) 23:1 Can J Human Sexuality 1; Tosh, "Zuck Off," *supra* note 32; Julia M Serano, "The Case against Autogynephilia" (2010) 12:3 Intl J Transgenderism 176; Jemma Tosh, *Perverse Psychology: The Pathologization of Sexual Violence and Transgenderism* (New York: Routledge, 2015); Jemma Tosh, *Psychology and Gender Dysphoria: Feminist and Transgender Perspectives* (New York: Routledge, 2016); Jemma Tosh, "Working Together for an Inclusive and Gender Creative Future: A Critical Lens on 'Gender Dysphoria'" in Meyer and Pullen-Sansfaçon, *ibid*, 27.

34 Robert L Spitzer, "The Diagnostic Status of Homosexuality in DSM-III: A Reformulation of the Issues" (1981) 138:2 Am J Psychiatry 210; American Psychiatric Association, *Diagnostic and Statistical Manual of Mental Disorders*, 5th ed (Washington, DC: American Psychiatric Association, 2013).

35 Zinck & Pignatiello, *supra* note 7 at 15.

36 Jack L Turban, Annelou LC de Vries & Kenneth J Zucker, "Gender Dysphoria and Gender Incongruence" in Andrés Martin, Michael H Bloch & Fred R Volkmar,

eds, *Lewis' Child and Adolescent Psychiatry*, 5th ed (Philadelphia: Wolters Kluwer, 2018) 632 at 639.

37 Sé Sullivan, *Conversion Therapy Ground Zero: Interrogating the Production of Gender as a Pathology in the United States* (PhD dissertation, California Institute of Integral Studies, 2017) at 54 [unpublished].

38 Quoted in Beth Schwartzapfel, "Born This Way?" *American Prospect* (March 14, 2013), online: <perma.cc/G5BS-TV3L>.

39 Robert Wallace & Hershel Russell, "Attachment and Shame in Gender-Nonconforming Children and Their Families: Toward a Theoretical Framework for Evaluating Clinical Interventions" (2013) 14:3 Intl J Transgenderism 113; Bauer et al, *supra* note 33.

40 See e.g. Jules Sherred, "I Underwent Conversion Therapy. It Stopped Me from Transitioning for Decades," *Daily Xtra* (October 26, 2020), online: <perma.cc/T5EP-6GLG>; Trevor Goodyear et al, "'They Want You to Kill Your Inner Queer but Somehow Leave the Human Alive': Delineating the Impacts of Sexual Orientation and Gender Identity and Expression Change Efforts" (2021) The Journal of Sex Research; Luke R Allen et al, "Well-Being and Suicidality among Transgender Youth after Gender-Affirming Hormones" (2019) 7:3 Clinical Practice in Pediatric Psychology 302; Center for the Study of Inequality, "What Does the Scholarly Research Say about the Effect of Gender Transition on Transgender Well-Being?" *What We Know Project at Cornell University* (2018), online: <perma.cc/S97J-Q5J2>.

41 Peter Gajdics, "I Experienced 'Conversion Therapy' – And It's Time to Ban It across Canada," *Maclean's* (June 6, 2018), online: <perma.cc/GLY3-X7QB>; Natasha Riebe, "'This Practice Is Evil': Edmonton to Ban Conversion Therapy," *CBC News* (August 21, 2019), online: <perma.cc/H8VW-YLZQ>; McDermott Will & Emery LLP, *The Pernicious Myth of Conversion Therapy: How Love in Action Perpetrated a Fraud on America* (Washington, DC: Mattachine Society, 2018) at 48; Christopher Romero, "Praying for Torture: Why the United Kingdom Should Ban Conversion Therapy" (2019) 51:1 Geo Wash Intl L Rev 201; Stephen Wright, "'Conversion Therapy' Is Medieval Torture Based on Ignorance" (2014) 28:33 Nursing Standard 17; Nico Lang, "Conversion Therapy Is 'Torture': LGBT Survivors Are Fighting to Ban 'Pray the Gay Away' Camps," *Salon* (March 21, 2017), online: <perma.cc/YFF9-TVQQ>; Ignatius Yordan Nugraha, "The Compatibility of Sexual Orientation Change Efforts with International Human Rights Law" (2017) 35:3 Netherlands Q Human Rights 176. The Office of the United Nations High Commissioner for Human Rights, *Discrimination and Violence against Individuals Based on Their Sexual Orientation and Gender Identity*, Doc A/HRC/29/23 (2015) at 11, observes that conversion therapy may breach the prohibition on torture and ill-treatment "when forced or otherwise involuntary." A similar view is espoused by the Independent Forensic Expert Group, "Statement on Conversion Therapy" (2020) 72 J Forensic & Legal Medicine 101930. It is considered torture, cruel, inhuman, or degrading treatment by UN Independent Expert Victor Madrigal-Borloz, *Practices of So-Called "Conversion Therapy,"* Doc

A/HRC/44/53 (2020). The assertion is most common in relation to sexual orientation and/or aversion practices, which have been more widely discussed, but similar rationales apply *mutatis mutandis* to gender identity and non-aversive techniques. See e.g. Douglas Haldeman, "Sexual Orientation Conversion Therapy for Gay Men and Lesbians: A Scientific Examination" in John C. Gonsiorek & James D. Weinrich, eds, *Homosexuality: Research Implications for Public Policy* (Thousand Oaks, CA: Sage Publications, 1991) 149.

42 US, *Report of the 2015 U.S. Transgender Survey*, by Sandy E James et al (Washington, DC: National Center for Transgender Equality, 2016) at 105, 112–14.

43 Jack L Turban et al, "Association between Recalled Exposure to Gender Identity Conversion Efforts and Psychological Distress and Suicide Attempts among Transgender Adults" (2019) 77:1 J American Medical Assoc Psychiatry 68.

44 Amy E Green et al, "Self-Reported Conversion Efforts and Suicidality among US LGBTQ Youths and Young Adults, 2018" (2020) 110:8 Am J Public Health 1221. The increases were similar for trans and cis participants. See also Lui Asquith et al, "2020 'Conversion Therapy' & Gender Identity Survey," (2020), online: Ozanne Foundation <perma.cc/SR3L-CKJS>; Ana María del Río-González et al, "Sexual Orientation and Gender Identity Change Efforts and Suicide Morbidity among Sexual and Gender Minority Adults in Colombia" (2021) LGBT Health.

45 CROP, *Perceptions, Interactions and Comfort Level of the Heterosexual Cisgender Population with Sexual Minorities* (Montréal: Fondation Jasmin Roy, 2017); Jessica Vomiero, "Is the World More Accepting of Transgender People? Yes, But Many People Still Aren't: Ipsos," *Global News* (January 29, 2018), online: <perma.cc/43XP-SKJH>; Florence Ashley, "Don't Be So Hateful: The Insufficiency of Anti-discrimination and Hate Crime Laws in Improving Trans Well-Being" (2018) 68:1 UTLJ 1; Serano, *Psychology, supra* note 32.

46 Herbert Blumer, "Society as Symbolic Interaction" in Nancy J Herman & Larry T Reynolds, eds, *Symbolic Interaction: An Introduction to Social Psychology* (Lanham, MD: AltaMira Press, 1994) 500; Kenneth Burke & Joseph R Gusfield, *On Symbols and Society* (Chicago: University of Chicago Press, 1989). In the context of law, see Christopher E Smith, "Law and Symbolism" (1997) Detroit College of Law at Michigan State University L Rev 935.

47 The minority stress model can help us understand why expressions of prejudice and devaluation can have a long-term negative effect on transgender people. Michael Hobbes, "The Epidemic of Gay Loneliness," *Highline* (March 2, 2017), online: <perma.cc/868D-F2PQ>; Brian A Rood et al, "Expecting Rejection: Understanding the Minority Stress Experiences of Transgender and Gender-Nonconforming Individuals" (2016) 1:1 Transgender Health 151.

48 Jack L Turban et al, "Psychological Attempts to Change a Person's Gender Identity from Transgender to Cisgender: Estimated Prevalence across US States, 2015" (2019) 109:10 American J Public Health 1452; James et al, *supra* note 42 at 108.

49 Trans PULSE Canada Team, "QuickStat #1 – Conversion Therapy," *Trans PULSE Canada* (December 20, 2019), online: <perma.cc/H6MC-N927>; Travis Salway et al, "Prevalence of Exposure to Sexual Orientation Change Efforts and Associated Sociodemographic Characteristics and Psychosocial Health Outcomes among Canadian Sexual Minority Men" (2020) 65:7 Can J Psychiatry 502; Travis Salway et al, "Experiences with Sexual Orientation and Gender Identity Conversion Therapy Practices among Sexual Minority Men in Canada, 2019–2020" (2021) PLoS ONE.

50 Amie Bishop, *Harmful Treatment: The Global Reach of So-Called Conversion Therapy* (New York: OutRight Action International, 2019) at 42 (Global: 36.9% minors); James et al, *supra* note 42 at 109 (United States: 51% minors); Asquith et al, *supra* note 44 (United Kingdom: 49% minors); Salway et al, "Experiences with Sexual Orientation and Gender Identity Conversion Therapy," *supra* note 49 (Canada: 72% under 20). An interim estimate from a Canadian study led by Travis Salway of Simon Fraser University (n = 43) as of 23 November 2020 found that 51.2% had experienced conversion practices prior to adulthood: Personal communication (January 11, 2021). In the latter estimate, 23.3% experienced conversion practices at 18 or 19 years old.

51 Eli Coleman et al, "Standards of Care for the Health of Transsexual, Transgender, and Gender-Nonconforming People, version 7" (2012) 13:4 Intl J Transgenderism 165 at 175.

52 Madrigal-Borloz, *supra* note 41. Independent expert Madrigal-Borloz's report defines conversion practices broadly and references an early draft of the present book when defining its scope. For a list of professional organisations, see the Appendix.

53 Interim estimate as of 23 November 2020 (n = 47). Travis Salway, Simon Fraser University, personal communication, January 4, 2021; Salway et al, "Experiences with Sexual Orientation and Gender Identity Conversion Therapy", *supra* note 49; Madrigal-Borloz, *supra* note 41 at 7. The interim estimate includes women and has a much larger proportion of trans people, which may explain the larger percentage of licensed providers compared to the other study by Salway and colleagues.

54 James et al, *supra* note 42 at 109.

55 For more on these debates, see Florence Ashley, "A Critical Commentary on 'Rapid-Onset Gender Dysphoria'" (2020) 68:4 Sociological Rev 779 [Ashley, "Critical Commentary"]; Florence Ashley, "Homophobia, Conversion Therapy, and Care Models for Trans Youth: Defending the Gender-Affirmative Model" (2019) 17:4 J LGBT Youth 361 [Ashley, "Homophobia"]; Florence Ashley, "Shifts in Assigned Sex Ratios at Gender Identity Clinics Likely Reflect Changes in Referral Patterns" (2019) 16:6 J Sexual Medicine 948; Arjee Javellana Restar, "Methodological Critique of Littman's (2018)" Parental-Respondents Accounts of 'Rapid-Onset Gender Dysphoria'" (2019) 49 Archives of Sexual Behavior 61; Natacha Kennedy, "Deferral: The Sociology of Young Trans People's Epiphanies and Coming Out" (2020) J LGBT Youth; Victoria Pitts-Taylor, "The Untimeliness of Trans Youth: The Temporal Construction of a Gender 'Disorder'" (2020) Sexualities; Global Board of Directors,

"WPATH Position on 'Rapid-Onset Gender Dysphoria (ROGD)'," *World Professional Association for Transgender Health* (September 4, 2018), online: <perma.cc/SQN6 -YFN5>; Australian Professional Association for Transgender Health, "Position Statement on 'Rapid-Onset Gender Dysphoria (ROGD)'," *AusPATH* (September 30, 2019), online: <perma.cc/MJD6-752R>; Coalition for the Advancement & Application of Psychological Science, "CAAPS Position Statement on Rapid Onset Gender Dysphoria (ROGD)," *CAAPS* (July 28, 2021), online: <perma. cc/53YY-V9BQ>.

56 Temple Newhook et al, *supra* note 33; Kelley Winters, "The '80% Desistance' Dictum: Is It Science?" in Arlene I Lev & Andrew R Gottlieb, eds, *Families in Transition: Parenting Gender Diverse Children, Adolescents, and Young Adults* (New York: Harrington Park Press, 2019) 88; Florence Ashley, "The Clinical Irrelevance of 'Desistance' Research for Transgender and Gender Creative Youth," (2021) Psychology of Sexual Orientation and Gender Diversity [Ashley, "The Clinical Irrelevance"].

57 Selin Gülgöz et al, "Similarity in Transgender and Cisgender Children's Gender Development" (2019) 116:49 Proceedings of the National Academy of Sciences 24480; James R Rae et al, "Predicting Early-Childhood Gender Transitions" (2019) 30:5 Psychological Science 669; Ashley, "Homophobia," *supra* note 55; Tessa Brik et al, "Trajectories of Adolescents Treated with Gonadotropin-Releasing Hormone Analogues for Gender Dysphoria" (2020) 49 Archives of Sexual Behavior 2611; Annelou LC de Vries et al, "Puberty Suppression in Adolescents with Gender Identity Disorder: A Prospective Follow-Up Study" (2011) 8:8 J Sexual Medicine 2276; Gaines Blasdel et al, "Description and Outcomes of a Hormone Therapy Informed Consent Model for Minors" (Poster presented at the 25th Biennial Symposium of the World Professional Association for Transgender Health in Buenos Aires, Argentina, November 3–6, 2018) [unpublished]; Skye Davies et al, "Rate of Detransition and Regret in an NHS Gender Identity Clinic" (Poster presented at the Third Biennial Conference of the European Professional Association for Transgender Health in Rome, Italy, April 11–13, 2019) [unpublished]; Diane Ehrensaft et al, "Prepubertal Social Gender Transitions: What We Know; What We Can Learn: A View from a Gender Affirmative Lens" (2018) 19:2 Intl J Transgenderism 251; *In re: Kelvin*, [2017] Fam CAFC 258 (Australia). See also Florence Ashley, "Thinking an Ethics of Gender Exploration: Against Delaying Transition for Transgender and Gender Creative Youth" (2019) 24:2 Clinical Child Psychology & Psychiatry 223 [Ashley, "Thinking an Ethics"].

58 Chase Strangio, "Conservative Legislators Want Transgender Kids' Lives as the New Battlefield in Their Culture War," *NBC Think* (January 17, 2021), online: <perma.cc/V5HC-GQNX>; Telfer et al, *supra* note 31; Rafferty, *supra* note 31; Lopez et al, *supra* note 31; Murchison, *supra* note 31; Oliphant et al, *supra* note 31.

59 *AB v CD and EF*, 2020 BCCA 11; *Bell v Tavistock*, [2020] EWHC 3274 [*Bell*]. In the latter case, the overly anti-trans organization Transgender Trend was granted intervener status, despite no trans community organization being granted the

same. See also Reubs J Walsh, "A blow to the rights of transgender children," *The Psychologist* (December 3, 2020), online: <perma.cc/4VTK-574C>; Heron Greene-smith, "Aberration of Common Sense," *Political Research Associates* (January 30, 2021), online: <perma.cc/8P55-6Q73>.

60 *Bell, supra* note 59.

61 Katelyn Burns, "The Rise of Anti-trans 'Radical' Feminists, Explained," *Vox* (September 5, 2019), online: <perma.cc/WJG8-RU3W>.

62 Bill C-6, *An Act to Amend the Criminal Code (Conversion Therapy)*, briefs submitted to the House of Commons Standing Committee on Justice and Human Rights in relation to 2nd Sess, 43rd Parl, 2020 (first reading 1 October 2020) [Bill C-6].

63 Bill 77, *supra* note 2.

64 *An Act to Amend the Criminal Code (Conversion Therapy)*, SC 2021, c 24.

65 Perlita Stroh, "Ottawa Rejects Plea for Nationwide Conversion Therapy Ban," *CBC News* (March 23, 2019), online: <perma.cc/V6NY-ZDCA>; House of Commons of Canada, Standing Committee on Health, *The Health of LGBTQIA2 Communities in Canada: Report of the Standing Committee on Health,* by Bill Casey (2019); Scott Johnston, "Liberal Justice Minister 'Committed' to Criminalizing Conversion Therapy, Says Edmonton MP," *Global News* (August 16, 2019), online: <perma.cc/8BGY-J3E6>.

66 Erika Muse, "Open Letter: Bill C-6 Excludes Conversion Therapy Practices That Target Trans People," *Centre for Gender and Sexual Health Equity* (June 25, 2020), online: <perma.cc/QQ4K-9D2V>. Her role with regard to the Ontario law is discussed in greater detail in Chapter 2.

67 "What We Do," *No Conversion Canada*, online: <perma.cc/6E7W-UP3H>.

68 Karl Bryant, "Making Gender Identity Disorder of Childhood: Historical Lessons for Contemporary Debates" (2006) 3:3 Sexuality Research & Social Policy 23; Pickstone-Taylor, *supra* note 1; Kenneth J Zucker, "Commentary on Langer and Martin's (2004) 'How Dresses Can Make You Mentally Ill: Examining Gender Identity Disorder in Children'" (2006) 23:5–6 Child & Adolescent Social Work J 533 [Zucker, "Commentary"]; Schwartzapfel, *supra* note 38.

69 Pickstone-Taylor, *supra* note 1; Zucker et al, *supra* note 8; Zucker, "Commentary," *supra* note 68; Langer & Martin, *supra* note 30; Tosh, "Zuck Off," *supra* note 32; Coleman et al, *supra* note 51; Temple Newhook et al, *supra* note 33; Kenneth J Zucker, "The Myth of Persistence: Response to 'A Critical Commentary on Follow-Up Studies and "Desistance" Theories about Transgender and Gender Non-conforming Children' by Temple Newhook et al (2018)" (2018) 19:2 Intl J Transgenderism 231.

70 Ashley, "Thinking an Ethics," *supra* note 57; Ashley, "The Clinical Irrelevance," *supra* note 56; Ashley, "Critical Commentary," *supra* note 55; Ashley, "Homo-phobia," *supra* note 55; Florence Ashley, "Gatekeeping Hormone Replacement Therapy for Transgender Patients Is Dehumanising" (2019) 45:7 J Medical Ethics 480.

71 Elizabeth Anne Riley et al, "The Needs of Gender-Variant Children and Their Parents: A Parent Survey" (2011) 23:3 Intl J Sexual Health 181 at 187; Edgardo J Menvielle, Catherine Tuerk & Michael S Jellinek, "A Support Group for Parents of Gender-Nonconforming Boys" (2002) 41:8 J American Academy Child & Adolescent Psychiatry 1010 at 1010.

72 ... to defeat conversion practices! There are so many layers to this Mulan reference in the trans conversion practices context, I don't even know where to start.

Chapter 1: What Are Trans Conversion Practices?

1 Diane Ehrensaft et al, "Prepubertal Social Gender Transitions: What We Know; What We Can Learn: A View from a Gender Affirmative Lens" (2018) 19:2 Intl J Transgenderism 251 at 8; Michelle M Telfer et al, *Australian Standards of Care and Treatment Guidelines for Trans and Gender Diverse Children and Adolescents*, version 1.1 (Melbourne: Royal Children's Hospital, 2018) at 5; US, *Report of the 2015 U.S. Transgender Survey*, by Sandy E James et al (Washington, DC: National Center for Transgender Equality, 2016) at 108; UK Council for Psychotherapy et al, "Memorandum of Understanding on Conversion Therapy in the UK," version 2 (October 2016), online: <perma.cc/8YY9-XNS5>; Ximena Lopez et al, "Statement on Gender-Affirmative Approach to Care from the Pediatric Endocrine Society Special Interest Group on Transgender Health" (2017) 29:4 Current Opinion in Pediatrics 475 at 476; Noah Adams et al, "Guidance and Ethical Considerations for Undertaking Transgender Health Research and Institutional Review Boards Adjudicating this Research" (2017) 2:1 Transgender Health 165 at 171; Laura Erickson-Schroth, ed, *Trans Bodies, Trans Selves: A Resource for the Transgender Community* (Oxford: Oxford University Press, 2014) at 612; Denise Medico, Joanie Heppell & Martin Blais, "Avis au public concernant les effets nocifs des thérapies dites de conversion ou thérapies réparatrices pour l'orientation sexuelle et le genre," *Ordre professionel des sexologues du Québec* (May 17, 2018), online: <perma. cc/K2TP-K385>.

2 William Byne, "Regulations Restrict Practice of Conversion Therapy" (2016) 3:2 LGBT Health 97 at 97, explains the evolution of definitions of conversion practices, which initially exclusively focused on sexual orientation.

3 Florence Ashley, "Homophobia, Conversion Therapy, and Care Models for Trans Youth: Defending the Gender-Affirmative Model" (2019) 17:4 J LGBT Youth 361 at 10ff [Ashley, "Homophobia"].

4 Diane Ehrensaft, "Found in Transition: Our Littlest Transgender People" (2014) 50:4 Contemporary Psychoanalysis 571 at 586 [Ehrensaft, "Found in Transition"]; Kristina R Olson, "Prepubescent Transgender Children: What We Do and Do Not Know" (2016) 55:3 J American Academy Child & Adolescent Psychiatry 155 at 156; Thomas D Steensma et al, "Factors Associated with Desistence and Persistence of Childhood Gender Dysphoria: A Quantitative Follow-Up Study" (2013) 52:6 J American Academy Child & Adolescent Psychiatry 582 at 588.

5 Ehrensaft, "Found in Transition," *supra* note 4 at 586; Diane Ehrensaft, "Exploring Gender Expansive Expressions versus Asserting a Gender Identity" in Colt Keo-Meier & Diane Ehrensaft, eds, *The Gender Affirmative Model: An Interdisciplinary Approach to Supporting Transgender and Gender Expansive Children*, Perspectives on Sexual Orientation and Diversity (Washington, DC: American Psychological Association, 2018) 34 at 40.

6 Florence Ashley, "Genderfucking Non-disclosure: Sexual Fraud, Transgender Bodies, and Messy Identities" (2018) 41:2 Dalhousie LJ 339; Florence Ashley, "Thinking an Ethics of Gender Exploration: Against Delaying Transition for Transgender and Gender Creative Youth" (2019) 24:2 Clinical Child Psychology & Psychiatry 223; Nova J Bradford & Moin Syed, "Transnormativity and Transgender Identity Development: A Master Narrative Approach" (2019) 81:5–6 Sex Roles 306.

7 James R Rae et al, "Predicting Early-Childhood Gender Transitions" (2019) 30:5 Psychological Science 669.

8 Julia Temple Newhook et al, "A Critical Commentary on Follow-Up Studies and 'Desistance' Theories about Transgender and Gender-Nonconforming Children" (2018) 19:2 Intl J Transgenderism 212 at 215; Florence Ashley, "The Clinical Irrelevance of 'Desistance' Research for Transgender and Gender Creative Youth," (2021) Psychology of Sexual Orientation and Gender Diversity [Ashley, "The Clinical Irrelevance"]; Ben Vincent, *Transgender Health: A Practitioner's Guide to Binary and Non-binary Trans Patient Care* (London: Jessica Kingsley Publishers, 2018) at 121–23; Kelley Winters, "The '80% Desistance' Dictum: Is It Science?" in Arlene I Lev & Andrew R Gottlieb, eds, *Families in Transition: Parenting Gender Diverse Children, Adolescents, and Young Adults* (New York: Harrington Park Press, 2019) 88; American Psychiatric Association, *Diagnostic and Statistical Manual of Mental Disorders*, 4th ed (Washington, DC: American Psychiatric Association, 2006); American Psychiatric Association, *Diagnostic and Statistical Manual of Mental Disorders*, 5th ed (Washington, DC: American Psychiatric Association, 2013). Throughout this book, "Gender Dysphoria" is capitalized when referring to the diagnosis of the *Diagnostic and Statistical Manual of Mental Disorders*, with lowercase being used to refer more broadly to discomfort or distress caused by the lack of correspondence between a person's gendered self-image and bodily traits.

9 Diane Ehrensaft, "Exploring Gender Expansive Expressions versus Asserting a Gender Identity" in Colt Keo-Meier & Diane Ehrensaft, eds, *The Gender Affirmative Model: An Interdisciplinary Approach to Supporting Transgender and Gender Expansive Children Perspectives on Sexual Orientation and Diversity* (Washington, DC: American Psychological Association, 2018) 34 at 40.

10 Beth Schwartzapfel, "Born This Way?" *American Prospect* (March 14, 2013), online: <perma.cc/G5BS-TV3L>.

11 Karl Bryant, "Making Gender Identity Disorder of Childhood: Historical Lessons for Contemporary Debates" (2006) 3:3 Sexuality Research & Social Policy 23 [Bryant, "Making Gender"].

12 Karl Bryant, "In Defence of Gay Children? 'Progay' Homophobia and the Production of Homonormativity" (2008) 11:4 Sexualities 455 at 466, 469; Damien W Riggs et al, "Transnormativity in the Psy Disciplines: Constructing Pathology in the Diagnostic and Statistical Manual of Mental Disorders and Standards of Care" (2019) 74:8 American Psychologist 912.

13 Jason Rafferty, "Ensuring Comprehensive Care and Support for Transgender and Gender-Diverse Children and Adolescents" (2018) 142:4 Pediatrics e20182162 at 4, 8; Gabe Murchison, *Supporting and Caring for Transgender Children* (Washington: Human Rights Campaign, American Academic of Pediatrics, and American College of Osteopathic Pediatricians, 2016) at 12; Substance Abuse and Mental Health Services Administration, *Ending Conversion Therapy: Supporting and Affirming LGBTQ Youth*, No 15-4928 (Rockville, MD: Substance Abuse and Mental Health Services Administration, 2015) at 1, 66; Sé Sullivan, *Conversion Therapy Ground Zero: Interrogating the Production of Gender as a Pathology in the United States* (PhD dissertation, California Institute of Integral Studies, 2017) at 3 [unpublished].

14 Temple Newhook et al, *supra* note 8 at 220. The definition bears similarities with the one found in the UK Memorandum of Understanding. UK Council for Psychotherapy et al, *supra* note 1 ("[f]or the purposes of this document 'conversion therapy' is an umbrella term for a therapeutic approach, or any model or individual viewpoint that demonstrates an assumption that any sexual orientation or gender identity is inherently preferable to any other, and which attempts to bring about a change of sexual orientation or gender identity, or seeks to supress an individual's expression of sexual orientation or gender identity on that basis"). See also Jake Pyne, "The Governance of Gender Non-conforming Children: A Dangerous Enclosure" (2014) 11 Annual Rev Critical Psychology 79 at 81 [Pyne, "Governance of Gender"].

15 For a detailed exploration of the conceptual apparatus underpinning trans conversion practices, see Sullivan, *supra* note 13. See also Jules Gill-Peterson, *Histories of the Transgender Child* (Minneapolis: University of Minnesota Press, 2018).

16 Jack L Turban, Annelou LC de Vries & Kenneth J Zucker, "Gender Dysphoria and Gender Incongruence" in Andrés Martin, Michael H Bloch & Fred R Volkmar, eds, *Lewis' Child and Adolescent Psychiatry*, 5th ed (Philadelphia: Wolters Kluwer, 2018) 632 at 639.

17 I borrow the term "corrective approach" from Pyne, "Governance of Gender," *supra* note 14. Bill 77, *Affirming Sexual Orientation and Gender Identity Act, 2015*, SO 2015, c 18.

18 Kenneth J Zucker, "The Myth of Persistence: Response to 'A Critical Commentary on Follow-Up Studies and "Desistance" Theories about Transgender and Gender Non-conforming Children' by Temple Newhook et al (2018)" (2018) 19:2 Intl J Transgenderism 231; Kelley Winters et al, "Learning to Listen to Trans and Gender Diverse Children: A Response to Zucker (2018) and Steensma and Cohen-Kettenis (2018)" (2018) 19:2 Intl J Transgenderism 246; Arlene I Lev, "Approaches to the

Treatment of Gender Nonconforming Children and Transgender Youth" in Arlene I Lev & Andrew R Gottlieb, eds, *Families in Transition: Parenting Gender Diverse Children, Adolescents, and Young Adults* (New York: Harrington Park Press, 2019); Diane Ehrensaft, "Psychoanalysis Meets Transgender Children: The Best of Times and the Worst of Times" (2021) 18:1 Psychoanalytic Perspectives 68 [Ehrensaft, "Psychoanalysis Meets"]; Bryant, "Making Gender," *supra* note 11.

19 Simon D Pickstone-Taylor, "Children with Gender Nonconformity" (2003) 42:3 J American Academy Child & Adolescent Psychiatry 266; Jemma Tosh, "'Zuck Off'! A Commentary on the Protest against Ken Zucker and His 'Treatment' of Child-hood Gender Identity Disorder" (2011) 13:1 Psychology of Women Section Rev 10; Pyne, "Governance of Gender," *supra* note 14; Winters et al, *supra* note 18 at 247; Ehrensaft et al, *supra* note 1; Ashley, "Homophobia," *supra* note 3; Ehrensaft, "Psychoanalysis Meets," *supra* note 18; cf. Susan J Bradley & Kenneth J Zucker, "Children with Gender Nonconformity" (2003) 42:3 J American Academy Child & Adolescent Psychiatry 266.

20 Kenneth J Zucker & Doug P VanderLaan, "The Self in Gender Dysphoria: A Developmental Perspective" in Michael Kyrios et al, eds, *The Self in Understanding and Treating Psychological Disorders* (Cambridge, UK: Cambridge University Press, 2016) 222 at 226.

21 Florence Ashley, "A Critical Commentary on 'Rapid-Onset Gender Dysphoria'" (2020) 68:4 Sociological Rev 779; Ashley, "Homophobia," *supra* note 3; Florence Ashley & Alexandre Baril, "Why 'Rapid-Onset Gender Dysphoria' Is Bad Science," *The Conversation* (March 22, 2018), online: <perma.cc/4JLX-2Z2E>; Kenneth J Zucker, Anne A Lawrence & Baudewijntje PC Kreukels, "Gender Dysphoria in Adults" (2016) 12:1 Annual Rev Clinical Psychology 217.

22 Turban, de Vries & Zucker, *supra* note 16 at 639; Zucker & VanderLaan, *supra* note 20 at 226.

23 Kenneth J Zucker & Susan J Bradley, *Gender Identity Disorder and Psychosexual Problems in Children and Adolescents* (New York: Guilford Press, 1995) at 269. It was also reiterated in similar terms in Kenneth J Zucker & Andrew G Epstein, "Prevention of Homosexuality in Adulthood," *Health.am* (March 30, 2006), online: <perma.cc/SVL3-AK8D> (revised June 22, 2011); Jack L Turban & Diane Ehrensaft, "Research Review: Gender Identity in Youth: Treatment Paradigms and Contro-versies" (2018) 59:12 J Child Psychology & Psychiatry 1228 at 1235.

24 Zucker & Bradley, *supra* note 23 at 269.

25 Turban & Ehrensaft, *supra* note 23 at 1235.

26 Alanna Rizza & Michelle McQuigge, "Former CAMH Psychologist Defends His Work at Youth Gender Identity Clinic," *CityNews* (October 9, 2018), online: <perma.cc/4CRB-JWCF>; Kenneth J Zucker et al, "A Developmental, Biopsychosocial Model for the Treatment of Children with Gender Identity Disorder" (2012) 59:3 J Homosexuality 369 at 383; Hanna Rosin, "A Boy's Life," *The Atlantic* (November 2008), online: <perma.cc/B558-PWT7>.

27 Zucker et al, *supra* note 26 at 392.

28 *Ibid* at 393.

29 See e.g. *Ibid* at 393–94.

30 On the diversity of often irreconcilable understandings of gender dysphoria, see Florence Ashley, "The Misuse of Gender Dysphoria: Toward Greater Conceptual Clarity in Transgender Health" (2019) Perspectives on Psychological Science; Zowie Davy & Michael Toze, "What Is Gender Dysphoria? A Critical Systematic Narrative Review" (2018) 3:1 Transgender Health 159.

31 Tey Meadow, *Trans Kids: Being Gendered in the Twenty-First Century* (Oakland: University of California Press, 2018) at 63.

32 Zucker & Bradley, *supra* note 23 at 273.

33 Kenneth J Zucker, "'I'm Half-Boy, Half-Girl': Play Psychotherapy and Parent Counseling for Gender Identity Disorder" in Robert L Spitzer, Miriam Gibbon, Andrew E Skodol, Janet BW Williams, & Michael B First, eds, *DSM-IV-TR Casebook: Experts Tell How They Treated Their Own Patients* (Washington, DC: American Psychiatric Publishing, 2006) 321; Zucker et al, *supra* note 26 at 388; Turban & Ehrensaft, *supra* note 23 at 8.

34 Zucker et al, *supra* note 26 at 374, 382; Diana Kuhl & Wayne Martino, "'Sissy' Boys and the Pathologization of Gender Non-conformity" in Susan Talburt, ed, *Youth Sexualities: Public Feelings and Contemporary Cultural Politics* (Santa Barbara, CA: Praeger, 2018) 31; Ehrensaft, "Psychoanalysis Meets," *supra* note 18.

35 Meadow, *supra* note 31 at 73.

36 Bradley & Zucker, *supra* note 19.

37 Richard Green, "Banning Therapy to Change Sexual Orientation or Gender Identity in Patients under 18" (2017) 45:1 J American Academy Psychiatry L 7.

38 American Psychological Association, *Report of the American Psychological Association Task Force on Appropriate Therapeutic Responses to Sexual Orientation* (Washington, DC: American Psychological Association, 2009); see also Lisa M Diamond & Clifford J Rosky, "Scrutinizing Immutability: Research on Sexual Orientation and US Legal Advocacy for Sexual Minorities" (2016) 53:4–5 J Sex Research 363.

39 Temple Newhook et al, *supra* note 8; Ashley, "The Clinical Irrelevance," *supra* note 8; Peter Hegarty, "Toward an LGBT-Informed Paradigm for Children Who Break Gender Norms: Comment on Drummond et al (2008) and Rieger et al (2008)" (2009) 45:4 Developmental Psychology 895; Winters, *supra* note 8; Vincent, *supra* note 8 at 121–23.

40 Byne, *supra* note 2 at 98.

41 Judd Marmor, ed, *Sexual Inversion: The Multiple Roots of Homosexuality* (New York: Basic Books, 1965).

42 For uses of the term in the 1970s, see Hugo Milne & Shirley J Hardy, eds, *Psychosexual Problems: Proceedings of the Congress Held at the University of Bradford 1974* (Baltimore: University Park Press, 1975) at 166; Harvey L Gochros, "Counseling Gay Husbands" (1978) 4:2 J Sex Education & Therapy 6; William H Masters &

Virginia E Johnson, *Homosexuality in Perspective* (Boston: Little, Brown, 1979). For a perspective on the debates, see Robert L Spitzer, "The Diagnostic Status of Homosexuality in DSM-III: A Reformulation of the Issues" (1981) 138:2 American J Psychiatry 210.

43 Eli Coleman et al, "Standards of Care for the Health of Transsexual, Transgender, and Gender-Nonconforming People, version 7" (2012) 13:4 Intl J Transgenderism 165 at 175.

Chapter 2: Interpreting the Scope of Bans

1 Bill 77, *Affirming Sexual Orientation and Gender Identity Act, 2015*, SO 2015, c 18 [Bill 77].

2 *Ibid* at 77.

3 *Regulated Health Professions Act, 1991*, SO 1991, c 18, s 29.1.

4 The statute also excluded conversion practices from insured services under the *Health Insurance Act*, RSO 1990, c H6.

5 *Rizzo & Rizzo Shoes Ltd (Re)*, [1998] 1 SCR 27, 154 DLR (4ᵗʰ) 193 [*Rizzo & Rizzo Shoes*].

6 Arguments of this kind are made by proponents of the unsupported hypothesis of Rapid-Onset Gender Dysphoria. Lisa Marchiano, "Outbreak: On Transgender Teens and Psychic Epidemics" (2017) 60:3 Psychological Perspectives 345; Lisa Littman, "Parent Reports of Adolescents and Young Adults Perceived to Show Signs of a Rapid Onset of Gender Dysphoria" (2018) 13:8 PLoS ONE e0202330. For critiques, see Florence Ashley, "A Critical Commentary on 'Rapid-Onset Gender Dysphoria'" (2020) 68:4 Sociological Rev 779; Arjee Javellana Restar, "Methodological Critique of Littman's (2018) Parental-Respondents Accounts of 'Rapid-Onset Gender Dysphoria'" (2019) 49 Archives of Sexual Behavior 61; Florence Ashley & Alexandre Baril, "Why 'Rapid-Onset Gender Dysphoria' Is Bad Science," *The Conversation* (March 22, 2018), online: <perma.cc/4JLX-2Z2E>; Natacha Kennedy, "Deferral: The Sociology of Young Trans People's Epiphanies and Coming Out" (2020) J LGBT Youth.

7 Kyle Kirkup, "The Origins of Gender Identity and Gender Expression in Anglo-American Legal Discourse" (2018) 68:1 UTLJ 80 at 87.

8 Robert J Stoller, "A Contribution to the Study of Gender Identity" (1964) 45 Intl J Psycho-Analysis 220 at 220.

9 Kirkup, *supra* note 7 at 94.

10 *Decision No 716/92*, 1993 CanLII 5958 (ON WSIAT).

11 *Sheridan v Sanctuary Investments Ltd (c.o.b BJ's Lounge)*, [1999] BCHRTD No 43, 33 CHRR D/467.

12 *Commission des droits de la personne et des droits de la jeunesse c Maison des jeunes A*, [1998] RJQ 2549, 33 CHRR 263 (QC TDP). Avoiding possible confusion, the adjudicator differentiated sexual identity from sexual orientation.

13 See e.g. *Forrester v Peel (Regional Municipality) Police Service Boards*, 2006 HRTO 13 [*Forrester*]; *Hogan v Ontario (Minister of Health & Long-Term Care)*, 2006 HRTO 32; *XY v Ontario (Government and Consumer Services)*, 2012 HRTO 726 [*XY*].

14 In Ontario case law, see *JPK v SE*, 2017 ONCJ 306; *TA v Ontario (Transportation)*, 2016 HRTO 17.

15 Eli Coleman et al, "Standards of Care for the Health of Transsexual, Transgender, and Gender-Nonconforming People, version 7" (2012) 13:4 Intl J Transgenderism 165 at 221.

16 *Yogyakarta Principles: Principles on the Application of International Human Rights Law in Relation to Sexual Orientation and Gender Identity* (2007) at 6.

17 Ontario Human Rights Commission (OHRC), *Policy on Preventing Discrimination because of Gender Identity and Gender Expression* (Toronto: OHRC, 2014) at 7.

18 *Human Rights Code*, RSO 1990, c H19, s 45.5(2).

19 Ruth Sullivan, *Statutory Interpretation: Essentials of Canadian Law*, 3rd ed (Toronto: Irwin Law, 2016) at 179, 182.

20 *Human Rights Code, supra* note 18, s 1.

21 *Vanderputten v Seydaco Packaging Corp*, 2012 HRTO 1977.

22 *Forrester, supra* note 13 at paras 444–46.

23 Service Ontario, *Application for a Change of Sex Designation on a Birth Registration of an Adult: 11325E* (Queen's Printer for Ontario, 2018). See also *XY, supra* note 13 at para 297.

24 Florence Ashley, "Gatekeeping Hormone Replacement Therapy for Transgender Patients Is Dehumanising" (2019) 45:7 J Medical Ethics 480.

25 *Canada 3000 Inc, Re; Inter-Canadian (1991) Inc (Trustee of)*, 2006 SCC 24 at para 36.

26 Cheri DiNovo, personal communication, October 5, 2018.

27 *Legislation Act, 2006*, SO 2006, c 21, s 64(1).

28 Sullivan, *supra* note 19 at 208; *R v Chartrand*, [1994] 2 SCR 864 at 880ff, 116 DLR (4th) 207 [*Chartrand*].

29 Legislative Assembly of Ontario, Standing Committee on Justice Policy, *Affirming Sexual Orientation and Gender Identity Act, 2015*, 41-1 (June 3, 2015) at JP-58 (Jake Pyne) [Legislative Assembly of Ontario, *Affirming Sexual Orientation*].

30 *Ibid* at JP-57.

31 Legislative Assembly of Ontario, "Affirming Sexual Orientation and Gender Identity Act, 2015," 2nd reading, *Official Report of Debates (Hansard)*, 41–1, No 65 (April 2, 2015) at 3345 (Hon Cheri DiNovo) [Legislative Assembly of Ontario, "Affirming Sexual Orientation"].

32 Legislative Assembly of Ontario, *Affirming Sexual Orientation, supra* note 29 at JP-63.

33 Sullivan, *supra* note 19 at 208; *Chartrand, supra* note 28 at 880ff.

34 Kenneth J Zucker et al, "A Developmental, Biopsychosocial Model for the Treatment of Children with Gender Identity Disorder" (2012) 59:3 J Homosexuality 369 at 393.

35 *Ibid* at 392.

36 Legislative Assembly of Ontario, "Affirming Sexual Orientation," *supra* note 31.

37 Jake Pyne, "Is CAMH Trying to Turn Trans Kids Straight?" *NOW Toronto* (April 1, 2015), online: <perma.cc/R7RP-8KXH>.

38 For my personal perspective on the constitution of gender identity, see Florence Ashley, "What Is It Like to Have a Gender Identity?" [under review], online: <perma. cc/HT2K-4HD8>.
39 *Schnarr v Blue Mountain Resorts Limited*, 2018 ONCA 313 at paras 52, 57.
40 *Ibid* at paras 52–56.
41 *Regulated Health Professions Act, 1991, supra* note 3, s 30(2).
42 American Psychological Association, *Report of the American Psychological Association Task Force on Appropriate Therapeutic Responses to Sexual Orientation* (Washington, DC: American Psychological Association, 2009).
43 *R v McIntosh*, [1995] 1 SCR 686, 36 CR (4th) 171 [*McIntosh*]; *Criminal Code*, RSC 1985, c C-46.
44 *McIntosh, supra* note 43 at para 25; see also Sullivan, *supra* note 19 at 182ff.
45 American Psychological Association, *supra* note 42 at v.
46 *Ibid* at 54.
47 American Psychiatric Association, *Diagnostic and Statistical Manual of Mental Disorders*, 5th ed (Washington, DC: American Psychiatric Association, 2013).
48 See Florence Ashley, "Homophobia, Conversion Therapy, and Care Models for Trans Youth: Defending the Gender-Affirmative Model" (2019) 17:4 J LGBT Youth 361.
49 American Psychological Association, *supra* note 42 at 55.
50 *Ibid*.
51 *Ibid* at 56.
52 US, *Report of the 2015 US Transgender Survey*, by Sandy E James et al (Washington, DC: National Center for Transgender Equality, 2016); Jeffrey H Herbst et al, "Estimating HIV Prevalence and Risk Behaviors of Transgender Persons in the United States: A Systematic Review" (2008) 12:1 AIDS & Behavior 1; Jaclyn M White Hughto, Sari L Reisner & John E Pachankis, "Transgender Stigma and Health: A Critical Review of Stigma Determinants, Mechanisms, and Interventions" (2015) 147 Social Science & Medicine 222; Greta R Bauer et al, "'I Don't Think This Is Theoretical; This Is Our Lives': How Erasure Impacts Health Care for Transgender People" (2009) 20:5 J Association of Nurses in AIDS Care 348.
53 Zucker et al, *supra* note 34.
54 American Psychological Association, *supra* note 42 at 57.
55 Providers should be mindful of the fact that cognitive-behavioural therapy is not always what their clients are talking about when they refer to "CBT."
56 American Psychological Association, *supra* note 42 at 59.
57 Miriam Rosenberg, "Children with Gender Identity Issues and Their Parents in Individual and Group Treatment" (2002) 41:5 J Am Academy of Child & Adolescent Psychiatry 619; Edgardo J Menvielle, Catherine Tuerk & Michael S Jellinek, "A Support Group for Parents of Gender-Nonconforming Boys" (2002) 41:8 J American Academy Child & Adolescent Psychiatry 1010; Edgardo Menvielle, "A Comprehensive Program for Children with Gender Variant Behaviors and Gender Identity

Disorders" (2012) 59:3 J Homosexuality 357. Gender Creative Kids Canada also hosts multiple support groups.

58 American Psychological Association, *supra* note 42 at 60.

59 *Ibid.*

60 *Ibid.*

61 *Ibid.*

62 I spoke about messy identities and my own complicated relationship to gender labels in Florence Ashley, "Genderfucking Non-disclosure: Sexual Fraud, Transgender Bodies, and Messy Identities" (2018) 41:2 Dalhousie LJ 339. Anecdotally, I know many trans people who have similarly complicated relationships to gender and yet have grown comfortable with this messiness.

63 American Psychological Association, *supra* note 42 at 61.

64 Kenneth J Zucker & Susan J Bradley, *Gender Identity Disorder and Psychosexual Problems in Children and Adolescents* (New York: Guilford Press, 1995) at 269.

65 Zucker et al, *supra* note 34 at 393.

66 *Rizzo & Rizzo Shoes, supra* note 5.

Chapter 3: Legal Variants across the Globe

1 Bill 77, *Affirming Sexual Orientation and Gender Identity Act, 2015*, SO 2015, c 18.

2 American Psychological Association, *Report of the American Psychological Association Task Force on Appropriate Therapeutic Responses to Sexual Orientation* (Washington, DC: American Psychological Association, 2009).

3 Michael K Lavers, "Argentina Joins Global LGBT Rights Initiative," *Washington Blade* (March 24, 2016), online: <perma.cc/8VAY-YSHM>.

4 *Transgender Person (Protection of Rights) Act 2018* (Pakistan).

5 People living in the District of Columbia have long sought statehood. In 2016, 85.69 percent of voters residing in the District of Columbia voted in support of statehood. See Jamal Holtz, "D.C. Needs Statehood More Than Ever, and the Capitol Riot Proves It," *Washington Post* (January 19, 2021), online: <perma.cc/SP9N-2H9N>.

6 Conselho Federal de Psicologia do Brazil, *Resolucao No 1, de 29 de Janeiro de 2018* (Brazil).

7 *Ley de salud mental,* Ley 19529 of 2017, s 4 (Uruguay) ("[e]n ningún caso podrá establecerse un diagnóstico en el campo de la salud mental sobre la base exclusiva de ... [o]rientación sexual e identidad de género") [author's translation, with the aid of Mauro Cabral].

8 *Ibid,* s 3(B) ("[l]a dignidad humana y los principios de derechos humanos constituyen el marco de referencia primordial de todas las medidas de carácter legislativo, judicial, administrativo, educativo y de cualquier otra índole y en todos los ámbitos de aplicación que guarden relación con la salud mental").

9 Jack Drescher and colleagues provide a list of attempted prohibitions of gay conversion practices within the United States, some of which also included attempted

bans on trans conversion practices. Jack Drescher et al, "The Growing Regulation of Conversion Therapy" (2016) 102:2 J Medical Regulation 7.

10 *An Act Respecting Sexual Orientation and Gender Identity Protection*, SNS 2018, c 28; *Regulated Health Professions Act, 1991*, SO 1991, c 18, s 29.1; *Regulated Health Professions Act*, RSPEI 1988, c R-101, s 90(4), 90(5). Although Manitoba is frequently cited as a province having prohibited conversion practices, no law or regulation appears to have been passed that would ban the practice. David Larkins, "Manitoba Bans Conversion Therapy," *Toronto Sun* (May 22, 2015), online: <perma.cc/F4KQ-628G>. The only apparent change on the books is a new page on the Manitoba government website that claims that conversion therapy has no place in the province's public healthcare system and calls on professional associations to ensure that conversion therapy is not practised. "Position on Conversion Therapy," *Manitoba Health, Seniors and Active Living*, online: <perma.cc/P9R7-4W4J>. The impact of such statements remains uncertain as they do not have any legal standing but may be accorded weight by regulatory colleges. Adjudicators regularly use sources that do not have the force of law in making their judgments. Lorne Sossin & Charles W Smith, "Hard Choices and Soft Law: Ethical Codes, Policy Guidelines and the Role of the Courts in Regulating Government" (2003) 40:4 Alberta L Rev 867. However, they are not accountable to those sources, unlike with laws, which may inhibit their consistent application.

11 Colorado: Colo Rev Stat § 12-240-104, 12-240-121, 12-245-202, 12-245-224; Connecticut: Conn Gen Stat § 19a-907 – 19a-907c; Delaware: Del Code tit 24 § 1702(b)(3), 1731(b)(24), 1731(25), 1902(g), 1922(a)(12), 3002(2), 3009(a)(11), 3009(a)(12), 3502(2), 3510(d), 3514(a)(13), 3514(a)(14), 3902(11), 3915(11), 3915(12); Del Code tit 19 § 9003(b); District of Columbia: DC Code § 7-1231.02, 7-1231.14a; Hawaii: Haw Rev Stat §453J-1; Maine: Me Rev Stat Ann tit 20-A § 13020; Me Rev Stat Ann tit 22 § 3174-DDD; Me Rev Stat Ann tit 32 § 59-C, 2112, 2600-D, 3300-G, 3837-B, 6223, 7006, 13800-B, 13866, 17311; Maryland: Md Code Ann, Health Occ § 1-212.1; Massachusetts: Mass Gen Laws ch 112 § 275; Nevada: Nev Rev Stat § 629.600; New Hampshire: NH Rev Stat Ann § 332-L; New Jersey: NJ Rev Stat § 45:1-54, 45:1-55; New Mexico: NM Stat § 61-1-3.3(A), 61-1-3.3(B), 61-3-28(A)(9), 61-3-28(G)(1), 61-6-15(D)(39), 61-6-15(E)(1), 61-9-13(A)(19), 61-9-13(C)(1), 61-9A-26(A)(12), 61-9A-26(E)(1), 61-10-15.1(A)(4), 61-10-15.1(D)(1), 61-31-17(A)(10), 61-31-17(C)(1); New York: NY Educ § 6509-e, 6531-a; Oregon: Or Rev Stat § 675.850; Puerto Rico: Boletín Administrativo Núm OE-2019-016; Rhode Island: RI Gen Laws § 29-94-1 – 29-94-5; Utah: Utah Admin Code R156-60-102(3), R156-60-502(23); Vermont: Vt Stat Ann tit 18, § 8351–8353; Vt Stat Ann tit 26 § 1354(a)(4), 1842(b)(13), 3016(11), 3210(a)(13), 3271(a)(8), 4042(a)(7), 4062(a)(7), 4132(a)(11); Virginia: Va Code Ann § 54.1-2409.5; Washington: Wash Rev Code § 18-130-020(4), 18-130-180(27).

12 *Ley 8/2017, de 28 de diciembre, para garantizar los derechos, la igualdad de trato y no discriminación de las personas LGTBI y sus familiares en Andalucía*, BOE, February 6, 2018, no 33, BOE-A-2018-1549 (Comunidad Autónoma de Andalucía); *Ley 3/2016, de 22 de julio, de Protección Integral contra LGTBIfobia y la Discriminación por Razón*

de Orientación e Identidad Sexual en la Comunidad de Madrid, BOE, November 25, 2016, no 285, BOE-A-2016-11096 (Comunidad de Madrid); *Ley 8/2016, de 27 de mayo, de igualdad social de lesbianas, gais, bisexuales, transexuales, transgénero e intersexuales, y de políticas públicas contra la discriminación por orientación sexual e identidad de género en la Comunidad Autónoma de la Región de Murcia*, BOE, June 25, 2016, 45833, BOE-A-2016-6170 (Comunidad Autónoma de la Región de Murcia); *Ley 8/2017, de 7 de abril, de la Generalitat, integral del reconocimiento del derecho a la identidad y a la expresión de género en la Comunitat Valenciana*, BOE, May 11, 2017, no 112, BOE-A-2017-5118 (Comunitat Valenciana).

13 *Affirmation of Sexual Orientation, Gender Identity and Gender Expression Act*, No LV (2016), c 567 (Malta) [*Gender Expression Act*].

14 American Psychological Association, *supra* note 2 at v.

15 *Yogyakarta Principles: Principles on the Application of International Human Rights Law in Relation to Sexual Orientation and Gender Identity* (2007).

16 *Ley 8/2017, de 28 de diciembre, para garantizar los derechos, la igualdad de trato y no discriminación de las personas LGTBI y sus familiares en Andalucía* (December 28, 2017), s 62 [author's translation].

17 The text of these laws aligns with AM Gill & Sam Ames, *Sample Legislation to Protect Youth from Conversion Therapy* (Washington, DC: Human Rights Campaign and National Center for Lesbian Rights, 2015).

18 Or Rev Stat § 675.850.

19 Del Code tit 19 § 710.

20 NM Stat § 61-1-3.3.

21 *Gender Expression Act, supra* note 13, s 2.

22 *Ibid*, s 4.

23 *Regulated Health Professions Act, 1991, supra* note 10.

24 *Gender Expression Act, supra* note 13, s 2.

25 The language of "likelihood of [gender dysphoria] persistence" is used by Kenneth J Zucker et al, "A Developmental, Biopsychosocial Model for the Treatment of Children with Gender Identity Disorder" (2012) 59:3 J Homosexuality 369 at 393.

26 *Gender Expression Act, supra* note 13, s 2.

27 Conn Gen Stat § 19a-907a.

28 Conn Gen Stat § 42-111d, 42-111o.

29 Conn Gen Stat § 42-111g.

30 Interim estimates (51.9 percent, n = 52) from a Canadian study led by Travis Salway of Simon Fraser University on 23 November 2020. Travis Salway, Simon Fraser University, personal communication, January 11, 2021.

31 Drescher et al, *supra* note 9 at 7.

32 *King v Christie*, 767 F (3d) 216 (3rd Cir 2014). See also *Doe v Christie*, 783 F (3d) 150 (3rd Cir 2015); *Pickup v Brown*, 740 F (3d) 1208 (9th Cir 2013).

33 Utah Admin Code R156-60-502.

34 *NAAP v California Bd of Psychology*, 228 F (3d) 1043 (9th Cir 2000).

Chapter 4: Opposition and Constitutional Challenges to Bans

1 Jacob M Victor, "Regulating Sexual Orientation Change Efforts: The California Approach, Its Limitations, and Potential Alternatives" (2014) 123:5 Yale LJ 1532 at 1552.

2 *Otto v City of Boca Raton, Florida*, 981 F (3d) 854 (11th Cir 2020) [*Otto*]; *Pickup v Brown*, 740 F (3d) 1208 (9th Cir 2013) [*Pickup*]; *King v Christie*, 767 F (3d) 216 (3rd Cir 2014) [*King*].

3 Part 1 of the *Constitution Act, 1982*, being Schedule B to the *Canada Act 1982* (UK), 1982, c 11 [*Charter*].

4 *Irwin Toy Ltd v Quebec (Attorney General)*, [1989] 1 SCR 927, 58 DLR (4th) 577 [*Irwin Toy*].

5 *R v Sharpe*, 2001 SCC 2 at paras 143, 150 [*Sharpe*].

6 *Ibid* at para 182.

7 *R v Oakes*, [1986] 1 SCR 103, 26 DLR (4th) 200.

8 See e.g. *Otto, supra* note 2; *King, supra* note 2; *Pickup, supra* note 2.

9 See e.g. *RAV v St Paul*, 505 US 377 (1992), which accorded free speech protection to racist cross burning.

10 *Pickup, supra* note 2 at 42.

11 See *King, supra* note 2; *Ward v Rock against Racism*, 491 US 781 (1989) [*Ward*]; *Florida Bar v Went For It*, 515 US 618 (1995).

12 *King, supra* note 2; *Otto, supra* note 2; *NIFLA v Becerra*, 585 U S ____ (2018) [*NIFLA*].

13 *Reed v Town of Gilbert*, 576 US ___ (2015); *NIFLA, supra* note 12.

14 Regarding safeguarding the well-being of minors, see *New York v Ferber*, 458 US 747 (1982) [*Ferber*].

15 The US Supreme Court has previously found that creating a diverse classroom environment is a compelling state interest under the Fourteenth Amendment. *Regents of the University of California v Bakke*, 438 US 265 (1978).

16 *Rumsfeld v Forum for Academic and Institutional Rights, Inc*, 547 US 47 (2006) [*Rumsfeld*].

17 *Lowe v SEC*, 472 US 181 (1985).

18 *Pickup, supra* note 2 at 32–33.

19 *Rumsfeld, supra* note 16.

20 *Ward, supra* note 11.

21 This fundamentally distinguishes it from the hypothetical, offered in *Otto, supra* note 2 at 11, of people being disallowed from engaging in a demonstration, which is an expressive practice, but being allowed to advocate for one such demonstration. According to the majority in *Otto*, this would not be a reasonable alternative since free speech is the right to speech itself, not the right to speak about banned speech. The ban on conversion practices is fundamentally different from that hypothetical, however, since conversion practitioners are allowed to express to patients the very same beliefs that motivates their practices – not just to advocate for being allowed to express them. It preserves the right to speech itself.

22 *Whitney v California*, 274 US 357 (1965) at 377.

23 In *Sharpe, supra* note 5 at para 5, the government conceded that prohibiting the possession of child pornography restricted freedom of expression.

24 *Irwin Toy, supra* note 4 at 976; *Sharpe, supra* note 5 at para 182 (L'Heureux-Dubé, Gonthier, and Bastarache JJ concurring).

25 *Turner Broadcasting Systems, Inc v FCC*, 512 US 622 (1994) [*Turner Broadcasting*].

26 *R v Keegstra*, [1990] 3 SCR 697 at 764, 117 NR 1.

27 *Irwin Toy, supra* note 4 at 976.

28 Edwin V Valdiserri, "Fear of AIDS: Implications for Mental Health Practice with Reference to Ego-dystonic Homosexuality" (1986) 56:4 American J Orthopsychiatry 634; Ilan H Meyer & Laura Dean, "Internalized Homophobia, Intimacy, and Sexual Behavior among Gay and Bisexual Men" in Gregory M Herek, ed, *Stigma and Sexual Orientation: Understanding Prejudice against Lesbians, Gay Men, and Bisexuals* (Thousand Oaks, CA: Sage Publications, 1998) 160; American Psychological Association, *Report of the American Psychological Association Task Force on Appropriate Therapeutic Responses to Sexual Orientation* (Washington, DC: American Psychological Association, 2009) [American Psychological Association, *Report*]; Brian A Rood et al, "Internalized Transphobia: Exploring Perceptions of Social Messages in Transgender and Gender-Nonconforming Adults" (2017) 18:4 Intl J Transgenderism 411.

29 Even though some wish to imagine him happy.

30 Such an approach is contemplated under section 3(c) and (d) of the model law discussed in Chapter 7.

31 My argument is reminiscent of the concurrence's argument in *Sharpe, supra* note 5 at para 185, that the possession of child pornography undermines self-fulfillment by "eroticising [children's] inferior social, economic and sexual status."

32 American Psychological Association, *Report, supra* note 28; Peter Gajdics, *The Inheritance of Shame: A Memoir* (Long Beach, CA: Brown Paper Press, 2017) [Gajdics, *Inheritance of Shame*]; Jules Sherred, "I Underwent Conversion Therapy. It Stopped Me from Transitioning for Decades," *Daily Xtra* (October 26, 2020), online: <perma. cc/T5EP-6GLG>; Sé Sullivan, *Conversion Therapy Ground Zero: Interrogating the Production of Gender as a Pathology in the United States* (PhD dissertation, California Institute of Integral Studies, 2017) [unpublished]; Beth Schwartzapfel, "Born This Way?" *American Prospect* (March 14, 2013), online: <perma.cc/G5BS-TV3L>; Luna M Ferguson, *Me, Myself, They: Life beyond the Binary* (Berkeley, CA: House of Anansi Press, 2019); Alex Cooper & Joanna Brooks, *Saving Alex* (New York: HarperOne, 2016); Garrard Conley, *Boy Erased: A Memoir* (New York: Riverhead Books, 2016); Daphne Scholinski & Jane Meredith Adams, *The Last Time I Wore a Dress* (New York: Riverhead Books, 1998).

33 Peter Gajdics, "I Experienced 'Conversion Therapy' – And It's Time to Ban It across Canada," *Maclean's* (June 6, 2018), online: <perma.cc/GLY3-X7QB>; Natasha Riebe, "'This Practice Is Evil': Edmonton to Ban Conversion Therapy," *CBC*

News (August 21, 2019), online: <perma.cc/H8VW-YLZQ>; McDermott Will & Emery LLP, *The Pernicious Myth of Conversion Therapy: How Love in Action Perpetrated a Fraud on America* (Washington, DC: Mattachine Society, 2018) at 48; Christopher Romero, "Praying for Torture: Why the United Kingdom Should Ban Conversion Therapy" (2019) 51:1 Geo Wash Intl L Rev 201; Stephen Wright, "'Conversion Therapy' Is Medieval Torture Based on Ignorance" (2014) 28:33 Nursing Standard 17; Nico Lang, "Conversion Therapy Is 'Torture': LGBT Survivors Are Fighting to Ban 'Pray the Gay Away' Camps," *Salon* (March 21, 2017), online: <perma.cc/YFF9 -TVQQ>; Ignatius Yordan Nugraha, "The Compatibility of Sexual Orientation Change Efforts with International Human Rights Law" (2017) 35:3 Netherlands Q Human Rights 176; Office of the United Nations High Commissioner for Human Rights, *Discrimination and Violence against Individuals Based on Their Sexual Orientation and Gender Identity*, Doc A/HRC/29/23 (2015) at 11; Independent Forensic Expert Group, "Statement on Conversion Therapy" (2020) 72 J Forensic & Legal Medicine 101930; UN Independent Expert Victor Madrigal-Borloz, *Practices of So-Called "Conversion Therapy,"* Doc A/HRC/44/53 (2020); Douglas Haldeman, "Sexual Orientation Conversion Therapy for Gay Men and Lesbians: A Scientific Examination" in John C. Gonsiorek & James D. Weinrich, eds, *Homosexuality: Research Implications for Public Policy* (Thousand Oaks, CA: Sage Publications, 1991) 149.

34 David J Kinitz et al, "'Conversion Therapy' Experiences in Their Social Contexts: A Qualitative Study of Sexual Orientation and Gender Identity and Expression Change Efforts in Canada" (2021) Can J Psychiatry; Trevor Goodyear et al, "'They Want You to Kill Your Inner Queer but Somehow Leave the Human Alive': Delineating the Impacts of Sexual Orientation and Gender Identity and Expression Change Efforts" (2021) The Journal of Sex Research; House of Commons of Canada, Standing Committee on Justice and Human Rights, *An Act to Amend the Criminal Code (Conversion Therapy)*, 43-2 (December 3, 2020) (Erika Muse) [House of Commons of Canada, Muse]; House of Commons of Canada, Standing Committee on Justice and Human Rights, *An Act to Amend the Criminal Code (Conversion Therapy)*, 43-2 (December 8, 2020) (Peter Gajdics) [House of Commons of Canada, Gajdics]; Sherred, *supra* note 32; Gajdics, *Inheritance of Shame, supra* note 32.

35 Amy E Green et al, "Self-Reported Conversion Efforts and Suicidality among US LGBTQ Youths and Young Adults, 2018" (2020) 110:8 Am J Public Health 1221 [Green et al, "Self-Reported Conversion Efforts"].

36 Jack L Turban et al, "Association between Recalled Exposure to Gender Identity Conversion Efforts and Psychological Distress and Suicide Attempts among Transgender Adults" (2019) 77:1 J American Medical Assoc Psychiatry 68; see also Ana María del Río-González et al, "Sexual Orientation and Gender Identity Change Efforts and Suicide Morbidity among Sexual and Gender Minority Adults in Colombia" (2021) LGBT Health.

37 Green et al, "Self-Reported Conversion Efforts," *supra* note 35. I took the percentage of each outcome among respondents who underwent conversion practices,

divided that number by the adjusted odds ratio – which accounts for demographic differences – and subtracted the calculated value from the initial percentage. For instance, the study reports that 62.6 percent of those who reported conversion practices seriously considered suicide, and an adjusted odds ratio of 1.76 compared to those who did not report conversion practices. Dividing 62.6 percent by 1.76 equals 35.57 percent. Subtracting 35.57 percent from 62.6 percent is 27.03 percent, or twenty-seven people out of one hundred when rounded to the nearest integer.

38 Jason Grossman & Fiona J Mackenzie, "The Randomized Controlled Trial: Gold Standard, or Merely Standard?" (2005) 48:4 Perspectives in Biology & Medicine 516.

39 Gordon CS Smith & Jill P Pell, "Parachute Use to Prevent Death and Major Trauma Related to Gravitational Challenge: Systematic Review of Randomised Controlled Trials" (2003) 327:7429 British Medical J 1459.

40 *Ferber, supra* note 14.

41 The US Supreme Court cited Ulrich C Schoettle, "Child Exploitation: A Study of Child Pornography" (1980) 19:2 J American Academy Child Psychiatry 289; Ulrich C Schoettle, "Treatment of the Child Pornography Patient" (1980) 137:9 American J Psychiatry 1109; Judianne Densen-Gerber, "Child Prostitution and Child Pornography: Medical, Legal, and Societal Aspects of the Commercial Exploitation of Children" in Barbara McComb Jones, Linda L Jenstrom & Kee MacFarlane, eds, *Sexual Abuse of Children: Selected Readings* (Washington, DC: National Center on Child Abuse and Neglect, 1980) 77; Vincent de Francis, "Protecting the Child Victim of Sex Crimes Committed by Adults" (1971) 35:3 Federal Probation 15; Norman S Ellerstein & J William Canavan, "Sexual Abuse of Boys" (1980) 134:3 Archives of Pediatrics & Adolescent Medicine 255; Ann Wolbert Burgess & Lynda Lytle Holmstrom, "Accessory-to-Sex: Pressure, Sex, and Secrecy" in Ann Wolbert Burgess et al, eds, *Sexual Assault of Children and Adolescents* (Lexington, MA: Lexington Books, 1978) 85; A Nicholas Groth, "Sexual Trauma in the Life Histories of Rapists and Child Molesters" (1979) 4:1 Victimology 10.

42 Paul Okami, "Self-Reports of 'Positive' Childhood and Adolescent Sexual Contacts with Older Persons: An Exploratory Study" (1991) 20:5 Archives of Sexual Behavior 437; Bruce Rind, Philip Tromovitch & Robert Bauserman, "A Meta-analytic Examination of Assumed Properties of Child Sexual Abuse Using College Samples" (1998) 124:1 Psychological Bulletin 22; J Michael Bailey, "How to Ruin Sex Research" (2019) 48:4 Archives of Sexual Behavior 1007 at 1007, n 1.

43 American Psychological Association, "Resolution on Gender Identity Change Efforts" (2021), online: <perma.cc/G462-TAUB> [American Psychological Association, "Resolution"].

44 *Turner Broadcasting, supra* note 25.

45 American Psychological Association, *Report, supra* note 28 at 2–3; Eli Coleman et al, "Standards of Care for the Health of Transsexual, Transgender, and Gender-Nonconforming People, version 7" (2012) 13:4 Intl J Transgenderism 165 at 186;

Julia Temple Newhook et al, "A Critical Commentary on Follow-Up Studies and 'Desistance' Theories about Transgender and Gender-Nonconforming Children" (2018) 19:2 Intl J Transgenderism 212; Florence Ashley, "The Clinical Irrelevance of 'Desistance' Research for Transgender and Gender Creative Youth" (2021) Psychology of Sexual Orientation and Gender Diversity.

46 *Otto, supra* note 2 at 39.

47 Benjamin Freedman, "Equipoise and the Ethics of Clinical Research" (1987) 317:3 New England J Medicine 141.

48 See the Appendix for a list of statements opposing conversion practices by prominent professional organizations.

49 *FCC v Fox Television Stations, Inc*, 556 US 502 (2009).

50 See Clay Calvert, "Testing the First Amendment Validity of Laws Banning Sexual Orientation Change Efforts on Minors: What Level of Scrutiny Applies after Becerra and Does a Proportionality Approach Provide a Solution?" (2020) 47:1 Pepperdine L Rev 1 at 44.

51 *Pickup, supra* note 2.

52 *King, supra* note 2.

53 *Otto, supra* note 2.

54 See also "*Otto v. City of Boca Raton*: Eleventh Circuit Invalidates Minor Conversion Therapy Bans," Case Comment, (2021) 134 Harv L Rev 2863.

55 On the balancing of equality rights against freedom of expression and religious freedom, see *Law Society of British Columbia v Trinity Western University*, 2018 SCC 32 [*Law Society*]; *Trinity Western University v Law Society of Upper Canada*, 2018 SCC 33 [*Trinity Western*]; *Ross v New Brunswick School District No 15*, [1996] 1 SCR 825, 133 DLR (4th) 1.

56 Bill C-16, *An Act to Amend the Canadian Human Rights Act and the Criminal Code*, SC 2017, c 13; *Canadian Human Rights Act*, RSC 1985, c H-6.

57 See e.g. Brenda Cossman, "Gender Identity, Gender Pronouns, and Freedom of Expression: Bill C-16 and the Traction of Specious Legal Claims" (2018) 68:1 UTLJ 37 at 42ff.

58 *Ibid* at 65.

59 See e.g. Richard Green, "Banning Therapy to Change Sexual Orientation or Gender Identity in Patients under 18" (2017) 45:1 J American Academy Psychiatry L 7 at 10 [Green, "Banning Therapy"].

60 Keith H Holland, "The Doctrine of Substantial Overbreadth: A Better Prescription for Strong Medicine in Missouri" (2014) 79:1 Missouri L Rev 185; Hamish Stewart, "Bedford and the Structure of Section 7" (2015) 60:3 McGill LJ 575.

61 William Byne, "Regulations Restrict Practice of Conversion Therapy" (2016) 3:2 LGBT Health 97 at 97; Bill 77, *Affirming Sexual Orientation and Gender Identity Act, 2015*, SO 2015, c 18.

62 Byne, *supra* note 61 at 98.

63 Coleman et al, *supra* note 45 at 175. For a list of organisations, see Appendix.

64 American Psychological Association, "Resolution," *supra* note 43.

65 Turban et al, *supra* note 36.

66 *Doe v Christie*, 33 F Supp (3d) 518 (2014), aff'd 783 F (3d) 150 (3rd Cir 2015) [*Doe*].

67 Contra Green, "Banning Therapy," *supra* note 59.

68 Pamela Hallquist Viale, "The Federal 'Right to Try' Act: An Answer to New Treatments during Terminal Illness?" (2017) 8:4 J Advanced Practitioner in Oncology 334. I discuss the right-to-try movement further in the next section.

69 Green, "Banning Therapy," *supra* note 59 at 8.

70 American Psychiatric Association, *Diagnostic and Statistical Manual of Mental Disorders*, 5th ed (Washington, DC: American Psychiatric Association, 2013) [*DSM, 5th ed*].

71 American Psychiatric Association, *Diagnostic and Statistical Manual of Mental Disorders*, 3rd ed (Washington, DC: American Psychiatric Association, 1980); American Psychiatric Association, *Diagnostic and Statistical Manual of Mental Disorders*, 4th ed (Washington, DC: American Psychiatric Association, 1994); American Psychiatric Association, *Diagnostic and Statistical Manual of Mental Disorders*, rev 4th ed (Washington, DC: American Psychiatric Association, 2000).

72 *DSM*, 5th ed, *supra* note 70.

73 Coleman et al, *supra* note 45 at 168; Lin Fraser et al, "Recommendations for Revision of the *DSM* Diagnosis of Gender Identity Disorder in Adults" (2010) 12:2 Intl J Transgenderism 80.

74 *DSM*, 5th ed, *supra* note 70 at 5.

75 World Health Organization (WHO), *The ICD-10 Classification of Mental and Behavioural Disorders: Clinical Descriptions and Diagnostic Guidelines* (Geneva: WHO, 1992); WHO, *The ICD-11 Classification of Mental and Behavioural Disorders: Clinical Descriptions and Diagnostic Guidelines* (Geneva: WHO, 2018).

76 Sam Winter, "Gender Trouble: The World Health Organization, the International Statistical Classification of Diseases and Related Health Problems (ICD)-11 and the Trans Kids" (2017) 14:5 Sexual Health 423 at 424.

77 Sam Winter et al, "The Proposed ICD-11 Gender Incongruence of Childhood Diagnosis: A World Professional Association for Transgender Health Membership Survey" (2016) 45:7 Archives of Sexual Behavior 1605 at 1611.

78 Byne, *supra* note 61 at 98.

79 *Charter*, *supra* note 3, s 15.

80 Peter W Hogg, *Constitutional Law of Canada*, 5th ed (Toronto: Thomson Reuters, 2007) at para 47.15.

81 See *R v Clay*, 2003 SCC 75 at para 40.

82 Green, "Banning Therapy," *supra* note 59 at 9.

83 *Ibid* at 10.

84 *AC v Manitoba (Director of Child and Family Services)*, [2009] 2 SCR 181, 309 DLR (4th) 581; *Jehovah's Witnesses in State of Wash v King County Hosp*, (1967) 278 F Supp 488 (Wash Dist Ct), affirmed 390 US 598 (1998).

85 Richard Green, "To Transition or Not to Transition? That Is the Question" (2017) 9:2 Current Sexual Health Reports 79 at 82.

86 On the balancing of religious freedom and equality rights in Canada, see *Law Society, supra* note 55; *Trinity Western, supra* note 55. For US law, see *King, supra* note 2; Ezra Ishmael Young, "What the Supreme Court Could Have Heard in *R.G. & G.R. Harris Funeral Homes v. EEOC and Aimee Stephens*" (2020) 11:9 Cal L Rev Online 9 at 48–49; *Masterpiece Cakeshop v Colorado Civil Rights Commission,* 584 US ___ at 16–18 (2018); *Trinity Lutheran Church of Columbia, Inc v Comer,* 582 US ___ at 8 (2017); *Hobby Lobby v Burwell,* 573 US 682 at 733 (2014) ; *Employment Division, Department of Human Resources of Oregon v Smith,* 494 US 872 (1990); *United States v Lee,* 455 US 252 at 261 (1982). For federal laws and in some states, the highest level of protection (strict scrutiny) may apply due to legislation. Bans on conversion practices have so far been at the state, rather than the federal, level.

87 *Pickup, supra* note 2 at 51–52.

88 Christian P Selinger, "The Right to Consent: Is It Absolute?" (2009) 2:2 British J Medical Practitioners 50.

89 *Criminal Code,* RSC 1985, c C-46, s 150.1; *R v Jobidon,* [1991] 2 SCR 714, 7 CR (4th) 233.

90 Kinitz et al, *supra* note 34; Goodyear et al, *supra* note 34; House of Commons of Canada, Muse, *supra* note 34; House of Commons of Canada, Gajdics, *supra* note 34; Sherred, *supra* note 32; Gajdics, *Inheritance of Shame, supra* note 32.

91 *Pickup, supra* note 2 at 51–52.

92 Tom L Beauchamp & James F Childress, *Principles of Biomedical Ethics,* 7th ed (New York: Oxford University Press, 2013).

93 *Criminal Code, supra* note 89.

94 *Carter v Canada,* 2015 SCC 5.

95 The comparison has notably been drawn by Jack Drescher et al, "The Growing Regulation of Conversion Therapy" (2016) 102:2 J Medical Regulation 7 at 9. On sexual and romantic relationships between doctors and patients, see Roger Collier, "When the Doctor–Patient Relationship Turns Sexual" (2016) 188:4 Can Medical Association J 247–48; *Norberg v Wynrib,* [1992] 2 SCR 226, 92 DLR (4th) 449 [*Norberg*]; *Criminal Code, supra* note 89, s 273.1(2)(c).

96 *Norberg, supra* note 95; *Criminal Code, supra* note 89, s 273.1(2)(c); *Code of Ethics of Physicians,* CQLR, c M-9, r 17, s 22.

97 Collier, *supra* note 95.

98 Ashley Austin & Revital Goodman, "The Impact of Social Connectedness and Internalized Transphobic Stigma on Self-Esteem among Transgender and Gender Nonconforming Adults" (2017) 64:6 J Homosexuality 825; Rood et al, *supra* note 28; Meyer & Dean, *supra* note 28; American Psychological Association, *Report, supra* note 28.

99 Madrigal-Borloz, *supra* note 33 at 6.

100 Goldwater Institute, "What Is Right To Try?" *Right to Try,* online: <perma.cc/EEU3-CK7E>; Viale, *supra* note 68.

101 Rebecca Dresser, "'Right to Try' Laws: The Gap between Experts and Advocates" (2015) 45:3 Hastings Center Report 9.

102 *Pickup, supra* note 2; *Doe, supra* note 66; *King, supra* note 2. The argument was not considered in *Otto, supra* note 2.

103 UN Committee on the Rights of the Child, *General Comment No 14 on the Right of the Child to Have His or Her Best Interests Taken as a Primary Consideration*, Doc CRC/C/GC/14 (2013).

104 SO 2017, c 14, ss 1(2), 74(3), 109(2), 179(2).

105 See e.g. Victoria Kolakowski, "Toward a Christian Ethical Response to Transsexual Persons" (1997) 1997:6 Theology & Sexuality 10; Chris Glaser, ed, *Gender Identity and Our Faith Communities: A Congregational Guide for Transgender Advocacy* (Washington, DC: Human Right Campaign Foundation, 2008); Susannah Cornwall, "Healthcare Chaplaincy and Spiritual Care for Trans People: Envisaging the Future" (2019) 7:1 Health & Social Care Chaplaincy 8; delfin bautista, Quince Mountain & Heath Mackenzie Reynolds, "Religion and Spirituality" in Laura Erickson-Schroth, ed, *Trans Bodies, Trans Selves: A Resource for the Transgender Community* (Oxford: Oxford University Press, 2014) 62. See also the Human Rights Campaign Foundation's Coming Home series, which includes guides specific to Catholicism, Islam, Judaism, Mormonism, and Evangelicalism. Human Rights Campaign Foundation, "Coming Home: To Faith, to Spirit, to Self" (2014), online: *Human Rights Campaign* <perma.cc/ R3D5-8F8H>

106 Florence Ashley, "Transgender Conversion Practices and the Ethical Burden of Justification" [under review], online: <perma.cc/T52W-XXLR>

107 Rood et al, *supra* note 28; Julia Raifman et al, "Difference-in-Differences Analysis of the Association between State Same-Sex Marriage Policies and Adolescent Suicide Attempts" (2017) 171:4 JAMA Pediatrics 350.

Chapter 5: Analyzing the Benefits and Limitations of Bans

1 Dean Spade, *Normal Life: Administrative Violence, Critical Trans Politics, and the Limits of Law*, rev ed (Durham, NC: Duke University Press, 2015) [Spade, *Normal Life*].

2 Legislative Assembly of Ontario, Standing Committee on Justice Policy, *Affirming Sexual Orientation and Gender Identity Act, 2015*, 41-1 (June 3, 2015) at JP-61 (Joyce Rowlands for the College of Registered Psychotherapists of Ontario) [Legislative Assembly of Ontario, *Affirming Sexual Orientation*]; Bill 77, *Affirming Sexual Orientation and Gender Identity Act, 2015*, SO 2015, c 18.

3 Legislative Assembly of Ontario, *Affirming Sexual Orientation, supra* note 2 at JP-65 (Jake Pyne).

4 Florence Ashley, "Suing for Conversion Therapy without a Statute? A Blueprint," *Law Matters* (2019), online: <perma.cc/LWZ9-EU4T> [Ashley, "Suing for Conversion Therapy"].

5 Legislative Assembly of Ontario, *Affirming Sexual Orientation, supra* note 2 at JP-61 (Joyce Rowlands); Suzanne Zinck & Antonio Pignatiello, *External Review of the Gender Identity Clinic of the Child, Youth and Family Services in the Underserved Populations Program at the Centre for Addiction and Mental Health* (Toronto: Centre for Addiction and Mental Health, 2015) at 13; Alice Dreger, "The Big Problem with Outlawing Gender Conversion Therapies," *Wired* (June 4, 2015), online: <perma.cc/ZR7K-WD6M>.

6 Marie-Amelie George, "Expressive Ends: Understanding Conversion Therapy Bans" (2017) 68:3 Alabama L Rev 793 at 828.

7 *Ibid* at 826.

8 Julia Raifman et al, "Difference-in-Differences Analysis of the Association between State Same-Sex Marriage Policies and Adolescent Suicide Attempts" (2017) 171:4 JAMA Pediatrics 350 [Raifman et al, "Difference-in-Differences"]; Julia Raifman et al, "Association of State Laws Permitting Denial of Services to Same-Sex Couples with Mental Distress in Sexual Minority Adults: A Difference-in-Difference-in-Differences Analysis" (2018) 75:7 JAMA Psychiatry 671.

9 Stefano Verrelli et al, "Minority Stress, Social Support, and the Mental Health of Lesbian, Gay, and Bisexual Australians during the Australian Marriage Law Postal Survey" (2019) 54:4 Australian Psychologist 336.

10 Evan Vipond, "Trans Rights Will Not Protect Us: The Limits of Equal Rights Discourse, Antidiscrimination Laws, and Hate Crime Legislation" (2015) 6:1 Western J Leg Studies art 3 at 19.

11 Zinck & Pignatiello, *supra* note 5 at 13.

12 George, *supra* note 6 at 826.

13 Ryan Conrad, *Against Equality: Queer Revolution, Not Mere Inclusion* (Chico, CA: AK Press, 2014); Dean Spade, "Under the Cover of Gay Rights" (2013) 37 NYU Rev of Law & Social Change 79.

14 Dean Spade, "Keynote Address: Trans Law and Politics in a Neoliberal Landscape" (2009) 18:2 Temp Pol & Civ Rits L Rev 353 at 372.

15 Evan Vipond, "Resisting Transnormativity: Challenging the Medicalization and Regulation of Trans Bodies" (2015) 8:2 Theory in Action 21; Dean Spade, "Mutilating Gender" in Susan Stryker & Stephen Whittle, eds, *The Transgender Studies Reader* (New York: Routledge, 2006) 315; Florence Ashley, "Gatekeeping Hormone Replacement Therapy for Transgender Patients Is Dehumanising" (2019) 45:7 J Medical Ethics 480.

16 American Psychiatric Association, *Diagnostic and Statistical Manual of Mental Disorders*, 5th ed (Washington, DC: American Psychiatric Association, 2013); World Health Organization (WHO), *The ICD-10 Classification of Mental and Behavioural Disorders: Clinical Descriptions and Diagnostic Guidelines* (Geneva: WHO, 1992); Sam Winter et al, "The Psycho-medical Case against a Gender Incongruence of Childhood Diagnosis" (2016) 3:5 The Lancet Psychiatry 404.

17 Florence Ashley, "Grounding Ourselves: On Bill C-16 and Symbolic Legislation," *University of Toronto Press Blog* (January 26, 2018), online: <perma.cc/8U62-B4G9>.

18 Raifman et al, "Difference-in-Differences," *supra* note 8.

19 For a discussion of disciplinary regimes and trans life, see Spade, *Normal Life, supra* note 1 at 50ff.

20 George, *supra* note 6 at 824–25.

21 Legislative Assembly of Ontario, "Affirming Sexual Orientation and Gender Identity Act, 2015," 2nd reading, *Official Report of Debates (Hansard)*, 41–1, No 65 (April 2, 2015) at 3345 (Hon Cheri DiNovo).

22 Amie Bishop, *Harmful Treatment: The Global Reach of So-Called Conversion Therapy* (New York: OutRight Action International, 2019) at 42.

23 Interim estimates (n = 43) as of November 23, 2020. Travis Salway, Simon Fraser University, personal communication, January 11, 2021. See also Travis Salway et al, "Prevalence of Exposure to Sexual Orientation Change Efforts and Associated Sociodemographic Characteristics and Psychosocial Health Outcomes among Canadian Sexual Minority Men" (2020) 65:7 Can J Psychiatry 502. This latter study does not include women and has a much smaller proportion of trans participants.

24 House of Commons of Canada, Standing Committee on Justice and Human Rights, *An Act to Amend the Criminal Code (Conversion Therapy)*, 43-2 (December 3, 2020) (Erika Muse); House of Commons of Canada, Standing Committee on Justice and Human Rights, *An Act to Amend the Criminal Code (Conversion Therapy)*, 43-2 (December 8, 2020) (Peter Gajdics). See also Jules Sherred, "I Underwent Conversion Therapy. It Stopped Me from Transitioning for Decades," *Daily Xtra* (October 26, 2020), online: <perma.cc/T5EP-6GLG>; Peter Gajdics, *The Inheritance of Shame: A Memoir* (Long Beach, CA: Brown Paper Press, 2017); Trevor Goodyear et al, "'They Want You to Kill Your Inner Queer but Somehow Leave the Human Alive': Delineating the Impacts of Sexual Orientation and Gender Identity and Expression Change Efforts" (2021) The Journal of Sex Research.

25 Jack Drescher et al, "The Growing Regulation of Conversion Therapy" (2016) 102:2 J Medical Regulation 7 at 9.

26 Melissa Ballengee Alexander, "Autonomy and Accountability: Why Informed Consent, Consumer Protection, and Defunding May Beat Conversion Therapy Bans" (2017) 55 U Louisville L Rev 283 at 310–13.

27 Vikki A Entwistle et al, "Supporting Patient Autonomy: The Importance of Clinician-Patient Relationships" (2010) 25:7 J General Internal Medicine 741; Rebecca Kukla, "Conscientious Autonomy: Displacing Decisions in Healthcare" (2005) 35:2 Hastings Center Report 34.

28 American Psychological Association, *Report of the American Psychological Association Task Force on Appropriate Therapeutic Responses to Sexual Orientation* (Washington, DC: American Psychological Association, 2009).

29 *Affirmation of Sexual Orientation, Gender Identity and Gender Expression Act*, No LV (2016), c 567 (Malta).

30 Interim estimates (n = 24) from a Canadian study led by Travis Salway of Simon Fraser University as of November 23, 2020. Travis Salway, Simon Fraser University, personal communication, January 11, 2021.

31 *Criminal Code*, RSC 1985, c C-46.
32 *R v McIntosh*, [1995] 1 SCR 686, 36 CR (4th) 171 at para 29. See also *R v DLW*, 2016 SCC 22, [2016] 1 SCR 402 at para 22; *R v SJL*, 2009 SCC 14, [2009] 1 SCR 426 at para 100.
33 *Bell ExpressVu Limited Partnership v Rex*, 2002 SCC 42.
34 Kent Roach et al, *Criminal Law and Procedure: Cases and Materials*, 11th ed (Toronto: Emond Publishing, 2015).
35 *Interpretation Act*, RSC 1985, c I-21, s 12.
36 Spade, *Normal Life*, *supra* note 1; Florence Ashley, "Don't Be So Hateful: The Insufficiency of Anti-discrimination and Hate Crime Laws in Improving Trans Well-Being" (2018) 68:1 UTLJ 1; Eric A Stanley & Nat Smith, eds, *Captive Genders: Trans Embodiment and the Prison Industrial Complex* (Oakland, CA: AK Press, 2011); Mimi E Kim, "From Carceral Feminism to Transformative Justice: Women-of-Color Feminism and Alternatives to Incarceration" (2018) 27:3 J Ethnic & Cultural Diversity in Social Work 219.
37 George, *supra* note 6 at 822; *Pickup v Brown*, 740 F (3d) 1208 (9th Cir 2013). In the United States, bans grounded in consumer protection acts may apply to unregulated practitioners. Alexander, *supra* note 26.
38 Legislative Assembly of Ontario, *Affirming Sexual Orientation*, *supra* note 2 at JP-61.
39 This interpretation is reminiscent of the legal principle that legislatures do not speak in vain. *AG (Que) v Carrières Ste-Thérèse Ltée*, [1985] 1 SCR 831 at 838, 20 DLR (4th) 602.
40 Conn Gen Stat § 19a-907b(b).
41 *Morin v Blais*, [1977] 1 SCR 570 at 580, 10 NR 489.
42 Legislative Assembly of British Columbia, *Motion 13 – Opposition to Conversion Therapy*, 41-4 (May 13, 2019) at 9196–97 (Spencer Chandra Herbert).
43 Nico Lang, "Utah's 'Conversion Therapy' Ban Is a Major Tipping Point for LGBTQ Rights," *Vox* (January 31, 2020), online: <web.archive.org/web/20210102201333/https://www.vox.com/identities/2020/1/31/21115408/utah-conversion-therapy-ban-lgbtq>.
44 Jack L Turban et al, "Psychological Attempts to Change a Person's Gender Identity from Transgender to Cisgender: Estimated Prevalence across US States, 2015" (2019) 109:10 American J Public Health 1452. I included California among states with a ban for the purposes of the analysis, even though it does not cover gender identity.
45 Travis Salway, Simon Fraser University, personal communication, December 31, 2019.
46 Hélène Frohard-Dourlent, Mauricio Coronel Villalobos & Elizabeth Sacwyc, *A Survey of Experiences with Surgery Readiness Assessment and Gender-Affirming Surgery among Trans People in Canada: Focus on British Columbia* (Vancouver: Stigma and Resilience among Vulnerable Youth Centre, School of Nursing, University of British Columbia, 2017) at 30–32; Florence Ashley, "Une meilleure couverture d'assurance pour les personnes trans," *Institute for Research on Public Policy Options*

Politiques (June 26, 2019), online: <perma.cc/Q4YF-NFUA>; Arjee Javellana Restar, *Breaking Barriers to Transgender Health Care: A Report on Health Challenges and Solutions for the Transgender Community* (New York: Amida Care, 2019); US, *Report of the 2015 US Transgender Survey*, by Sandy E James et al (Washington, DC: National Center for Transgender Equality, 2016) at 93ff.

47 Ashley, "Suing for Conversion Therapy," *supra* note 4; Florence Ashley, "Corriger nos pratiques: les approches thérapeutiques pour intervenir auprès des enfants trans examinées dans une perspective juridique" in Annie Pullen Sanfaçon & Denise Medico, eds, *Les interventions affirmatives auprès des enfants et jeunes trans : perspectives multidisciplinaires* (Montréal and Paris: Éditions Remue-Ménage and Médecine et Hygiène, 2021) 89; see also Craig Purshouse & Illias Trispiotis, "Is 'Conversion Therapy' Tortious?" (2021) Legal Studies.

48 *Michael Ferguson et al v JONAH et al*, No L-5473-12 (NJ Super Ct Law Div 2015).

Chapter 6: Developing an Affirmative Professional Culture

1 Various associations have observed that conversion practices violate professional obligations. Canadian Association of Social Workers & Canadian Association for Social Work Education, "Joint Statement on the Affirmation of Gender Diverse Children and Youth" (January 9, 2015), online: <perma.cc/G6LD-C8Z5>; Alberta College of Social Workers, "Practice Statement on Reparative or Conversion Therapy" (February 21, 2020), online: <perma.cc/Z8T9-E4VK>; New Brunswick Association of Social Workers, "Standards Regarding Conversion Therapy" (September 14, 2019), online: <perma.cc/9YYF-8CF2>; Manitoba College of Social Workers, "'Conversion Therapy' Position Statement" (May 2020), online: <perma.cc/MVZ9-Q6DE>.

2 Alexis Marcoux Rouleau, Annie Pullen Sansfaçon & Edward Ou Jin Lee, "Pratiques anti-oppressives auprès des jeunes trans," online: *OTSTCFQ* <perma.cc/4X6Z-6XQA>.

3 Canadian Association of Social Workers & Canadian Association for Social Work Education, *supra* note 1; Ordre des travailleurs sociaux et des thérapeutes conjugaux et familiaux du Québec, "L'Ordre appuie la déclaration de la CASWE-ACFTS et l'ACTS" (January 10, 2019), online: *OTSTCFQ* <perma.cc/4N8Q-DSQX>.

4 *Professional Code*, CQLR, c C-26, s 23.

5 Nina Mazar, On Amir & Dan Ariely, "The Dishonesty of Honest People: A Theory of Self-Concept Maintenance" (2008) 45:6 J Marketing Research 633 at 633.

6 *Ibid* at 634.

7 *Ibid*.

8 *Ibid* at 634–35.

9 Suzanne Zinck & Antonio Pignatiello, *External Review of the Gender Identity Clinic of the Child, Youth and Family Services in the Underserved Populations Program at the Centre for Addiction and Mental Health* (Toronto: Centre for Addiction and Mental Health, 2015) at 13.

10 Michael Davis, "Thinking Like an Engineer: The Place of a Code of Ethics in the Practice of a Profession" (1991) 20:2 Philosophy & Public Affaires 150; Denise du Toit, "A Sociological Analysis of the Extent and Influence of Professional Socialization on the Development of a Nursing Identity among Nursing Students at Two Universities in Brishane, Australia" (1995) 21 J Advanced Nursing 164; Gretchen B Sechrist & Charles Stangor, "Perceived Consensus Influences Intergroup Behavior and Stereotype Accessibility" (2001) 80:4 J Personality & Social Psychology 645.

11 See e.g. Ontario Human Rights Commission (OHRC), *Policy on Preventing Discrimination because of Gender Identity and Gender Expression* (Toronto: OHRC, 2014).

12 Francesca Gino, Shahar Ayal & Dan Ariely, "Contagion and Differentiation in Unethical Behavior: The Effect of One Bad Apple on the Barrel" (2009) 20:3 Psychological Science 393.

13 *Ibid* at 394.

14 *Ibid* at 397–98.

15 *Ibid.*

16 Jemma Tosh, "'Zuck Off'! A Commentary on the Protest against Ken Zucker and His 'Treatment' of Childhood Gender Identity Disorder" (2011) 13:1 Psychology of Women Section Rev 10.

17 Andrew Brien, "Professional Ethics and the Culture of Trust" (1998) 17:4 J Business Ethics 391.

18 *Ibid* at 402.

19 Josianne Crête & Annie Pullen Sansfaçon, "Étudier le développement de l'identité professionnelle en travail social: les défis de combiner diverses approches méthodologiques" (2015) 17 Recherches Qualitatives, Hors-Série 4; Florence Ashley, "Don't Be So Hateful: The Insufficiency of Anti-discrimination and Hate Crime Laws in Improving Trans Well-Being" (2018) 68:1 UTLJ 1; Annie Pullen Sansfaçon, Isabelle Marchand & Josianne Crête, "Explorer l'identité professionnelle chez les travailleurs sociaux en devenir: Une étude de l'expérience des étudiants québécois finissants" (2014) 27:1 Nouvelles pratiques sociales 137 at 150.

20 Crête & Pullen Sansfaçon, *supra* note 19 at 45.

21 *Ibid* at 44.

22 du Toit, *supra* note 10 at 169.

23 Alexandra Kalev, Frank Dobbin & Erin Kelly, "Best Practices or Best Guesses? Assessing the Efficacy of Corporate Affirmative Action and Diversity Policies" (2006) 71:4 American Sociological Rev 589 at 606.

24 Josianne Crête, Annie Pullen Sanfaçon & Isabelle Marchand, "L'identité professionnelle de travailleurs sociaux en devenir: de la formation à la pratique" (2015) 61:1 Service social 43 at 50.

25 Davis, *supra* note 10 at 166–67.

26 Herminia Ibarra, "Provisional Selves: Experimenting with Image and Identity in Professional Adaptation" (1999) 44:4 Administrative Science Q 764 at 781.

27 *Ibid* at 774.

28 Gino, Ayal & Ariely, *supra* note 12; Kinnon Ross MacKinnon, Lesley A Tarasoff & Hannah Kia, "Predisposing, Reinforcing, and Enabling Factors of Trans-Positive Clinical Behavior Change: A Summary of the Literature" (2016) 17:2 Intl J Transgenderism 83 at 88.

29 Sechrist & Stangor, *supra* note 10 at 651.

30 Crête & Pullen Sansfaçon, *supra* note 19; Pullen Sansfaçon, Marchand & Crête, *supra* note 19 at 145; du Toit, *supra* note 10.

31 Ibarra, *supra* note 26 at 765; Crête & Pullen Sansfaçon, *supra* note 19 at 44; MacKinnon, Tarasoff & Kia, *supra* note 28.

32 Samuel N Dubin et al, "Transgender Health Care: Improving Medical Students' and Residents' Training and Awareness" (2018) 9 Advances in Medical Education & Practice 377.

33 Sand C Chang, Anneliese A Singh & lore m dickey, *A Clinician's Guide to Gender-Affirming Care: Working with Transgender and Gender-Nonconforming Clients* (Oakland, CA: Context Press, 2018); Madeline B Deutsch, *Guidelines for the Primary and Gender-Affirming Care of Transgender and Gender Nonbinary People*, 2nd ed (San Francisco: University of California San Francisco Center for Excellence for Transgender Health, 2016); Marcoux Rouleau, Pullen Sansfaçon & Ou Jin Lee, *supra* note 2; Michelle M Telfer et al, *Australian Standards of Care and Treatment Guidelines for Trans and Gender Diverse Children and Adolescents*, version 1.1 (Melbourne: Royal Children's Hospital, 2018); Ximena Lopez et al, "Statement on Gender-Affirmative Approach to Care from the Pediatric Endocrine Society Special Interest Group on Transgender Health" (2017) 29:4 Current Opinion in Pediatrics 475; Jason Rafferty, "Ensuring Comprehensive Care and Support for Transgender and Gender-Diverse Children and Adolescents" (2018) 142:4 Pediatrics e20182162; Jeannie Oliphant et al, *Guidelines for Gender Affirming Healthcare for Gender Diverse and Transgender Children, Young People and Adults in Aotearoa, New Zealand* (Hamilton, NZ: Transgender Health Research Lab, University of Waikato, 2018); Gabe Murchison, *Supporting and Caring for Transgender Children* (Washington: Human Rights Campaign, American Academic of Pediatrics, and American College of Osteopathic Pediatricians, 2016); Florence Ashley, "Thinking an Ethics of Gender Exploration: Against Delaying Transition for Transgender and Gender Creative Youth" (2019) 24:2 Clinical Child Psychology & Psychiatry 223.

34 Timothy W Jones et al, *Healing Spiritual Harms: Supporting Recovery from LGBTQA+ Change and Suppression Practices* (Melbourne: Australian Research Centre in Sex, Health and Society, La Trobe University, 2021); Tiffany M Lange, "Trans-affirmative Narrative Exposure Therapy (TA-NET): A Therapeutic Approach for Targeting Minority Stress, Internalized Stigma, and Trauma Reactions among Gender Diverse Adults" (2020) 5:3 Practice Innovations 230; Jessica Horner, "Undoing the Damage: Working with LGBT Clients in Post-Conversion Therapy" (2010) 8 Columbia Social Work Rev 8; Douglas C Haldeman, "Therapeutic Antidotes: Helping Gay and Bisexual Men Recover from Conversion Therapies" (2002) 5:3–4 J Gay & Lesbian

Psychotherapy 117; Aritra Chatterjee & Tilottama Mukherjee, "On Conversion Talk in Indian Clinical Contexts: A Pilot Venture" (2021) Journal of Psychosexual Health.

35   Dubin et al, *supra* note 32 at 385.

36   Nancy S Elman, Joyce Illfelder-Kaye & William N Robiner, "Professional Development: Training for Professionalism as a Foundation for Competent Practice in Psychology" (2005) 36:4 Professional Psychology: Research and Practice 367 at 373. For a discussion of quality of moral education in continuing professional development, see David AJ Richards, "Moral Theory, the Developmental Psychology of Ethical Autonomy and Professionalism" (1981) 31 J Legal Education 359.

37   Gino, Ayal & Ariely, *supra* note 12 at 394.

38   *Ibid* at 397–98.

39   *Professional Code, supra* note 4, s 128.

40   *Ibid*, s 122.

41   *Health Professions Procedural Code, Schedule II of the Regulated Health Professions Act, 1991*, SO 1991, c 18, s 25.

42   *Ibid*, s 75.

43   *Ibid*.

44   Ibarra, *supra* note 26; Kalev, Dobbin & Kelly, *supra* note 23.

Chapter 7: Annotated Model Law for Prohibiting Conversion Practices

1   Peter Gajdics, "I Experienced 'Conversion Therapy' – And It's Time to Ban It across Canada," *Maclean's* (June 6, 2018), online: <perma.cc/GLY3-X7QB>; Natasha Riebe, "'This Practice Is Evil': Edmonton to Ban Conversion Therapy," *CBC News* (August 21, 2019), online: <perma.cc/H8VW-YLZQ>; McDermott Will & Emery LLP, *The Pernicious Myth of Conversion Therapy: How Love in Action Perpetrated a Fraud on America* (Washington, DC: Mattachine Society, 2018) at 48; Christopher Romero, "Praying for Torture: Why the United Kingdom Should Ban Conversion Therapy" (2019) 51:1 Geo Wash Intl L Rev 201; Stephen Wright, "'Conversion Therapy' Is Medieval Torture Based on Ignorance" (2014) 28:33 Nursing Standard 17; Nico Lang, "Conversion Therapy Is 'Torture': LGBT Survivors Are Fighting to Ban 'Pray the Gay Away' Camps," *Salon* (March 21, 2017), online: <perma.cc/YFF9-TVQQ>; Ignatius Yordan Nugraha, "The Compatibility of Sexual Orientation Change Efforts with International Human Rights Law" (2017) 35:3 Netherlands Q Human Rights 176; Office of the United Nations High Commissioner for Human Rights (OHCHR), *Discrimination and Violence against Individuals Based on Their Sexual Orientation and Gender Identity*, Doc A/HRC/29/23 (2015) at 11; Independent Forensic Expert Group, "Statement on Conversion Therapy" (2020) 72 J Forensic & Legal Medicine 101930; UN Independent Expert Victor Madrigal-Borloz, *Practices of So-Called "Conversion Therapy,"* Doc A/HRC/44/53 (2020); Douglas Haldeman, "Sexual Orientation Conversion Therapy for Gay Men and

Lesbians: A Scientific Examination" in John C. Gonsiorek & James D. Weinrich, eds, *Homosexuality: Research Implications for Public Policy* (Thousand Oaks, CA: Sage Publications, 1991) 149.

2 Jack L Turban et al, "Psychological Attempts to Change a Person's Gender Identity from Transgender to Cisgender: Estimated Prevalence across US States, 2015" (2019) 109:10 American J Public Health 1452; US, *Report of the 2015 U.S. Transgender Survey*, by Sandy E James et al (Washington, DC: National Center for Transgender Equality, 2016) at 108.

3 Trans PULSE Canada Team, "QuickStat #1 – Conversion Therapy," *Trans PULSE Canada* (December 20, 2019), online: <perma.cc/H6MC-N927>; Travis Salway et al, "Prevalence of Exposure to Sexual Orientation Change Efforts and Associated Sociodemographic Characteristics and Psychosocial Health Outcomes among Canadian Sexual Minority Men" (2020) 65:7 Can J Psychiatry 502.

4 Christy Mallory, Taylor NT Brown & Kerith J Conron, *Conversion Therapy and LGBT Youth* (Los Angeles: Williams Institute on the Study of Sexual Orientation and Gender Identity, 2018).

5 United Kingdom, *National LGBT Survey: Research Report*, by Government Equalities Office (Manchester: UK Government Equalities Office, 2018) at 88 [*UK National LGBT Survey*].

6 *Ibid* at 89.

7 Luna M Ferguson, *Me, Myself, They: Life beyond the Binary* (Berkeley, CA: House of Anansi Press, 2019); Peter Gajdics, *The Inheritance of Shame: A Memoir* (Long Beach, CA: Brown Paper Press, 2017); Alex Cooper & Joanna Brooks, *Saving Alex* (New York: HarperOne, 2016); Garrard Conley, *Boy Erased: A Memoir* (New York: Riverhead Books, 2016); Daphne Scholinski & Jane Meredith Adams, *The Last Time I Wore a Dress* (New York: Riverhead Books, 1998); Samantha Allen, "I Wasn't Ready for the Intersex Surgery I Had as a Child," *The Daily Beast* (February 9, 2019), online: <perma.cc/6P3W-ZH5F>; Karl Bryant, "Making Gender Identity Disorder of Childhood: Historical Lessons for Contemporary Debates" (2006) 3:3 Sexuality Research & Social Policy 23 [Bryant, "Making Gender"]; Beth Schwartzapfel, "Born This Way?" *American Prospect* (March 14, 2013), online: <perma.cc/G5BS -TV3L>; Sé Sullivan, *Conversion Therapy Ground Zero: Interrogating the Production of Gender as a Pathology in the United States* (PhD dissertation, California Institute of Integral Studies, 2017) [unpublished]; Jules Sherred, "I Underwent Conversion Therapy. It Stopped Me from Transitioning for Decades," *Daily Xtra* (October 26, 2020), online: <perma.cc/T5EP-6GLG>.

8 Sullivan, *supra* note 7 at 54.

9 Schwartzapfel, *supra* note 7.

10 American Psychological Association, *Report of the American Psychological Association Task Force on Appropriate Therapeutic Responses to Sexual Orientation* (Washington, DC: American Psychological Association, 2009); Robert Wallace & Hershel Russell, "Attachment and Shame in Gender-Nonconforming Children and Their Families:

Toward a Theoretical Framework for Evaluating Clinical Interventions" (2013) 14:3 Intl J Transgenderism 113; Greta R Bauer et al, "Intervenable Factors Associated with Suicide Risk in Transgender Persons: A Respondent Driven Sampling Study in Ontario, Canada" (2015) 15:1 BMC Public Health art 525 [Bauer et al, "Intervenable Factors"]; Darryl B Hill et al, "An Affirmative Intervention for Families with Gender Variant Children: Parental Ratings of Child Mental Health and Gender" (2010) 36:1 J Sex & Marital Therapy 6; Trevor Goodyear et al, "'They Want You to Kill Your Inner Queer but Somehow Leave the Human Alive': Delineating the Impacts of Sexual Orientation and Gender Identity and Expression Change Efforts" (2021) The Journal of Sex Research; Jack L Turban et al, "Association between Recalled Exposure to Gender Identity Conversion Efforts and Psychological Distress and Suicide Attempts among Transgender Adults" (2019) 77:1 J American Medical Assoc Psychiatry 68.

11 James et al, *supra* note 2 at 110.

12 Turban et al, *supra* note 10.

13 Amy E Green et al, "Self-Reported Conversion Efforts and Suicidality among US LGBTQ Youths and Young Adults, 2018" (2020) 110:8 Am J Public Health 1221. See also Ana María del Río-González et al, "Sexual Orientation and Gender Identity Change Efforts and Suicide Morbidity among Sexual and Gender Minority Adults in Colombia" (2021) LGBT Health.

14 Bauer et al, "Intervenable Factors," *supra* note 10; Kristina R Olson et al, "Mental Health of Transgender Children Who Are Supported in Their Identities" (2016) 137:3 Pediatrics e20153223; Lily Durwood, Katie A McLaughlin & Kristina R Olson, "Mental Health and Self-Worth in Socially Transitioned Transgender Youth" (2017) 56:2 J American Academy Child Adolescent Psychiatry 116; Annie Pullen Sansfaçon et al, "Digging beneath the Surface: Results from Stage One of a Qualitative Analysis of Factors Influencing the Well-Being of Trans Youth in Quebec" (2018) 19:2 Intl J Transgenderism 184; Center for the Study of Inequality, "What Does the Scholarly Research Say about the Effect of Gender Transition on Transgender Well-Being?" *What We Know Project at Cornell University* (2018), online: <perma.cc/S97J-Q5J2>; Jon Arcelus et al, "Risk Factors for Non-suicidal Self-Injury among Trans Youth" (2016) 13:3 J Sexual Medicine 402.

15 See the Appendix for a list.

16 American Psychological Association, *supra* note 10; Julia Temple Newhook et al, "A Critical Commentary on Follow-Up Studies and 'Desistance' Theories about Transgender and Gender-Nonconforming Children" (2018) 19:2 Intl J Transgenderism 212; Florence Ashley, "The Clinical Irrelevance of 'Desistance' Research for Transgender and Gender Creative Youth," (2021) Psychology of Sexual Orientation and Gender Diversity.

17 Ariel Shidlo & Michael Schroeder, "Changing Sexual Orientation: A Consumers' Report" (2002) 33:3 Professional Psychology: Research & Practice 249; Eli Coleman et al, "Standards of Care for the Health of Transsexual, Transgender, and Gender-Nonconforming People, version 7" (2012) 13:4 Intl J Transgenderism 165 at 175.

18 Florence Ashley, "Transgender Conversion Practices and the Ethical Burden of Justification" [under review], online: <perma.cc/T52W-XXLR>.

19 See Chapter 3 for a list.

20 *Yogyakarta Principles: Principles on the Application of International Human Rights Law in Relation to Sexual Orientation and Gender Identity* (2007), Principle 18 on Protection from Medical Abuses [*Yogyakarta Principles*].

21 Madrigal-Borloz, *supra* note 1 at 21–22.

22 Suzanne Zinck & Antonio Pignatiello, *External Review of the Gender Identity Clinic of the Child, Youth and Family Services in the Underserved Populations Program at the Centre for Addiction and Mental Health* (Toronto: Centre for Addiction and Mental Health, 2015) at 13.

23 *Change or Suppression (Conversion) Practices Prohibition Bill 2020* (Victoria) [*Conversion Practices Bill*]; Sumeyya Ilanbey & Paul Sakkal, "Gay Conversion Therapy Banned in Victoria after Marathon Debate," *The Age* (February 4, 2021), online: <perma.cc/GE72-968W>.

24 Jack Drescher, "I'm Your Handyman: A History of Reparative Therapies" (1998) 36:1 J Homosexuality 19 at 20; Kelley Winters et al, "Learning to Listen to Trans and Gender Diverse Children: A Response to Zucker (2018) and Steensma and Cohen-Kettenis (2018)" (2018) 19:2 Intl J Transgenderism 246; Arlene I Lev, "Approaches to the Treatment of Gender Nonconforming Children and Transgender Youth" in Arlene I Lev & Andrew R Gottlieb, eds, *Families in Transition: Parenting Gender Diverse Children, Adolescents, and Young Adults* (New York: Harrington Park Press, 2019); Florence Ashley, "Homophobia, Conversion Therapy, and Care Models for Trans Youth: Defending the Gender-Affirmative Model" (2019) 17:4 J LGBT Youth 361 [Ashley, "Homophobia"]; American Psychological Association, *supra* note 10; Jake Pyne, "The Governance of Gender Non-conforming Children: A Dangerous Enclosure" (2014) 11 Annual Rev Critical Psychology 79 at 81 [Pyne, "Governance of Gender"]; Amie Bishop, *Harmful Treatment: The Global Reach of So-Called Conversion Therapy* (New York: OutRight Action International, 2019) at 7, 11.

25 Jonathan Foiles, "Conversion 'Therapy' Isn't Therapy at All," *Psychology Today* (January 31, 2018), online: <perma.cc/7BVT-UP33>; Lara Embry, "'Conversion Therapy': Therapy That Isn't," *Los Angeles Times* (August 27, 2012), online: <https://web.archive.org/web/20210301111441/www.latimes.com/opinion/la-xpm-2012-aug-27-la-oe-embry-gay-conversion-20120827-story.html>.

26 *Affirmation of Sexual Orientation, Gender Identity and Gender Expression Act*, No LV (2016), c 567 (Malta) [*Gender Expression Act*].

27 Ashley, "Homophobia," *supra* note 24 at 10.

28 Madrigal-Borloz, *supra* note 1 at 12; Kenneth J Zucker, "Commentary on Langer and Martin's (2004) 'How Dresses Can Make You Mentally Ill: Examining Gender Identity Disorder in Children'" (2006) 23:5–6 Child & Adolescent Social Work J 533 at 544, 549 [Zucker, "Commentary"]; Kenneth J Zucker et al, "A Developmental,

Biopsychosocial Model for the Treatment of Children with Gender Identity Disorder" (2012) 59:3 J Homosexuality 369 at 375, 377; Susan J Bradley & Kenneth J Zucker, "Gender Identity Disorder and Psychosexual Problems in Children and Adolescents" (1990) 35:6 Can J Psychiatry 477 at 478.

29 Coleman et al, *supra* note 17 at 166.

30 American Psychiatric Association, *Diagnostic and Statistical Manual of Mental Disorders*, 5th ed (Washington, DC: American Psychiatric Association, 2013).

31 Zucker et al, *supra* note 28 at 382.

32 Elizabeth Reis, *Bodies in Doubt: An American History of Intersex* (Baltimore: Johns Hopkins University Press, 2012) at 59, 70, 72, 79; Jemma Tosh, *Body and Consent in Psychology, Psychiatry, and Medicine: A Therapeutic Rape Culture* (New York: Routledge, 2020) at 24–25; Nadia Guidotto, "Monsters in the Closet: Biopolitics and Intersexuality" (2007) 4 Wagadu 48 at 55.

33 *Proyecto de Ley Sobre Proteccion Integral de Las Caracteristicas Sexuales*, 5864-D-2020 (Cámara de Diputados de la Nación Argentina) [*Proyecto de ley Sobre Proteccion*].

34 See Erika Muse, "Open Letter: Bill C-6 Excludes Conversion Therapy Practices That Target Trans People," *Centre for Gender and Sexual Health Equity* (June 25, 2020), appendix, online: <perma.cc/QQ4K-9D2V>. I have updated the language to make it read more fluidly. I also added the sentence clarifying that the provision does not serve to limit the contexts under which no consent is obtained.

35 *Criminal Code*, RSC 1985, c C-46; *Gender Expression Act, supra* note 26.

36 James et al, *supra* note 2 at 109; *UK National LGBT Survey, supra* note 5 at 93; Mallory, Brown & Conron, *supra* note 4; Tracy N Hipp et al, "From Conversion toward Affirmation: Psychology, Civil Rights, and Experiences of Gender-Diverse Communities in Memphis" (2019) 74:8 American Psychologist 882.

37 Bradley & Zucker, *supra* note 28; Tey Meadow, *Trans Kids: Being Gendered in the Twenty-First Century* (Oakland: University of California Press, 2018) at 73; Kenneth J Zucker, "'I'm Half-Boy, Half-Girl': Play Psychotherapy and Parent Counseling for Gender Identity Disorder" in Robert L Spitzer & American Psychiatric Publishing, eds, *DSM-IV-TR Casebook: Experts Tell How They Treated Their Own Patients* (Washington, DC: American Psychiatric Publishing, 2006) 321 at 325 [Zucker, "I'm Half-Boy, Half-Girl"].

38 Bryant, "Making Gender," *supra* note 7; Lev, *supra* note 24; Sullivan, *supra* note 7; Karl Bryant, "In Defence of Gay Children? 'Progay' Homophobia and the Production of Homonormativity" (2008) 11:4 Sexualities 455 at 466, 469 [Bryant, "In Defence of Gay Children"]; Damien W Riggs et al, "Transnormativity in the Psy Disciplines: Constructing Pathology in the Diagnostic and Statistical Manual of Mental Disorders and Standards of Care" (2019) 74:8 American Psychologist 912.

39 Sonali Kohli, "Gender Behavior Therapy and Gay Conversion: UCLA's Past, California's Future," *Daily Bruin* (November 15, 2012), online: <perma.cc/CVQ9-38LK>; George A Rekers & O Ivar Lovaas, "Behavioral Treatment of Deviant Sex-Role Behaviors in a Male Child" (1974) 7:2 J Applied Behavior Analysis 173; Richard

Green, *The "Sissy Boy Syndrome" and the Development of Homosexuality* (New Haven, CT: Yale University Press, 1987).

40 Bryant, "Making Gender," *supra* note 7 at 30–31.

41 Zucker et al, *supra* note 28 at 388–89; Kenneth J Zucker & Susan J Bradley, *Gender Identity Disorder and Psychosexual Problems in Children and Adolescents* (New York: Guilford Press, 1995) at 270–71, 273; Madrigal-Borloz, *supra* note 1 at 11.

42 Zucker et al, *supra* note 28 at 382.

43 Zucker, "Commentary," *supra* note 28 at 543–44.

44 *Ibid* at 543.

45 Edwin V Valdiserri, "Fear of AIDS: Implications for Mental Health Practice with Reference to Ego-dystonic Homosexuality" (1986) 56:4 American J Orthopsychiatry 634.

46 Harold I Lief & Helen S Kaplan, "Ego-dystonic Homosexuality" (1986) 12:4 J Sex & Marital Therapy 259.

47 Warren Throckmorton, "Efforts to Modify Sexual Orientation: A Review of Outcome Literature and Ethical Issues" (1998) 20:4 J Mental Health Counseling 283.

48 Ilan H Meyer & Laura Dean, "Internalized Homophobia, Intimacy, and Sexual Behavior among Gay and Bisexual Men" in Gregory M Herek, ed, *Stigma and Sexual Orientation: Understanding Prejudice against Lesbians, Gay Men, and Bisexuals* (Thousand Oaks, CA: Sage Publications, 1998) 160; American Psychological Association, *supra* note 10.

49 Jack L Turban, Annelou LC de Vries & Kenneth J Zucker, "Gender Dysphoria and Gender Incongruence" in Andrés Martin, Michael H Bloch & Fred R Volkmar, eds, *Lewis' Child and Adolescent Psychiatry*, 5th ed (Philadelphia: Wolters Kluwer, 2018) 632 at 369; Richard Green, "Banning Therapy to Change Sexual Orientation or Gender Identity in Patients under 18" (2017) 45:1 J American Academy of Psychiatry L 7 at 8; Zucker & Bradley, *supra* note 41 at 266; Bryant, "Making Gender," *supra* note 7 at 29; Susan J Langer & James I Martin, "How Dresses Can Make You Mentally Ill: Examining Gender Identity Disorder in Children" (2004) 21:1 Child and Adolescent Social Work J 5 at 11.

50 American Psychiatric Association, *Diagnostic and Statistical Manual of Mental Disorders*, 4th ed (Washington, DC: American Psychiatric Association, 1994); American Psychiatric Association, *Diagnostic and Statistical Manual of Mental Disorders*, rev 4th ed (Washington, DC: American Psychiatric Association, 2000).

51 Bradley & Zucker, *supra* note 28; Meadow, *supra* note 37 at 73; Zucker, "I'm Half-Boy, Half-Girl," *supra* note 37 at 325.

52 Jessica Horner, "Undoing the Damage: Working with LGBT Clients in Post-conversion Therapy" (2010) 8 Columbia Social Work Rev 8 at 8; Douglas C Haldeman, "The Practice and Ethics of Sexual Orientation Conversion Therapy" in Linda Garnets & Douglas C Kimmel, eds, *Psychological Perspectives on Lesbian, Gay, and Bisexual Experiences*, 2nd ed (New York: Columbia University Press, 2003) 681 at 689; American Psychological Association, *supra* note 10 at 35, 61.

53 American Psychological Association, *supra* note 10 at 35; Brandon Ambrosino, "Gay Celibacy Is the New Ex-gay Therapy," *Daily Beast* (April 14, 2017), online: <web.archive.org/web/20210610052035/https://www.thedailybeast.com/gay-celibacy -is-the-new-ex-gay-therapy>; Gabriel Arana, "My So-Called Ex-gay Life," *The American Prospect* (April 11, 2012), online: <perma.cc/C5CM-NJNK>.

54 American Psychological Association, *supra* note 10 at 35, 61.

55 Madrigal-Borloz, *supra* note 1 at 10.

56 Peggy T Cohen-Kettenis & Friedemann Pfäfflin, *Transgenderism and Intersexuality in Childhood and Adolescence: Making Choices* (Thousand Oaks, CA: Sage Publications, 2003); Zucker et al, *supra* note 28 at 376–81; Lisa Marchiano, "Outbreak: On Transgender Teens and Psychic Epidemics" (2017) 60:3 Psychological Perspectives 345; Lisa Littman, "Parent Reports of Adolescents and Young Adults Perceived to Show Signs of a Rapid Onset of Gender Dysphoria" (2018) 13:8 PLoS ONE e0202330; Diana Kuhl, *Death of the Clinic: Trans-Informing the Clinical Gaze to Counter Epistemic Violence* (PhD dissertation, University of Western Ontario, 2019) at 87ff [unpublished]; Diane Ehrensaft, "Psychoanalysis Meets Transgender Children: The Best of Times and the Worst of Times" (2021) 18:1 Psychoanalytic Perspectives 68.

57 Cohen-Kettenis & Pfäfflin, *supra* note 56.

58 Sherred, *supra* note 7; Florence Ashley, "A Critical Commentary on 'Rapid-Onset Gender Dysphoria'" (2020) 68:4 Sociological Rev 779 [Ashley, "Critical Commentary"]; Ashley, "Homophobia," *supra* note 24.

59 Wallace & Russell, *supra* note 10 at 120; Zucker et al, *supra* note 28 at 389.

60 Wallace & Russell, *supra* note 10 at 120.

61 Noah Adams et al, "Guidance and Ethical Considerations for Undertaking Transgender Health Research and Institutional Review Boards Adjudicating This Research" (2017) 2:1 Transgender Health 165 at 170; Ben Vincent, "Studying Trans: Recommendations for Ethical Recruitment and Collaboration with Transgender Participants in Academic Research" (2018) 9:2 Psychology & Sexuality 102.

62 Turban, de Vries & Zucker, *supra* note 49 at 639; Zucker, "I'm Half-Boy, Half-Girl," *supra* note 37; Zucker et al, *supra* note 28 at 382, 388.

63 Zucker et al, *supra* note 28; Diana Kuhl & Wayne Martino, "'Sissy' Boys and the Pathologization of Gender Non-conformity" in Susan Talburt, ed, *Youth Sexualities: Public Feelings and Contemporary Cultural Politics* (Santa Barbara, CA: Praeger, 2018) 31; Kuhl, *supra* note 56 at 87ff.

64 Marchiano, *supra* note 56; Michael Laidlaw, Michelle Cretella & Kevin Donovan, "The Right to Best Care for Children Does Not Include the Right to Medical Transition" (2019) 19:2 American J Bioethics 75.

65 Carol Lloyd, "Is a Sex Change Operation Liberating or Mutilating?" *Salon* (August 3, 2007), online: <perma.cc/UR6A-LSKS>.

66 Florence Ashley, "Thinking an Ethics of Gender Exploration: Against Delaying Transition for Transgender and Gender Creative Youth" (2019) 24:2 Clinical Child Psychology & Psychiatry 223 at 230 [Ashley, "Thinking an Ethics"].

67 Katherine Rachlin, "Medical Transition without Social Transition" (2018) 5:2 Transgender Studies Q 228.

68 Richard Green, "To Transition or Not to Transition? That Is the Question" (2017) 9:2 Current Sexual Health Reports 79 at 82; Zucker & Bradley, *supra* note 41 at 266; Langer & Martin, *supra* note 49 at 14.

69 Olson et al, *supra* note 14; Durwood, McLaughlin & Olson, *supra* note 14.

70 Zucker, "Commentary," *supra* note 28 at 543; Marchiano, *supra* note 56 at 346.

71 American Psychological Association, "Resolution on Gender Identity Change Efforts" (2021), online: <perma.cc/G462-TAUB>.

72 Olson et al, *supra* note 14; Diane Ehrensaft et al, "Prepubertal Social Gender Transitions: What We Know; What We Can Learn: A View from a Gender Affirmative Lens" (2018) 19:2 Intl J Transgenderism 251; Winters et al, *supra* note 24 at 248; Temple Newhook et al, *supra* note 16 at 218–19; Diane Ehrensaft, "Found in Transition: Our Littlest Transgender People" (2014) 50:4 Contemporary Psychoanalysis 571 at 579; Ruth Pearce, *Understanding Trans Health: Discourse, Power and Possibility* (Bristol, UK: Policy Press, 2018) at 157; Bauer et al, "Intervenable Factors," *supra* note 10; Michelle M Telfer et al, *Australian Standards of Care and Treatment Guidelines for Trans and Gender Diverse Children and Adolescents*, version 1.1 (Melbourne: Royal Children's Hospital, 2018) at 17.

73 Ashley, "Thinking an Ethics," *supra* note 66; Kristina R Olson, "Prepubescent Transgender Children: What We Do and Do Not Know" (2016) 55:3 J American Academy of Child & Adolescent Psychiatry 155; Gaines Blasdel et al, "Description and Outcomes of a Hormone Therapy Informed Consent Model for Minors" (Poster presented at the 25th Biennial Symposium of the World Professional Association for Transgender Health in Buenos Aires, Argentina, 3-6 November 2018) [unpublished]; Madeline B Deutsch, "Use of the Informed Consent Model in the Provision of Cross-Sex Hormone Therapy: A Survey of the Practices of Selected Clinics" (2012) 13:3 Intl J Transgenderism 140; Tim C van de Grift et al, "Surgical Satisfaction, Quality of Life, and Their Association after Gender-Affirming Surgery: A Follow-Up Study" (2018) 44:2 J Sex & Marital Therapy 138; Chantal M Wiepjes et al, "The Amsterdam Cohort of Gender Dysphoria Study (1972–2015): Trends in Prevalence, Treatment, and Regrets" (2018) 15:4 J Sexual Medicine 582; Annelou LC de Vries et al, "Young Adult Psychological Outcome after Puberty Suppression and Gender Reassignment" (2014) 134:4 Pediatrics 696; Florence Ashley, "Gender (De)Transitioning before Puberty? A Response to Steensma and Cohen-Kettenis (2011)" (2019) 48:3 Archives of Sexual Behavior 679; Anne A Lawrence, "Factors Associated with Satisfaction or Regret Following Male-to-Female Sex Reassignment Surgery" (2003) 32:4 Archives of Sexual Behavior 299.

74 Susan Bewley, Lucy Griffin & Richard Byng, "Safeguarding Adolescents from Premature, Permanent Medicalisation," *BMJ Rapid Responses* (February 11, 2019), online: <perma.cc/HRC7-5AN5>; Marchiano, *supra* note 56; Littman, *supra* note 56; Debra Soh, "The Unspoken Homophobia Propelling the Transgender

Movement in Children," *Quillette* (October 23, 2018), online: <perma.cc/DW3W
-LTYX>; Kathleen Stock, "Stonewall's New Definition of 'Conversion Therapy'
Raises a Few Questions," *The Article* (November 15, 2018), online: <perma.cc/
NGN8-NDDX>.

75 Ashley, "Homophobia," *supra* note 24; Ashley, "Critical Commentary," *supra* note
58; James et al, *supra* note 2 at 59. See also Bryant, "In Defence of Gay Children,"
supra note 38.

76 Alan D Miller & Ronen Perry, "The Reasonable Person" (2012) 87:2 NYUL Rev
323; Elizabeth L Shoenfelt, Allison E Maue & JoAnn Nelson, "Reasonable Person
versus Reasonable Woman: Does It Matter?" (2002) 10:3 Am UJ Gender, Soc Pol'y
& Law 633.

77 *R v Tran*, 2010 SCC 58 at para 34.

78 Mark Hayter, "Is Non-judgemental Care Possible in the Context of Nurses' Attitudes
to Patients' Sexuality?" (1996) 24:4 J Advanced Nursing 662; M Johnston, "On
Becoming Non-judgmental: Some Difficulties for an Ethics of Counselling" (1999)
25:6 J Medical Ethics 487.

79 Y Gavriel Ansara & Peter Hegarty, "Cisgenderism in Psychology: Pathologising
and Misgendering Children from 1999 to 2008" (2012) 3:2 Psychology & Sexuality
137; Y Gavriel Ansara & Peter Hegarty, "Methodologies of Misgendering: Recom-
mendations for Reducing Cisgenderism in Psychological Research" (2014) 24:2
Feminism & Psychology 259; Alexandre Baril & Kathrym Trevenen, "Exploring
Ableism and Cisnormativity in the Conceptualizsation of Identity and Sexuality
'Disorders'" (2014) 11 Annual Rev Critical Psychology 389; Nova J Bradford &
Moin Syed, "Transnormativity and Transgender Identity Development: A Master
Narrative Approach" (2019) 81:5–6 Sex Roles 306; Kristen Schilt & Laurel West-
brook, "Doing Gender, Doing Heteronormativity: 'Gender Normals,' Transgender
People, and the Social Maintenance of Heterosexuality" (2009) 23:4 Gender &
Society 440; Brenda A LeFrançois, "Queering Child and Adolescent Mental Health
Services: The Subversion of Heteronormativity in Practice" (2013) 27:1 Children
& Society 1.

80 Coleman et al, *supra* note 17.

81 Nicola Davis, "Trans Patients in England Face 'Soul Destroying' Wait for Treatment," *The Guardian* (February 26, 2019), online: <perma.cc/7DEZ-GGM7>; *Eld-
ridge v British Columbia (Attorney General)*, [1997] 3 SCR 624, 151 DLR (4th) 577;
Auton (Guardian ad litem of) v British Columbia (Attorney General), 2004 SCC 78.

82 *Snell v Farrell*, [1990] 2 SCR 311, 72 DLR (4th) 289; *McGhee v National Coal Board*,
[1972] 3 All ER 1008, [1972] UKHL 7.

83 See e.g. *Proyecto de ley Sobre Proteccion, supra* note 33.

84 Alesdair Ittelson, Sylvan Fraser & M Dru Levasseur, *Providing Ethical and Compassionate Health Care to Intersex Patients: Intersex-Affirming Hospital Policies* (New York:
Lambda Legal and interACT Advocates, 2018) at 9; *Proyecto de ley Sobre Proteccion,
supra* note 33. See also US, SB 201, *Medical Procedures: Treatment or Intervention:*

Sex Characteristics of a Minor, 2019-20, Reg Sess, Cal, 2019 [SB 201]; *Gender Identity, Gender Expression and Sex Characteristics Act,* Act XI of 2015 (Malta).

85 Reis, *supra* note 32 at 59, 70, 72, 79; Tosh, *supra* note 32 at 24–25; Guidotto, *supra* note 32 at 55.

86 Catherine Clune-Taylor, "Securing Cisgendered Futures: Intersex Management under the 'Disorders of Sex Development' Treatment Model" (2019) 34:4 Hypatia 690.

87 Birgit Köhler et al, "Satisfaction with Genital Surgery and Sexual Life of Adults with XY Disorders of Sex Development: Results from the German Clinical Evaluation Study" (2012) 97:2 J Clinical Endocrinology & Metabolism 577; Janik Bastien-Charlebois, "The Medical Treatment of Intersex Bodies and Voices" (Paper delivered at Sanctioned Sex(ualiti)es, ILGA International World Congress, 2015); Cheryl Chase, "'Cultural Practice' or 'Reconstructive Surgery'? US Genital Cutting, the Intersex Movement, and Medical Double Standards" in Stanlie M James & Claire C Robertson, eds, *Genital Cutting and Transnational Sisterhood: Disputing US Polemics* (Urbana: University of Illinois Press, 2002) 126; Morgan Holmes, "Rethinking the Meaning and Management of Intersexuality" (2002) 5:2 Sexualities 159; M Joycelyn Elders, David Satcher & Richard Carmona, *Re-thinking Genital Surgeries on Intersex Infants* (Santa Barbara, CA: Palm Center, 2017); Tiffany Jones et al, *Intersex: Stories and Statistics from Australia* (Cambridge, UK: Open Book Publishers, 2016) at 99ff.

88 Jones et al, *supra* note 87 at 110; Tosh, *supra* note 32 at 28–32; Nancy Ehrenreich & Mark Barr, "Intersex Surgery, Female Genital Cutting, and the Selective Condemnation of 'Cultural Practices'" (2005) 40 Harv CR-CLL Rev 71 at 107; Anne Fausto-Sterling, *Sexing the Body: Gender Politics and the Construction of Sexuality* (New York: Basic Books, 2000) at 86; Suzanne J Kessler, *Lessons from the Intersexed* (New Brunswick, NJ: Rutgers University Press, 1998) at 59–60.

89 Rachel Sloth-Nielsen, "Gender Normalisation Surgery and the Best Interest of the Child in South Africa" (2018) 29:1 Stellenbosch L Rev 48.

90 Köhler et al, *supra* note 87; *Malta Declaration,* December 1, 2013, online: OII Europe <perma.cc/36Y3-LEL6>; Silvian Agius, *Human Rights and Intersex People: Issue Paper* (Strasbourg: Council of Europe, 2017); Ittelson, Fraser & Levasseur, *supra* note 84; Elders, Satcher & Carmona, *supra* note 87; OHCHR, *supra* note 1; *Yogyakarta Principles plus 10: Additional Principles and State Obligations on the Application of International Human Rights Law in Relation to Sexual Orientation, Gender Identity, Gender Expression and Sex Characteristics to Complement the Yogyakarta Principles* (2017) at 10, 19 [*Yogyakarta Principles plus 10*]; Sloth-Nielsen, *supra* note 89.

91 *Ley 8/2017, de 28 de diciembre, para garantizar los derechos, la igualdad de trato y no discriminación de las personas LGTBI y sus familiares en Andalucía,* December 28, 2017, s 29; *Ley 3/2016, de 22 de julio, de Protección Integral contra LGTBIfobia y la Discriminación por Razón de Orientación e Identidad Sexual en la Comunidad de Madrid,* July 22, 2016, s 7(2); *Ley 8/2016, de 27 de mayo, de igualdad social de lesbianas,*

gais, bisexuales, transexuales, transgénero e intersexuales, y de políticas públicas contra la discriminación por orientación sexual e identidad de género en la Comunidad Autónoma de la Región de Murcia, May 27, 2016, s 16.

92 Georgiann Davis, *Contesting Intersex: The Dubious Diagnosis* (New York: New York University Press, 2015) [Davis, *Contesting Intersex*]; Bastien-Charlebois, *supra* note 87.

93 Bastien-Charlebois, *supra* note 87; Janik Bastien-Charlebois & Vincent Guillot, "Medical Resistance to Criticism of Intersex Activists: Operations on the Frontline of Credibility" in Erik Schneider & Christel Baltes-Löhr, eds, *Normed Children: Effects of Gender and Sex Related Normativity on Childhood and Adolescence* (Bielefeld, Germany: Transcript-Verlag, 2018) 257.

94 Florence Ashley, "Qui est-ille ? Le respect langagier des élèves non-binaires, aux limites du droit" (2017) 63:2 Service social 35 [Ashley, "Qui est-ille"].

95 Heath Fogg Davis, *Beyond Trans: Does Gender Matter?* (New York: New York University Press, 2017) [Davis, *Beyond Trans*].

96 Johann S Koehle & Sharleen O'Brien, *LGBTQIA+ Health and Healthcare at UCSB 2018–2019* (Santa Barbara, CA: University of Santa Barbara Department of Health and Wellness, 2021).

97 Kevin A McLemore, "A Minority Stress Perspective on Transgender Individuals' Experiences with Misgendering" (2018) 3:1 Stigma & Health 53; Kevin A McLemore, "Experiences with Misgendering: Identity Misclassification of Transgender Spectrum Individuals" (2015) 14:1 Self & Identity 51; Stephanie Julia Kapusta, "Misgendering and Its Moral Contestability" (2016) 31:3 Hypatia 502; Stephen T Russell et al, "Chosen Name Use Is Linked to Reduced Depressive Symptoms, Suicidal Ideation, and Suicidal Behavior among Transgender Youth" (2018) 63:4 J Adolescent Health 503; Bauer et al, "Intervenable Factors," *supra* note 10.

98 Madeline B Deutsch & David Buchholz, "Electronic Health Records and Transgender Patients: Practical Recommendations for the Collection of Gender Identity Data" (2015) 30:6 J General Internal Medicine 843 at 844; Lauren Freeman & Saray Ayala López, "Sex Categorization in Medical Contexts: A Cautionary Tale" (2018) 28:3 Kennedy Institute of Ethics J 243 at 258; Hale M Thompson, "Patient Perspectives on Gender Identity Data Collection in Electronic Health Records: An Analysis of Disclosure, Privacy, and Access to Care" (2016) 1:1 Transgender Health 205 at 212.

99 Florence Ashley, "Recommendations for Institutional and Governmental Management of Gender Information" (2021) 44:4 NYU Rev L & Soc Change 489; Davis, *Beyond Trans, supra* note 95 at 90; Commission scolaire de Montréal, "Lignes directrices relatives aux élèves transgenres de la Commission scolaire de Montréal" (February 23, 2017) at 11–12, online: <perma.cc/ACH3-33LX>.

100 Ashley, "Qui est-ille," *supra* note 94.

101 American Psychiatric Association, *Diagnostic and Statistical Manual of Mental Disorders*, 5th ed (Washington, DC: American Psychiatric Association, 2013); World

Health Organization (WHO), *The ICD-10 Classification of Mental and Behavioural Disorders: Clinical Descriptions and Diagnostic Guidelines* (Geneva: WHO, 1992). But see also Florence Ashley, "The Misuse of Gender Dysphoria: Toward Greater Conceptual Clarity in Transgender Health" (2019) Perspectives on Psychological Science.

102 Sam Winter et al, "The Proposed ICD-11 Gender Incongruence of Childhood Diagnosis: A World Professional Association for Transgender Health Membership Survey" (2016) 45:7 Archives of Sexual Behavior 1605; Amets Suess Schwend et al, "Depathologising Gender Diversity in Childhood in the Process of ICD Revision and Reform" (2018) 13:11 Global Public Health 1585; Zowie Davy & Michael Toze, "What Is Gender Dysphoria? A Critical Systematic Narrative Review" (2018) 3:1 Transgender Health 159; Jack Drescher, Peggy Cohen-Kettenis & Sam Winter, "Minding the Body: Situating Gender Identity Diagnoses in the ICD-11" (2012) 24:6 Intl Rev Psychiatry 568; Françoise Askevis-Leherpeux et al, "Why and How to Support Depsychiatrisation of Adult Transidentity in ICD-11: A French Study" (2019) 59 European Psychiatry 8; Zowie Davy, "The DSM-5 and the Politics of Diagnosing Transpeople" (2015) 44:5 Archives of Sexual Behavior 1165; Florence Ashley, "Gatekeeping Hormone Replacement Therapy for Transgender Patients Is Dehumanising" (2019) 45:7 J Medical Ethics 480.

103 American Psychological Association, *supra* note 10.

104 *Ibid* at 55.

105 *Ibid* at 57.

106 *Ibid* at 59.

107 Madrigal-Borloz, *supra* note 1 at 9, 13.

108 American Psychological Association, *supra* note 10 at 60.

109 *Ibid*.

110 *Ibid*; British Psychological Society, "Guidelines for Psychologists Working with Gender, Sexuality and Relationship Diversity" (July 4, 2019) at 6, online: <perma. cc/G3E7-LFBE>.

111 Madrigal-Borloz, *supra* note 1 at 17; Hipp et al, *supra* note 36; Mark A Yarhouse & Warren Throckmorton, "Ethical Issues in Attempts to Ban Reorientation Therapies" (2002) 39:1 Psychotherapy: Theory, Research, Practice, Training 66; Throckmorton, *supra* note 47. See also the earlier discussion of the ego-dystonic homosexuality diagnosis.

112 British Psychological Society, *supra* note 110 at 6.

113 Timothy W Jones et al, *Healing Spiritual Harms: Supporting Recovery from LGBTQA+ Change and Suppression Practices* (Melbourne: Australian Research Centre in Sex, Health and Society, La Trobe University, 2021); Susannah Cornwall, "Healthcare Chaplaincy and Spiritual Care for Trans People: Envisaging the Future" (2019) 7:1 Health & Social Care Chaplaincy 8; delfin bautista, Quince Mountain & Heath Mackenzie Reynolds, "Religion and Spirituality" in Laura Erickson-Schroth, ed, *Trans Bodies, Trans Selves: A Resource for the Transgender Community* (Oxford: Oxford

University Press, 2014) 62; Aiyyana Maracle, "A Journey in Gender" (2000) 2 tor-quere: J Can Lesbian & Gay Studies Assoc 36; Victoria Kolakowski, "Toward a Christian Ethical Response to Transsexual Persons" (1997) 1997:6 Theology & Sexuality 10. See also the Human Rights Campaign Foundation's Coming Home series, which includes guides specific to Catholicism, Islam, Judaism, Mormonism, and Evangelicalism. Human Rights Campaign Foundation, "Coming Home: To Faith, to Spirit, to Self" (2014), online: *Human Rights Campaign* <perma.cc/ R3D5-8F8H>.

114 Bill 56-1, *Conversion Practices Prohibition Legislation Bill* 2021 (NZ), 53rd Parl (first reading 30 July 2021).

115 *Yogyakarta Principles, supra* note 20.

116 Andrew Park, *Comment on the Definition of Sexual Orientation and Gender Identity Submitted to the Drafting Committee, Yogyakarta Principles on the Application of International Human Rights Law to Sexual Orientation and Gender Identity* (Los Angeles: Williams Institute on the Study of Sexual Orientation and Gender Identity, 2017).

117 Talia Mae Bettcher, "When Selves Have Sex: What the Phenomenology of Trans Sexuality Can Teach about Sexual Orientation" (2014) 61:5 J Homosexuality 605.

118 Ashley, "Homophobia," *supra* note 24.

119 Sarah Hunt, *An Introduction to the Health of Two-Spirit People: Historical, Contemporary and Emergent Issues* (Prince George, BC: National Collaborating Centre for Aboriginal Health, 2016) at 7; Arielle Twist, "On Translating the Untranslatable," *Canadian Art* (June 20, 2018), online: <perma.cc/6X3F-ENDH>; Saylesh Wesley, "Twin-Spirited Woman: *Sts'iyóye smestíyexw slhá:li*" (2014) 1:3 Transgender Studies Q 338 at 343; Chelsea Vowel, *Indigenous Writes: A Guide to First Nations, Métis, and Inuit Issues in Canada* (Winnipeg: HighWater Press, 2016) at 108; Kai Pyle, "Naming and Claiming: Recovering Ojibwe and Plains Cree Two-Spirit Language" (2018) 5:4 Transgender Studies Q 574 at 577; Angela Sterritt, "Indigenous Languages Recognize Gender States Not Even Named in English," *Globe and Mail* (March 10, 2016), online: <perma.cc/WU4D-XQDZ>. See also Marie Laing, *Urban Indigenous Youth Reframing Two-Spirit* (New York: Routledge, 2021).

120 *Yogyakarta Principles, supra* note 20.

121 G Nic Rider et al, "The Gender Affirmative Lifespan Approach (GALA): A Framework for Competent Clinical Care with Nonbinary Clients" (2019) 20:2–3 Intl J Transgenderism 275.

122 *Yogyakarta Principles plus 10, supra* note 90 at 10.

123 SB 201, *supra* note 84.

124 Emilie K Johnson et al, "Attitudes towards 'Disorders of Sex Development' Nomenclature among Affected Individuals" (2017) 13:6 J Pediatric Urology 608.e1; Davis, *Contesting Intersex, supra* note 92.

125 *Yogyakarta Principles plus 10, supra* note 90 at 10.

126 Georgiann Davis, Jodie M Dewey & Erin L Murphy, "Giving Sex: Deconstructing Intersex and Trans Medicalization Practices" (2016) 30:3 Gender & Society 490; *Malta Declaration, supra* note 90; Agius, *supra* note 90; Bastien-Charlebois, *supra* note 87; Chase, *supra* note 87; Holmes, *supra* note 87; Ittelson, Fraser & Levasseur, *supra* note 84; Elders, Satcher & Carmona, *supra* note 87; OHCHR, *supra* note 1.

127 Melissa Ballengee Alexander, "Autonomy and Accountability: Why Informed Consent, Consumer Protection, and Defunding May Beat Conversion Therapy Bans" (2017) 55 U Louisville L Rev 283 at 319–20, n 183.

128 *Ibid.*

129 *Orden ejecutiva del Gobernador de Puerto Rico, Hon. Ricardo A. Rosselló Nevares, para prohibir terapias de conversión o reparativas para cambiar la orientación sexual o de identidad de género de menores de edad,* Boletín Administrativo No OE-2019-016 (March 27, 2019).

130 Travis Salway et al, "Experiences with Sexual Orientation and Gender Identity Conversion Therapy Practices among Sexual Minority Men in Canada, 2019–2020" (2021) PLoS ONE; Greta Bauer et al, "Who Are Trans People in Ontario?" (2010) 1:1 Trans PULSE e-Bulletin, online: <perma.cc/UVP4-SMQY> [Bauer et al, "Who Are Trans People"]; James et al, *supra* note 2 at 55–56; MV Lee Badgett, Laura E Durso & Alyssa Schneebaum, *New Patterns of Poverty in the Lesbian, Gay, and Bisexual Community* (Los Angeles: Williams Institute on the Study of Sexual Orientation and Gender Identity, 2013).

131 *Norberg v Wynrib,* [1992] 2 SCR 226 at 263, 92 DLR (4th) 449 ; *Hill v Church of Scientology of Toronto,* [1995] 2 SCR 1130 at paras 188–89, 126 DLR (4th) 129; *Elkow v Sana,* 2020 ABCA 350 at paras 31–32.

132 *Michael Ferguson et al v JONAH et al,* No L-5473-12 (NJ Super Ct Law Div 2015).

133 Bauer et al, "Who Are Trans People," *supra* note 130; James et al, *supra* note 2 at 55–56; Badgett, Durso & Schneebaum, *supra* note 130.

134 *Conversion Practices Bill, supra* note 23; Ilanbey & Sakkal, *supra* note 23.

135 See also the full recommendations of Madrigal-Borloz, *supra* note 1 at 21–22.

Conclusion

1 Florence Ashley, "Suing for Conversion Therapy without a Statute? A Blueprint," *Law Matters* (2019), online: <perma.cc/LWZ9-EU4T>; Florence Ashley, "Corriger nos pratiques: les approches thérapeutiques pour intervenir auprès des enfants trans examinées dans une perspective juridique" in Annie Pullen Sanfaçon & Denise Medico, eds, *Les interventions affirmatives auprès des enfants et jeunes trans : perspectives multidisciplinaires* (Montréal and Paris: Éditions Remue-Ménage and Médecine et Hygiène, 2021) 89.

2 *Michael Ferguson et al v JONAH et al,* No L-5473-12 (NJ Super Ct Law Div 2015).

Index

accountability, peer, 10, 19
accountability structures, 124, 127–29
adjudicators, 113–14
Administrative Procedure Act, 85
adulthood, 142
advertising, 58, 133, 138, 139,
   167, 170
affirmative practices: in Bill 77, 44, 45;
   commitment to in education, 125;
   increasing availability of, 117; in
   legal terms, 47–48; in model law,
   136, 155–56; in *Task Force report*,
   50–51
affirmative therapeutic interventions,
   47–48
*Affirming Sexual Orientation and
   Gender Identity Act*, 3, 27, 33
age in conversion bans, 56, 58, 62,
   108–10, 142
Alcorn, Leelah, 40
ambiguity in gender identity, 24
American Academy of Pediatrics, 84
American Medical Association, 84
American Psychiatric Association, 88

American Psychological Association,
   30, 84, 85, 88, 90, 147
*An Act to Amend the Canadian Human
   Rights Act and the Criminal Code*.
   See Bill C-16
*An Act to Amend the Criminal Code
   (Conversion Therapy)*, 16
anatomical features, 163
Andalucía, 55, 56, 57, 66, 152
anti-discrimination policies, 15, 166
anti-trans views and activism, 6,
   15–16. *See also* transantagonism
anxiety, 11, 49, 84, 115. *See also* harm
Argentina, 54, 142, 152
Ariely, Dan, 123
assessments, comprehensive, 49
Australia, 170
Australian and New Zealand
   Professional Association for
   Transgender Health, 84
authority, 18
autonomy, 93–102, 108, 109–10.
   See also religion
Ayal, Shahar, 122–23

backlashes, 15–16
bans, on conversion practices: age
    and, 56, 58, 62, 108–10, 142;
    benefits of, 20, 104–8; Bill 77 as a
    case study, 34; calls for governments
    to, 14; Canadian, 56; constitutionality
    of, 102; and criminal laws, 111–12;
    effects on professional practice, 21,
    104–5; focus on trans communities
    in, 17; freedom of expression and,
    72; funding of conversion
    practices, 115–16; importance of,
    16, 174, 175; lack of compensation
    for survivors, 114–15; limitations
    of, 104; in Ontario, 3–5, 10;
    opposition to, 71, 113–14, 122;
    overbreadth critique of, 87–93;
    policy objectives of, 101–2; to
    prevent harm, 74; in Spain, 56–57;
    texts of, 56, 110–11; unregulated
    practitioners, 112–13; unwillingness
    to adopt, 116–18
behavioural approaches, 10, 26, 29,
    59, 144
belief expression, 159–60
Bell v Tavistock, 15, 197*n*59
Bill 77 Ontario: applicability of, 53; as
    a ban case study, 33, 51–52; date of,
    3; definitions of "seeks to change,"
    39, 42, 44; denying contradictions
    to, 121–22; exceptions, 44–45;
    expressive elements of, 106; focus on
    gender identity, 33–34; impact on
    CAMH clinic closure, 10, 27, 88,
    105; interpretation of, 37; legislative
    history of, 37–38; removing "or
    direct," 39–40; restriction to minors
    only, 108; subsections 29.1(1) and
    29.1(2), 62; text of, 34–35, 43; viewed
    as unnecessary, 104
Bill C-6 (Canada), 16
Bill C-16 (Canada), 87

billing codes, 115–16. *See also*
    insurance coverage
Binnie, Ian, 38
bioethics, 97
birth certificates, 161–62
blood transfusions, 94–95, 96, 100
Bolt, Vincent, 40
Bradley, Susan, 4, 28
brainwashing, 79
Brandeis, Justice Louis, 77–78
British Columbia, 36, 115
Bryant, Karl, 11, 25, 131
Byne, William, 6, 30, 88, 92

California, 55, 86, 96, 105, 116
California Senate Bill 201, 162
Canada: bans on conversion therapy,
    56, 64; federal government of, 15,
    16; freedom of expression in, 72–73,
    87; suicide law in, 98. *See also* Bill 77
    Ontario
Canadian Association for Social Work
    Education, 121
Canadian Association of Social
    Workers, 121
*Canadian Charter of Rights and
    Freedoms*, 72–73, 78, 92
Canadian Human Rights Act, 87
Canadian Psychiatric Association, 84
Canadian Psychological Association, 84
Carter v Canada, 98
celibacy, 147
Centre for Addiction and Mental
    Health (CAMH) Board of Trustees, 6
Centre for Addiction and Mental
    Health (CAMH) Gender Identity
    Clinic for Children and Youth: ban
    on conversion practices and, 71;
    closure as case study, 175; closure of,
    3, 6–8, 10, 88, 103, 119; controversy
    around conversion practices of, 22,
    32; corrective approaches of, 5, 41;

experiences of conversion practices at, 16–17; external review of, 33; history of, 4; settlement with Zucker, 6–7
Child, Youth and Family Services Act, 2017 (Ontario), 101
child development, 23, 24
childhood gender diversity, 4
child pornography, 83
child protection law, 134
chosen names, 153–54
Church of Jesus Christ of Latter-Day Saints, 116
cisgender identification, 25, 28, 78, 80, 100–1
civil cause of action, 168–69
civil liability, 68, 150, 166
Clarke Institute, 3, 4, 36
client-centred approaches, 48, 155. *See also* affirmative practices
clinical goals and outcomes, 4, 5, 25–26
cognitive-behavioural therapy, 5, 49, 156, 206*n*55
College of Registered Psychotherapists of Ontario, 104, 114
Colorado, 55, 57
compensation from harm, 114–15, 139, 168–69
concept logic, 29–30
conduct, 74–75, 78, 81
conformity, encouraging, 25–26, 28
Connecticut, 55, 57, 67, 68, 114–15
consensus on conversion practice harm, 8, 30–31, 80, 81, 84, 88, 124–25
consent: to conversion practices, 82, 97, 98–99, 100, 109–10, 142, 152–53; to medical transition, 163–64; sexual, 143
conservative governments, 117
conservative views, 6, 80. *See also* anti-trans views

consistent and uniform assertion, 60
constitutionality, 71, 86, 94–95, 113, 140, 165–67, 172, 175
consumer fraud law, 109, 118, 170, 176
content, expressive, 74, 77, 78–79, 81, 86
conversion practices: in adults, 109, 142; advertising of, 58, 133, 138, 139, 167, 170; alternative terms for, 140–41; broader social context of, 13; CAMH engaging in, 3; changing ethics of, 14; as conduct not speech, 74–75, 78, 81; consent to, 82, 97, 98–99, 100, 109–10, 142, 152–53; criminalization of, 16; definitions of, 22, 26, 57, 58, 88; efficacy of, 132; evaluation of freedom of expression, 78–81; experienced as hurtful, 130, 131; first-hand experiences of, 11, 41–42; gay, 25, 59; harm from, 11–13, 23, 25, 41, 74, 77–78, 80–85, 92, 97; increases in, 13–15, 16, 116–18; lack of professional support for, 83–84; under Malta's ban, 61–64; model law definition of, 134–36, 140–43; news coverage of from bans, 105; organizational stances against, 83; political weight and meaning of term, 22; religious motivations for, 95; review uncovering, 33; statistics on, 130–31; systematic nature of, 143–44, 159–60; therapy, 30, 31; as unethical, 132
coping strategies, 49, 136, 156–58
corporate dissolution, 139, 169–70
corrective approaches: academic analysis of, 9; addressed in Bill 77, 44; vs affirming approaches, 8; in Bill 77, 33, 43, 45–48, 51; concept logic of, 29–30; as conversion practices, 22, 26–32
Cossman, Brenda, 87
counselling, 58, 69

Court of Appeal for the Eleventh
Circuit, 86
Court of Appeal for the Ninth
Circuit, 86
Court of Appeal for the Seventh
Circuit, 96
Court of Appeal for the Third
Circuit, 86
Criminal Code, 46, 111, 143, 160
criminalization, 112
cross-gender identification: notes on
in model law, 146–47
cultural changes, 105–8, 171, 173, 175
cultural sensitivity, 160

damages, 168–69. *See also*
compensation from harm; harm
debates, 8–9, 18, 27, 80
defamation, 6–8
defendants, 111
definitions, 22, 26, 57, 58, 61, 88,
160–65, 201*n*14
Delaware, 55, 57, 58, 59, 60
depression, 11, 12, 41, 49, 82. *See also*
harm
de Vries, Annelou L.C., 27
diagnosis and assessment in model
law, 154–55
*Diagnostic and Statistical Manual of
Mental Disorders (DSM)*: diagnosis and
assessment and, 154–55; Ego-dystonic
Homosexuality in, 145; on Gender
Dysphoria, 28; on gender identity, 24,
47, 90–92, 107, 141; Gender Identity
Disorder in, 146; on homosexuality, 9,
31; in model law, 136
DiNovo, Cheri, 39, 40, 41, 108
disallowed practices, 145
disciplinary law, 176
discrimination, 138, 139, 165–68
disorders of sexual development
(DSDs), 162

District of Columbia, 55, 57, 59, 207*n*5
diversity. *See* human variation
Dobbin, Frank, 128
doctor-patient sexual relationships,
98–99
Doe v Christie, 89
Drescher, Jack, 109

easy lives, 95
education, 124–26, 171, 173
effectiveness of law, 176
Ego-dystonic Homosexuality, 145, 157
Ehrensaft, Diane, 24–25, 28
ejusdem generis principle, 45, 46, 47
electroshock therapy, 75–76
employment law, 7–8
enforcement, visible, 127
equality, 92
Equal Opportunity and Human
Rights Commission of Victoria
(Australia), 170
equipoise, 85
ethical contagion, 122–23
ethics, research, 85–86, 90
etiological lens, 147–48
evidence, scientific, 83, 84, 85–86,
131, 132
evidence of gender identity, 60
exceptions and exclusions in bans, 46,
47–48, 51, 62
executive orders, 55
experience, clinical with trans
people, 122
expression, freedom of, 73–74, 78
expressio unius est exclusio alterius
principle, 45, 47–48
external reviews, 4, 5, 6–7, 33, 119

faith-based practices, 25–26
family, 159–60. *See also* parents
Ferguson v JONAH, 170
fines, 66, 167, 170

First Amendment, US Constitution, 73
flourishing, human, 80, 81. *See also* harm
fluidity of identity, 30, 50, 140, 207*n*62
free choice, 163–64
freedom of expression, 71–72, 75, 78,
    80–81, 87
freedom of religion. *See* religion
freedom of speech, 85, 87
funding for conversion practices,
    115–16, 139, 168

Gajdics, Peter, 109
gap in services, 6
gay conversion practices, 25, 59.
    See also conversion practices
gender-affirmative approaches, 8–10,
    16, 49–50, 51, 92
gender binaries, 29, 161
gender-creative children, 4, 23–25, 27,
    31, 50, 88, 144
gender dysphoria, 12, 27, 90–92, 150,
    155–56
Gender Dysphoria (diagnosis), 24,
    28–29, 47, 63, 91, 92
gender expression: conflated with
    gender identity, 59–61, 63–64;
    definition in model law, 138,
    162–63; definition in *Yogyakarta
    Principles*, 161; efforts to change, 88;
    notes on model law, 144–45
gender identity: ambiguity in, 23–24;
    conflated with gender expression,
    59–61, 63–64; definitions, 35–39, 63,
    137, 161; history of, 35–37; notes on
    in model law, 146; respect for,
    153–54; self-identified, 35–39; well-
    defined, 24
Gender Identity Clinic for Children
    and Youth. *See* Centre for Addiction
    and Mental Health (CAMH)
    Gender Identity Clinic for Children
    and Youth

Gender Identity Disorder, 24, 36, 47,
    63, 91, 146
*Gender Identity Disorder and
    Psychosexual Problems in Children
    and Adolescents* (Zucker and
    Bradley), 4
Gender Identity Disorder of
    Childhood, 91
Gender Incongruence in Childhood,
    91, 92
gender markers, 154
gender non-conforming children, 15,
    23, 144
gender non-conformity, 23, 25, 29,
    144, 147, 163, 164
gender norms, 23, 29, 141. *See also*
    norms
George, Marie-Amelie, 105–6
Gino Francesca, 122–23
Global North, 54
Global South, 54
good lives, 95
Green, Amy, 12, 82
Green, Richard, 90, 91–92, 94, 95
Greeson, Ralph, 36

harm: to adults, 142; compensation
    for, 114–15, 139, 168–69; consensus
    on, 84–85; consent and, 97; duty to
    refrain from, 96–97; experiences of,
    130–31; justifying bans, 95–96;
    nature and severity of, 82–84; from
    non-consensual medical treatments,
    152; personal understanding of,
    172; of prejudice and devaluation,
    195*n*47; preventing through
    regulation, 89–90; prevention of, 74,
    77, 78; risk of, 89; self-harm, 98;
    statistics on, 82–83, 131;
    understanding scope of, 174
Hawaii, 55, 57, 58, 59
healing, 81, 126

healthcare, access to, 155
Health Care Consent Act, 1996, 34
healthcare professionals, 68
Health Products and Food Branch of
   Health Canada, 89–90
*Health Professionals Procedural
   Code*, 127
Herbert, Spencer Chandra, 115
hierarchy of identities, 25
Hippocratic Oath, 97. *See also* harm
HIV (human immunodeficiency
   viruses), 59, 112, 145
homoantagonism, 77, 80–81, 87, 100,
   145–46, 150, 157
homosexuality, 9, 31, 90
hormonal interventions, 28, 136,
   151, 152
House of Commons Standing
   Committee on Health, 16
Human Rights Code, 37
human rights complaints, 166
human variation, 4, 9, 47, 81, 90, 91

Ibarra, Herminia, 125
Icahn School of Medicine at Mount
   Sinai, 30
identity, professional, 124, 125, 128
identity exploration and development,
   50, 137, 158–59
ideology, 9
Illinois, 55
imprisonment, 66, 112
ineffectiveness of therapies, 89–90
inequality, 92
Inquiries, Complaints and Reports
   Committee, 127
insurance coverage, 67–68, 117, 139,
   168
integrated personal identity, 158–59
InterACT, 152
*International Classification of Diseases
   (ICD)*, 91, 92, 107, 136

International Commission of
   Jurists, 37
International Federation of Social
   Workers, 84
International Psycho-Analytic
   Congress, 36
International Service for Human
   Rights, 37
intersex genitals, 152
intersex people, 141–42, 151–52, 162
intersex traits, 137, 141–42, 151–53, 162
interventions in the naturalistic
   environment, 5, 148
invalidation, 11, 25

Jehovah's Witnesses, 94
Joint Statement on the Affirmation of
   Gender Diverse Children and Youth
   of the Canadian Association for
   Social Work Education, 120–21
judgment: non-judgmental practices,
   48, 149, 150–51, 155, 156; value, 9
jurisdictions, 166, 171–72, 176. *See also*
   individual jurisdictions

Kalev, Alexandra, 128
Kay, Barbara, 6
Kelly, Erin, 128
King v Christie, 86, 89

Lambda Legal, 152
Lamer, Justice Antonio, 46–47, 111
language of bans, 110–11, 172
laws: child protection, 134;
   comparison of, 53; confusion
   around, 132–33; consumer fraud,
   118; efficacy of, 132; positive
   cultural impact of, 105–8; role of in
   behaviours, 18, 19. *See also*
   model law
legal aid, 139, 169, 170
legal fees, 139

legalization of same-sex marriage, 106
legal names, 154
legal research, 176
Legislative Assembly of Ontario, 108
legislative history, 51–52
legislative intent, 37, 40, 43, 47, 51, 109
Liberal Party, 39
licensure, 18, 140, 170–71
limitations of bans, 104, 108–17
linguistic scope of research, 54
linguistic shifts, 91
lists, exhaustive and illustrative, 45, 46
lives, good vs easy, 95
London Business School, 125

Madrid, Spain, 55, 56, 57, 66, 152
Maine, 55, 57, 58
malleability in gender identity, 27, 30,
    41. *See also* fluidity of identity
malleability of norms, 121, 122.
    See also norms
Malta, 55, 61–64, 66, 68, 108, 111,
    141, 143
Manitoba, 208*n*10
marginalization, 81, 158
marriage equality. *See* same-sex
    marriage legalization
Maryland, 55, 57
Massachusetts, 55, 57, 58, 59, 60, 67, 68
Meadow, Tey, 8, 29
medical models of illness, 11
mens rea, 111
mental disorders, 4, 9, 29–30, 62–63
mental health outcomes, 11–12,
    105–8
methodology, research, 54–55
mindfulness-based therapy, 49, 156
misattributing orientation, 153–54
misgendering, 153–54
model law: consent to conversion
    practices in, 142–43; definition of
    sexual orientation in, 160–61; notes

for paragraph 1(2)(c), 147–48; notes
    for paragraph 1(2)(d), 148; notes for
    paragraph 1(2)(e), 149; notes for
    paragraph 1(2)(f), 149–51; notes for
    paragraph 1(2)(g), 151–53; notes for
    paragraph 1(2)(h), 153–54; notes for
    section 14, 172; notes for sections
    7–11, 168; notes on section 12,
    170–71; notes on section 13, 171–72;
    notes on sections 2–6, 165–68; notes
    on subsection 1(3), 154–60; notes on
    subsection 1(11), 165; purpose and
    background of, 21, 128–29, 133–34;
    role of, 172–73; text of, 134–40
Montreal Sex Garage raid, 112
morality, 87
moral psychology, 121
Mormon Church, 116
municipal bans, 55
Murcia, Spain, 55, 56, 66, 152
Muse, Erika, 16–17, 40–42, 51, 109
mutatis mutandis principle, 52

names, 153–54
narrative therapy, 49, 157
National Post, 6
naturalistic environments, 148
negligence, 68, 138, 139, 150, 165, 166,
    167–68
Nevada, 55, 57
New Hampshire, 55, 57
New Jersey, 55, 58, 59, 86, 89, 116, 170
New Jersey Superior Court, 170
New Mexico, 55, 58, 59, 60
news coverage, 105
New York State, 55, 58, 59
New York v Ferber, 83
New Zealand, 160
No Conversion Canada, 17
non-binary label, 153–54, 161
non-consensual interventions relating
    to intersex traits, 151–53

non-judgmental care, 48, 149, 150, 151, 155–56
non-maleficence, principle of, 92, 97
norms: ethical, 121, 123, 124–25; gender, 23, 29, 141; social, 25–26, 59, 121, 123, 164
Nova Scotia, 55, 56, 68
NOW Toronto, 42

Ontario, 3–5, 9, 16, 55–56, 70, 101, 115, 127. *See also* Bill 77 Ontario
Ontario Human Rights Commission, 35–37, 122
Ontario Human Rights Tribunal, 37
Order of Social Workers, Family, and Marriage Therapists of Québec (OTSTCFQ), 120
Ordre des travailleurs sociaux et des thérapeutes conjugaux et familiaux du Québec, 120
Oregon, 55, 58–59
organizations against conversion practices, 83–84
Otto v City of Boca Raton, 85, 86, 210n21
overbreadth critique of bans, 87–93

Pakistan, 54
parents: counselling for, 29; impact of conversion practices by, 11; in model law, 135, 148, 159–60, 166; parental rights, 94; perspectives of, 94, 101; teachings about gender, 24
participation, in social or political decision-making, 79
patient perspectives, 94
peer pressure, 122–25, 171, 175
permitted practices, 154–60
permitted practices in model law: acceptance and support 1(3) (B), 155–56; coping strategies paragraph 1(3) (C), 156–58; diagnosis and

assessment paragraph 1(3) (A), 154–55; integrated personal identity paragraph 1(3) (D), 158–59; mere speech paragraph 1(3) (E), 159–60
personal identity, 158–59
Pickup v Brown, 86, 96, 97
Pignatiello, Antonio, 4
play therapy, 5, 29
police violence, 112
Policy on Preventing Discrimination because of Gender Identity and Gender Expression (OHRC), 37
political will, 175
poverty, 169, 170
practitioners, unlicensed, 65, 66, 68, 112–13
prevention of trans identities, 4, 9–10, 28, 40, 42–43, 51, 144, 146
primum non nocere principle, 97
Prince Edward Island, 55, 56
prison sentences, 66
professional associations: against conversion practices, 83–84; disciplinary sanctions and, 65; discipline from, 139; enforcing bans, 107; importance of to conversion bans, 18; regulations within, 104, 114; role in model law, 170–71; tone-setting role of, 128
professional culture, 19, 119–20
professional education, 124–26
professional guidelines, clear, 120–24
professional identity, 124, 125, 128
professional malpractice, 176
professional misconduct, 165, 167
professionals, healthcare, 68
professionals, licensed: conversion practices of, 14; disciplinary sanctions for, 65, 68; lacking right to harm, 102; in model law, 143, 166, 170–71; peer pressure among, 122–24; regulation of, 18;

resentment toward bans, 113–14;
self-fulfillment of, 80
professional speech, 73–74
prohibited acts in model law, 165–68
pronouns, 153–54
protogay children, 24–25
*Providing Ethical and Compassionate
Health Care to Intersex Patients:
Intersex-Affirming Hospital Policies*
(Lambda Legal and InterACT), 152
Proyecto de Ley Sobre Proteccion
Integral de Las Caracteristicas
Sexuales, 142, 152
pseudoscientific practices, 89
psychoeducation, 156
psychopathologization: assessments
as, 155; as basis of corrective
approaches, 27, 32, 34, 141; covered
in Maltese ban, 62–63; freedom of
speech and, 87; of gender creativity,
24; limitations of bans to prevent,
77–78; practices in model law,
145–46; reduction in, 91–93
psychosocial interventions, 51
puberty, 4, 12, 15, 30, 138, 163
public awareness, 15
Puerto Rico, 55, 58, 59, 68
Pyne, Jake, 8, 9, 42, 104–5

Québec, 36, 112, 127
queerness, 23, 31

Rainbow Health Alliance, 4
randomized controlled trials, 83,
85–86
reasonability, 150, 151, 158, 159
Re Canada 3000, 38
regret, 15
Regulated Health Professions Act, 1991,
34–35, 62
regulation, legal, 18, 77, 89, 90, 97, 133,
170–71

Rekers, George Alan, 144
religion, 69, 94, 100–1, 113, 157–59
reparative therapy, 23, 30, 31
*Report of the American Psychological
Association Task Force on Appropriate
Therapeutic Responses to Sexual
Orientation. See Task Force report*
respectability politics, 106–7
re-transition, 15
reviews, external, 4–7, 33
Rhode Island, 55, 58
rights and protections in bans, 57
right to refuse treatment, 97
right-to-try movement, 99–100
risk, 89
Rowlands, Joyce, 104, 114
Royal College of Psychiatrists, 84
*Rumfeld v Forum for Academic &
Institutional Rights*, 76
Russell, Hershel, 148
R v McIntosh, 46, 47, 111

same-sex intimacy, 112, 141,
146–47, 152
same-sex marriage legalization,
106, 107
sanctions: administrative, 66;
corporate dissolution, 139; criminal,
66; for deceptive trade practices,
66–67; disciplinary sanctions, 65;
funding restrictions, 67–68; penal,
65–67; possible avenues for, 176;
social, 124–25; targets of, 68–70;
threats of, 127–28; understanding
bans through, 64–70
scholarship, 175
scientific process, 83, 90
Seattle University, 107
self-acceptance, 146, 156
self-fulfillment, individual, 80, 81
self-image, 49
self-incrimination, right against, 111–12

self-reporting and identification, 37–39, 165
Serano, Julia, 9
service gaps, 88
settlements, legal, 6–7
severability, 172
sex assigned at birth, 137, 147, 161–62
sexual assault, 83, 152, 172
sexual contact with therapists, 109
Sexual Disorder Not Otherwise Specified, 145
Sexual Inversion: The Multiple Roots of Homosexuality, 31
sexual orientation: affirmative practices for, 47; conversion practices for, 23, 25–26, 145; definition in model law, 137, 160–61; as distinct from gender, 24–25, 175; fluidity of, 30; as focus of bans on conversion practices, 33
shame, 11, 48, 131, 156
Sheridan v Sanctuary Investments Ltd, 36
social contagion, 14–15, 27, 164–65
socialization, professional, 124
social support, 49–50, 59
Spade, Dean, 107
Spain, 55–57, 64, 66, 68, 152
specificity of bans, 121–22
speech: explanatory, 76–77; freedom of, 15, 28–29, 57, 76; in model law, 159–60; professional, 73–74
Standing Committee on Justice Policy, 39, 40, 41, 42, 104, 114
statistics, 82
statutes, 55
stigma, 49, 109, 127, 156, 158
Stoller, Robert, 36
substantive due process rights, 96
suicidality: experiences of, 11, 40, 41; reduced through legalization of same-sex marriage, 106, 108; statistics on, 12, 82–83, 131

Sullivan, Sé, 11, 131
support groups, 49–50
Supreme Court of Canada, 46, 47, 72–73, 98, 111
surgery, 96–97, 151, 152, 164
surveillance, 128
symbolic effects of bans, 105–8
symbolic interactionism, theory of, 13

talk therapy, 74, 76–77
targeted characteristics, 155–56, 157–58
Task Force report: as basis of conversion bans, 48, 49–50, 53–54, 59, 110; connection to Maltese ban, 62; use in Canadian bans, 46, 47, 56, 64
taxes, 139, 167–68
Temple Newhook, Julia, 25–26, 197n59, 201n14
terminology. *See* definitions
testimonies, 40–41
TG Innerselves, 40
therapeutic approach. *See* corrective approaches
therapy types in conversion practices, 26, 140–41
time frames of bans, 171–72
Toronto, ON, 3, 4, 112. *See also* Centre for Addiction and Mental Health (CAMH) Gender Identity Clinic for Children and Youth
Toronto bathhouse raids, 112
tort law, 166
torture, 12, 82
Tosh, Jemma, 9
trade, deceptive or unfair practices in, 66–67, 138, 167
trans-affirmative views, 17–18
transantagonism: compared with homoantagonism, 150; freedom of expression and, 87; inherent in conversion practices, 75, 92;

internalized, 81, 99, 146, 157; pervasiveness of, 49, 51, 80; in speech, 77

trans conversion practices. *See* conversion practices

trans health, 3, 4, 125–26. *See also* transitions, medical

trans-inclusive policies, 15

transitioning: avoiding, 28–29; care for, 4, 117; delaying or impeding, 149–51

transitions, medical: delaying or impeding, 12, 41, 149–51; in model law, 135, 136, 138, 163–65; in *Task Force report*, 48; viewed as extreme, 145

transitions, social: delaying or impeding, 149–51; in model law, 135, 138, 149, 163–65

transitude, 4, 92, 95

TransPULSE research project, 9

trauma, 49, 147–48, 152, 172

trust, culture of, 123–24

truth, pursuit of, 78–79

Turban, Jack, 27, 28, 82, 116

tutors, 135, 148

Two-Spirit people, 160, 161

United Kingdom, 15, 131

United Nations Committee on the Rights of the Child *General Comment No. 14*, 101

United Nations Independent Expert on Sexual Orientation and Gender Identity, 14, 132

United States, 13–14, 15, 57–61, 64, 69–70, 72–73

university courses, 124–26

University of California Los Angeles Gender Identity Clinic, 25, 144

University of Toronto, 87

University of Toronto Press Blog, 107–8

Uruguay, 55

US Supreme Court, 73–74, 76–78, 83, 85, 86, 96, 210*n*15

Utah, 55, 58, 59, 69, 116

València, Spain, 55, 56, 57

values, religious, 94, 96

Vermont, 55, 58

Victoria, Australia, 170

Vipond, Evan, 106

Virginia, 55, 58

Wake Forest University, 105

Wallace, Robert, 148

Washington State, 55, 58

washrooms, 36

Whitney v California, 78

Williams Institute, 131

Workers' Compensation Appeal Tribunal, 36

World Professional Association for Transgender Health, 14, 36, 84, 88, 91, 151

Yogyakarta Principles, 36–37, 56–57, 63, 132, 160, 161

Yogyakarta Principles plus 10, 162

York University, 106

Zinck, Suzanne, 4

Zucker, Kenneth, 4–8, 27, 28